Involving Parents in Their Children's Learning

SECOND EDITION

Involving Parents in Their Children's Learning

SECOND EDITION

Margy Whalley

and the

Pen Green Centre Team

Paul Chapman Publishing

Paul Chapman Publishing
A SAGE Publications Company
1 Oliver's Yard
55 City Road
London EC1Y 1SP

SAGE Publications Inc
2455 Teller Road
Thousand Oaks
California 91320

SAGE Publications India Pvt Ltd
B1/I1 Mohan Cooperative Industrial Area
Mathura Road, Post Bag 7
New Delhi 110044

SAGE Publications
Asia-Pacific Pte Ltd
33 Pekin Street #02-01
Four East Square
Singapore 048763

Library of Congress Control Number: 2007921673

A catalogue record for this book is available from the British Library

ISBN 978-1-4129-3500-5
ISBN (pbk) 978-1-4129-3501-2

Typeset by Pantek Arts Ltd, Maidstone, Kent
Printed in Great Bntain by Athenaeum Press, Gateshead, Tyne and Wear
Printed on paper from sustainable resources

Contents

Notes on the Team

Cath Arnold is an education consultant at the Pen Green Centre for under fives and their families. She has over 30 years' experience in both private and public sector childcare and education. She is a qualified teacher, has a master's degree in education, and is currently completing a PhD. Cath is a parent and grandparent, and has published two books about her grandchildren.

Trevor Chandler trained as a social worker. He worked at Pen Green for 20 years, originally as Deputy Head and subsequently as Head of Centre. He has completed an MA in education with care. Trevor has two children, Rachel and David.

Annette Cummings is a teacher/senior family worker in the nursery and the parent of two children. She originally became involved with the work of the Pen Green Centre as a parent and returned to university in 1996/97 to gain a PGCE. Annette has undertaken a number of practitioner research projects with staff in the Research Base at Pen Green and has a master's degree in early education with care.

Marcus Dennison was a family worker at Pen Green for seven years and also worked as a researcher in the Pen Green Research Base for a further three years. He ran groups at Pen Green for parents during the day and in the evening. Marcus has four children, and he left to care for his youngest daughter.

Kate Hayward trained to be a teacher after being involved in the early education of her three children, Tom, Hannah and Emily. Previously she worked in community development projects and health programmes in Britain, Kenya and Papua New Guinea. She is currently a researcher at the Pen Green Research Base, leading on pedagogical support and the professional development programme on parental involvement.

Eddie McKinnon is a principal researcher at Pen Green. He is a qualified teacher with an MA in mass communications. Eddie is married with two daughters. Eddie is responsible for conducting evaluation work at the Pen Green Centre and is currently leading on supporting the development of children's centres in Northamptonshire.

Colette Tait is a researcher at the Pen Green Research Base and runs a number of groups for parents and young children. She has two children, Georgia and Harry, who both attended the Pen Green Nursery. Colette is currently completing an MA in integrated provision for children and families.

Margy Whalley has a 27-year-old daughter and has worked for over 34 years in education and community projects in Britain, Brazil and Papua New Guinea. She is a qualified teacher with an MA in community education and a doctorate in leadership within early years settings. She is currently directing the research programme at the Pen Green Research Base.

Acknowledgements

We would like to acknowledge our huge debt to Chris Athey, who directed the Froebel Early Education Project 1973–8, and Professor Tina Bruce, who worked alongside her. They were the pioneers, and they have inspired and supported us.

We also want to acknowledge Professor Ferre Laevers, Professor Chris Pascal, Dr Tony Bertram and Professor Colwyn Trevarthen, and thank them for sharing their work with us.

Finally, we want to thank the Esmee Fairbairn Charitable Trust, who funded this project; our Advisory Group, who have supported and sustained us over the years; and the staff, parents and children at Pen Green who became so deeply involved.

Preface

This book is just one of the outcomes of a five-year research and development project at the Pen Green Centre for under fives and their families. In it we describe the rich and challenging dialogue that can develop when early years practitioners, supported by colleagues in institutions of higher education, work collaboratively with children and families.

Small-scale innovative projects such as this one, with its focus on involving parents, have a major contribution to make, not just to the community which they serve but also to the wider early years community (Oliver, Smith and Barker, 1998). Practitioner research can inform the wider debate about the ethical dimension of research and can demonstrate how much more effective it is to work in a genuine research partnership with those who have traditionally been the objects of research (Pascal, 1996).

This research project was set up in 1995. It was part funded during 1996 by the Teacher Training Agency and subsequently was fully funded from 1997 to 2000 by the Esmee Fairbairn Charitable Trust; we are very grateful to our funders for giving us the opportunity to work so closely and thoughtfully with parents and children. The full research report is available from the Pen Green Research, Training and Development Base. A VHS video illustrating much of this project has also been produced with support from the Department for Education and Employment (DfEE). This video is now distributed as part of a training programme delivered by staff and parents at the Pen Green Centre: the Parents' Involvement in Their Children's Learning (PICL) programme.

Early years educators rarely have enough non-contact time to develop their skills as reflective practitioners. When we embarked on this research and development project in the mid-1990s, our vision for the future was that there would be many early years centres across the public, private and voluntary sector where staff could develop innovative projects with the same kind of support that we had received:

Imagine early years centres where all staff are beginning to be assertive, self-critical and supportively critical of other, where the staff are deeply attached to each other, work cooperatively, respect each other's strengths, and celebrate each other's successes and failures. Centres in which the adults, parents and staff are rigorous thinkers, focused and analytical, and yet aware of the rhythms of the organisation and their personal lives; where the work is rooted in the local community but staff also reach out, make their views known and challenge local and central government over important issues. These would be centres in which children's rich emotional lives were acknowledged and supported, where children were encouraged and cognitively challenged and their learning was promoted. In such centres children could truly become the managers of their own possibilities.

(Adapted from Whalley, 1999a, p. 336)

Today, as this second edition goes to press, there are staff and parents in settings across many local authorities working within the same conceptual framework in creative and challenging partnerships.

To my daughter Natasha, now aged 27 and very much a
'shining light powerful beyond measure'

CHAPTER 1

New Forms of Provision, New Ways of Working – the Pen Green Centre

Margy Whalley

The Pen Green Centre for children and their families opened in 1983. It was set up as a multifunctional service for children and families and was staffed by a multidisciplinary team. The centre was financed by Northamptonshire County Council and was jointly managed by the Education and Social Services Departments and the local health authority. In 1983, Pen Green had six staff and worked with 50 children; today the centre is a designated children's centre (June 2004) and has more than 110 staff, including teachers, nursery nurses, social workers, play workers, midwives, health workers and support staff, and we work with over 1200 families.

Corby, where the centre is based, was a steel town in the 1930s with a teeming population of steelworkers who had come down from Scotland and across from central Europe to find work. By the 1980s, when the Pen Green Centre opened, the steelworks had closed, the housing estates were boarded up, shops were barricaded with wire grills, and 43 per cent of the male population was unemployed. Poor nutrition, inadequate housing and high infant mortality rates were all major factors influencing the lives of young families. There were minimal statutory services for parents and young children and very few of the traditional voluntary services for families in need of support.

In Corby in the early 1980s, as in some parts of the UK today, there was no choice of services for parents wanting nursery education, childcare or 'time out' to study. There was no partnership between the public, private and voluntary sectors because there was so little provision. There was only one private day nursery, a small number of registered childminders and a few playgroups. The part-time nursery education that was provided in nursery units attached to primary schools was hugely oversubscribed, and these nursery sessions did not help parents who wanted to attend college or go back to work.

There was also a social services children's centre in Corby, which was perceived by local parents as a resource exclusively for 'problem families'.

The Pen Green Centre was set up in what was formerly a comprehensive school built in the 1930s to provide an education for the children of the steelworkers. The houses that surround the centre were once steelworkers' homes. Sixty feet away stood the last of the blast furnaces that had transformed a small Northamptonshire village into a steel town (Whalley, 1994).

Problems and contradictions

Corby in the 1980s exemplified many of the problems and contradictions inherent in education and day-care services in the UK at this time. These were some of the issues which staff at Pen Green had to face:

1 *Simplistic demarcation lines:* crude divisions remained between those that saw themselves as providers for the educational needs of the child (the local education authority (LEA)) and those supporting the child in terms of welfare and childcare (Social Services, the private sector).
2 *Separatism:* there was no tradition of working in an integrated way with other agencies such as health and the Adult Education Services, both of which have a critical role in working with children and their families.
3 *Over-professionalism:* the contribution of the voluntary sector had been underestimated, and the energy and commitment of the local community was largely unrecognised.
4 *Monoculturalism:* when setting up early childhood services, there had been no attempt to learn from other European countries, such as Scandinavia or Italy, where integrated services for young children have a long history.
5 *Europhobia:* the only 'models' generally recognised as successful in the 1980s were those that had been transplanted from the USA. There was very little recognition of the importance of a local diagnosis of need.
6 *Compensatory models:* because professionals who worked with parents were still assuming a 'deficit' model of parenting based on the premise that some parents are ineffective and that they can become more effective by being taught a set of 'parenting skills'.
7 *Political will:* most early years educators did not recognise the political nature of early years work and had little experience of engaging in political debate.
8 *Lack of accountability:* this was manifested as a general lack of awareness of the changing needs of families, and the need for flexible and responsive services. There had also been a failure locally to recognise the issues of the stakeholders' children, parents, families and the wider community.

9 *Poor conditions of service and training:* although early childhood educators were powerful advocates for children and families, they were traditionally fairly passive in relation to their own conditions of service. Staff were accustomed to working long hours with poor pay, inadequate training and little if any non-contact time to be able to plan and reflect on children's learning.

Working with the community

Pen Green, as a centre for children and families, developed from a perspective 'which regards early childhood services as a need and right for all communities and families, and as an expression of social solidarity with children and parents' (Moss, 1992, p. 43). However, this social solidarity was born, in the first instance, out of conflict.

When the centre was set up, staff had to work with a very vocal and often hostile group of people, since the strongest voluntary group in the local community was a parents' action group *against* the centre. This group comprised local residents who felt that there had not been enough consultation between those setting up the new early years service and those who were expected to use it. They were afraid that the local authority planned to set up a day-care service for vulnerable families, and this was not what they wanted. They were clear that what was needed in their community was a radically new kind of service.

The visions and principles behind the services that were set up at Pen Green were carved out by this 'local action group', local politicians, local authority officers and the newly appointed staff group. Their big idea, their vision for the future, was that in this small community there should be a service for children aged under five and their families, a service which would honour the needs of young children and celebrate their existence. It would also support families however they were constituted within the community.

This vision was underpinned by the belief that:

- the most effective way of delivering coherent education, health and social services to young families was through an integrated centre which would be easily accessible (i.e. at pram-pushing distance);
- services should be flexible and responsive to the needs of all local children and their extended families;
- education and care are indivisible, that the early years curriculum offered in these services should be developmentally appropriate for children aged up to five years and should recognise the central position of play in early learning;
- services should respect and value children and parents' individual differences and celebrate ethnic, linguistic and cultural diversity;

- education begins at birth, and services must recognise the key role parents play as their child's first educators, and parents' commitment to their children's early education;
- parent education and adult community education should be made available to parents *within* services for early childhood education and care;
- all the staff working in these settings need to be highly trained, reflective practitioners with equitable conditions of service, adequate pay, appropriate non-contact time, in-service training, supervision, opportunities for promotion, etc.; and
- workers in early childhood settings need to be concerned with power sharing and community regeneration.

Principles

The staff group appointed to work at Pen Green in the early 1980s were committed to engaging parents as decision-makers in the planning and implementation of work at the centre. They knew that working in this way was not about compensating for disadvantage. Instead it was about acknowledging the impact of poverty on the lives of local children and their families, and encouraging families to take an equal and active role in developing responsive services.

The principles that underpin the work at Pen Green are the principles of community education. Community education should:

- be concerned with individuals' capacity to be self-directing;
- help individuals to gain more control over their lives;
- be about raising self-esteem;
- promote learning as a lifelong experience;
- be about equal opportunities;
- be about pushing boundaries;
- be about constructive discontent and not having to put up with things the way they are;
- encourage people to feel they have the power to change things; and
- be about self-fulfilment (adapted from Whalley, 1994).

A one-stop shop

Chris Athey (1990) describes the conceptual gulf that exists when groups of people who lack shared experience begin to work together. The newly appointed staff at Pen Green adopted an 'open-door' approach, which helped to bridge the gap between these local parents and the new service. Parents were invited into the centre before the concrete was even dry. They shared the experience of transforming a derelict comprehensive school, which many of them had attended, into a stimulating and secure environment for very young children and their families. They shared the responsibility for establishing priorities, allocating space and developing the work. Over the next 14 years, the centre developed the following strands of activity:

Early years education.

Extended hours, extended year provision to support families.

Inclusive, flexible, education with care for children in need and children with special educational needs.

Adult community education and family support services.

Voluntary work and community regeneration.

Training and support for early years practitioners.

Research and development.

The centre became a 'one-stop shop' for families with young children in the local community (Audit Commission, 1994). What we at the centre provided for children and families was as follows:

- a high-quality, developmentally appropriate, early childhood education with care provision for young children;
- a place where children could meet, learn and grow; where staff worked hard to meet children's affective and cognitive needs; where there was appropriate provision for children in need;
- an inclusive service for children with special educational needs;
- a seamless provision for parents, with accessible adult education, health and social welfare services all on one site; the centre became a focus for lifelong learning in the community; and
- a centre where parents were engaged in an equal, active and responsible partnership, and shared their concerns about their children's development.

The changing political agenda

By 1997, the need to involve parents actively in their children's education was high on the political agenda of the newly elected Labour government. Two of the main reasons for this were that the role of parents as their children's first and most consistent educators was by now firmly established (Barber, 1996, p. 244). The link between parents' own experiences of the education system, their attitudes and expectations, and their children's achievement was also acknowledged as a factor of even greater significance than school improvement (OECD, 1997).

In 1997, the government recommended that there should be a fully integrated approach to early years education and care across the public, private and voluntary sector. Supporting parents and training parents were identified as major tasks for early childhood educators in all settings (DfEE, 1996,1997).

Early excellence centres

In December 1997, the government launched its Centres of Excellence programme (DfEE, 1997), offering financial support and defining standards for those individual centres or networks where flexible, high-quality, early years education and care were offered alongside education and training for parents. This government initiative acted as a catalyst, inspiring many local authorities to bid for funding to improve existing services or to initiate projects.

Pen Green was one of the first centres designated by the government as a Centre of Excellence. The additional financial support the centre received meant that we could increase our educational services to both children and their parents with new after-school programmes for school-aged children and for family education. The government acknowledged the work of the centre in providing local and national training: 'The centre is ... a focal point for training early years educators in the public, private and voluntary sectors and is playing a major role in the dissemination of good practice in early years provision' (DfEE, 1998, p. 19). Under the Early Excellence Programme, Pen Green was allocated funding for a new family education annex, which provided badly needed accommodation and space in which to set up our research and development work.

Education Action Zones

Another government initiative that had an immediate impact on the Pen Green Centre and on Corby was the establishment of Education Action Zones. Early Action Zones (EAZs) were set up to galvanise local schools and improve educational achievement. Most EAZs focused on work in the secondary phase, but some had an early years component. All EAZs had as a primary task the raising of parental expectations. Data generated from the schools in Corby in 1997 identified the area as one in which children were significantly under-achieving. Corby had three schools in special measures and in 1999 was declared an Education Action Zone.

Statistics showed that there were very few adults in Corby who had undertaken further or higher education, and this was confirmed by interviews that we had completed with parents using the centre. Eighteen out of the 22 parents who completed our interview schedules had left school at, or before, age 16. The majority of the parents who responded felt that 'school had not brought out the best in them'. Perhaps because so few parents in Corby had continued their education after 16, and because most parents experienced education as a disempowering force in their own lives, a culture of low expectations had developed.

Corby Sure Start

In 1999, the government introduced another major initiative, the national Sure Start programme (DfEE, 1999a). This programme was designed to offer comprehensive support to families with children under 4 years in disadvantaged neighbourhoods. A Sure Start Unit accountable to both the Minister for Health and the Minister for Education was set up. Identified communities were invited to prepare proposals for innovative multidisciplinary work. The programme had a strong community development strand, and there was an expectation that local people would be involved in developing local bids.

Pen Green became the lead partner for Corby Sure Start and worked in collaboration with all the other statutory and voluntary agencies concerned with family support. A particular feature of the Corby Sure Start programme was that large numbers of parents were involved in conceptualising the local targets and programmes of work. Parents who had been involved in Pen Green for several years became powerful advocates for other parents living in the extended catchment area that was the 'Sure Start community'. A parent-led needs assessment was immediately set up to assess the effectiveness of local services for the 103 new families whose children were born in the previous year. Parents were recruited, paid and trained in interview techniques. They constructed an interview schedule collaboratively with staff and then went out and conducted informal interviews (Pen Green Research Base Report, 2000; McKinnon, 2005). This provided rich data for the new Sure Start programme, data which were analysed and then shared with local agencies. Parents presented the data at local seminars and conferences, and professionals were able to use very creatively the constructive feedback they were given. Within a few months, professionals were already beginning to make services more accessible and responsive to families.

A learning community

By the late 1990s, what we had created at Pen Green was an environment in which:

- children, parents and staff were encouraged to be good decision-makers, able to question, challenge and make choices;

- there were opportunities for staff to become highly trained reflective practitioners, with good levels of support and supervision, in an environment where they could build satisfactory relationships and feel valued personally and professionally;
- staff consulted with and felt accountable to all the stakeholders – children, parents, staff, the local community, the LEA and local authority; and
- parents had become advocates for their children and were beginning to share their understanding of their children's learning at home with nursery staff.

Over 17 years, we had been able to develop a comprehensive parent partnership programme. More than 6,000 local parents had been involved (Whalley, 1997b), and staff had established a model of cooperative working that respected both the learning and support needs of parents, and the children's right to high-quality early years education with care.

Our work with parents was underpinned by the belief that all parents had a critical role to play as their child's primary educators. We were aware that young children achieve more and are happier when early years educators work together with parents and share views on how to support and extend children's learning (Athey, 1990; Meade, 1995). The belief that parents' involvement should be a key feature of any high-quality early years provision has been well supported in government reports from the Plowden Report in 1967 to *Excellence in Schools* in 1997 (DfEE, 1997).

The concept of a 'triangle of care' was developed in the Start Right report (Ball, 1994), which described a new kind of partnership between parents and professionals. Through this equal and active partnership, a secure, warm and stimulating environment could be created for children. Parents, for the first time, were described as having their own proper competence, and parents' deep commitment to their children's learning was finally acknowledged.

The Start Right report made it clear that the key issue for early childhood educators in education and care settings was to develop a strong relationship with parents as the child's first and enduring educators. The role of early childhood settings was to support parents through:

- exemplifying good practice;
- providing information about current research;
- offering appropriate parent education and professional support; and
- helping parents to develop and sustain their sense of self-esteem and self-efficacy.

Research showed that a large number of parents wanted to be involved in their children's early school experiences (Smith, 1990). The involvement of parents in the Froebel Early Education Project (1973–8) provided evidence of deep commitment on the part of parents, who were consulted on professional concerns rather than 'peripheral issues' (Athey, 1990, p. 206).

Research also indicated that children made significant gains when their parents were involved in early childhood programmes (Lazar, 1983). However, researchers were still unclear about just 'how' parental involvement actually benefits children in nursery settings (Meade, 1995).

Setting up a research base in a centre for children and families

Building on our long tradition of parental involvement, we decided in 1996 to establish a research base at Pen Green in partnership with parents, early years practitioners and researchers in higher education. We realised we had underestimated the enthusiasm which parents demonstrated for a deeper and more extended dialogue about their children's learning. We began to see that teaching and learning and curriculum issues, which had previously been the fairly uncontested domain of professional staff, needed to be opened up for a wider discussion with parents in the early years community.

What we needed was a rich and relevant dialogue between parents and nursery staff which could be sustained over time, a dialogue which focused on the children's learning and achievements and our own pedagogic practice.

CHAPTER 2

Developing Evidence-Based Practice

Margy Whalley

> I would like to see the research world opening its doors much more fully to practice and practitioners, embracing the messy chaotic world of the young child and trying to work with it in order to understand it more fully.

(Pascal, 1996, p. 5)

As a committed group of reflective practitioners concerned with both institutional development and professional development, staff at Pen Green had naturally developed a commitment to the research process. Because the service we were offering was innovatory, there was a great deal of interest in the centre, from social scientists and educationalists in universities and research institutions both in the UK and overseas. Staff, parents and children grew accustomed to being the object of other people's research programmes. These research exercises helped us to become better-informed practitioners. At Pen Green, the staff, like early childhood educators in Reggio Emilia and in Sweden (Edwards, Gandini and Forman, 1998), are convinced that 'pedagogic practice demands continuous adaptation and reflection if it is to evolve' (Dahlberg, at 1998 seminar). Although these research exercises helped us to become better-informed practitioners, being the objects of research, rather than participants in it, proved to be problematic at times.

Our early years curriculum has evolved dynamically over the years and is very much concerned with the 'researching child' capable of performing 'heroic feats' (Dahlberg, 1998). We worked hard to encourage the children to become effective decision-makers, able to reflect deeply on their own experiences. We also encouraged staff to become more reflective practitioners. Increasingly, because of their involvement with higher education and further education studies and our centre-based in-service training programme, staff took on small-scale action research projects addressing their own questions and concerns. These in the main were concerned with children's development and parental involvement (Arnold, 1990, 1999; Malcolm, 1993). Staff learnt a great deal from these small-scale research projects about children's well-being, their learning strategies and the importance of observation. They also developed a deeper understanding of the kinds of intervention that women valued as parents and why fathers found it harder to get involved. The fact that all staff consistently received high levels of support and supervision made it possible for them to receive critical input from parents, colleagues and visitors, and to be positively self-critical without feeling overwhelmed by guilt when things were not going well.

At this stage the decision was made that we should formalise our research partnerships with our critical friends from higher-education institutions and with the children and their parents (Hargreaves, 1996). We decided to start taking ourselves more seriously as practitioner researchers. During 1995–6, we established a small-scale, research development and training base with two key research posts. Funding, in the first instance, came from income generated by training and development work, and, subsequently, the Early Excellence Centre pilot, and from research grants. Over the next 10 years, the research base developed significantly. With DfES support, we were able to construct a leadership centre and research base on the same campus as the children's centre and nursery school (www.pengreen.org). This research base has comprehensive facilities so that Pen Green staff can undertake practitioner research. It also accommodates our growing number of MA students and participants on training courses and the evolving leadership programme (Whalley, 2005).

Our aims in our initial research project in 1995/96 were to:

- develop an effective dialogue with parents about their children's learning at home and at nursery;
- develop a style of working with parents that empowers rather than deskills;
- develop a greater understanding of how parents were encouraging their children to learn at home;
- compare and contrast the styles that nursery staff and parents adopt when engaging children in learning experiences; and
- produce materials to assist parents to get actively involved in recording and understanding their children's development.

Partners, not victims

Building on our own previous experience, we felt it was important that the research was not about doing things to people. We wanted to adopt a research methodology where the forms of investigation were enabling and participative. Young families and early years practitioners are both marginalised groups, often living on low incomes. A large number of the families using Pen Green had no choice in the 1980s and early 1990s but to depend on welfare benefit and welfare services. Bob Holman (1987) makes the point that research is largely about, on or for the poor and is rarely designed or written by, or with, the poor. One of the central concerns of our research was that it would help families living in poverty. Throughout the life of the project, we were concerned with involving parents as equal and active partners in the research process. We adopted a timescale and methodology that were acceptable to them. In this way, our research project fits the category that Holman (1987) defines as 'research from the underside'.

We also made it clear to parents that this research was not undertaken with the view that the parenting they were demonstrating was of a 'deficit model'. Our experience was that the parents using the nursery at Pen Green had a passionate commitment to their children. Their deep insight into their own children's development had often provided nursery staff with essential information. In this way parents had helped us to develop a more effective pedagogical approach, and a more relevant and responsive curriculum.

Our shared code of ethics was as follows. Research at Pen Green should always:

- be positive for all the participants;
- provide data that are open to, accountable to and interpreted by all the participants;
- focus on questions that the participants themselves (parents, children and staff) are asking;
- be based on a relationship of trust where people's answers are believed; and
- produce results which are about improving practice at home and at nursery, or at least sustaining it.

First attempts at involving parents, 1995

Our initial dialogue with parents about their involvement in their children's learning was fairly unfocused. During this period nursery parents were encouraged to keep records of their children's play and development at home, using diaries and video cameras. Small numbers of parents got involved. Often parents found it difficult to decide what was noteworthy. While a few parents made insightful observations of their children playing at home that were very useful for nursery staff, other parents simply recorded amusing incidents or family events such as birthday parties. Parents behaved like nursery staff when they first used the camcorder and tended to go for quantity rather than quality. That summer we had more than 30 hours of videotape to watch and analyse. Parents were also hungry for feedback. Although these vignettes of family life helped parents to maintain a creative dialogue with nursery staff and gave us useful information about the children's rich social lives, they did not help us to consistently support and extend the children's learning in the nursery.

Having a second 'shot', 1996: parents and early childhood educators engaging children in learning

With new funding from the Teacher Training Agency (TTA) (Whalley and Arnold, 1997a), we spent five months looking closely at the different ways that nursery staff and parents engaged with the children in the nursery. Initially, we worked with a group of 10 families who had already shown an interest in their children's development through discussions with the nursery staff. The families involved were all going to be using the nursery during the summer holidays and throughout the following academic year, and were all able to commit time to the project. They included employed and unemployed parents, single parents, reconstituted families where one parent was a step-parent, and married and unmarried couples. Eight of the families were white European. Two parents were from minority ethnic groups.

At the first informal meeting between parents, nursery staff, and research staff the parents were asked if they were willing to be videotaped settling their children into nursery and playing alongside their children at the beginning of the day. The parents were also asked if they would keep a diary (or make an audiotape) about how their children played at home. We discussed with them their willingness to let staff either video them at home or help them set up the video so that they could film themselves interacting with their child. It was important that all the parents made their own decisions about the nature and level of their involvement.

Developing a shared language

Teachers of young children could make a revolutionary move forward in developing a pedagogy of the early years if they recorded how they conceptualised and shared their professional concepts with parents.

(Athey, 1990, p. 206)

It seemed to us that if parents were to be able to enter into a dialogue about their children's learning, then nursery staff and parents needed to have a shared conceptual framework. We felt it was essential to spend time developing this framework for thinking with parents, not because there is only one way to think about learning and teaching but because it is critically important to develop a shared language with parents (Drummond, 1989; Dahlberg, Moss and Pence, 1999). Using a shared language, we could discuss the ways in which children learn and how adults can effectively intervene to support and extend children's learning. When adults intervene, they adopt a particular pedagogical approach, and this approach is underpinned by a particular philosophy. At Pen Green, our philosophy is that early childhood educators are interactionists (Bruce, 1997, p. 10). They base their interventions on careful observations of the children, they spend time watching children and work alongside them to support and extend their learning, they teach skills when appropriate, and they reflect deeply and make links between child development theory and their own practice.

When we observe the children in the nursery at Pen Green, we also do so from within a conceptual framework. We set up training sessions to help parents find a focus for their observations of their children at home, sharing with them our understanding of the work of Susan Isaacs at the Malting House (Isaacs, 1936), whose open-ended observations and celebration of children's cognitive competence had made a real impact on our staff group. In Chapter 8, this approach is described in more detail.

Deep-level learning

In one of the training sessions, we explained to the parents how we used the Leuven involvement scale in our observations of children in the nursery (Laevers, 1994). We shared our understanding of this scale, which is not designed to make judgements about children's performance, but rather as a tool to assess whether the provision that adults are offering to children is sufficiently stimulating to support and extend their learning: 'The child's closely focused attention usually suggests that a good match has been made between an adult's stimulus and some particular or general concern in the child' (Athey, 1990, p. 63). When a child is 'deeply involved', he or she scores 4–5 on the scale. The provision is appropriate and the pedagogical approach is supportive. When the child is scoring at a low level, there is something wrong with the provision; the adult may be intervening inappropriately or the child's well-being may be low.

Parents found these sessions fascinating and quickly picked up the idea that if their children were deeply involved, then it would be appropriate to record what they were doing, using the camcorder or their diaries. Chris Athey comments on how the parents in the Froebel Early Education Project responded in a similar vein: 'Nothing gets under a parent's skin more quickly and more permanently than the illumination of his or her own child's behaviour. The effect of participation can be profound' (Athey, 1990, p. 66).

Adult engagement styles

The parents became equally absorbed in a subsequent training session on adult engagement styles (Pascal and Bertram, 1997). The adult engagement style is a methodology designed to assess adults' ability to engage children effectively in a learning situation. It is described in detail in the work of Pascal and Bertram, who direct the National Effective Early Learning Project. Staff at Pen Green, who had been involved in the Effective Early Learning project since 1993, were accustomed to recording the way that adults in a nursery interact with children in terms of the degree to which they stimulate the children and the sensitivity with which they engage them. We wanted parents to have the same kind of information and understanding as staff about these *pedagogical* approaches.

In Chapter 4, Cath Arnold describes in much more detail the training sessions that we set up and suggests how these concepts could be shared in other settings.

What we all learnt: levels of commitment vary

Parents were given a lot of time and space to express their anxieties about the research project in general, and the training programme in particular. All 10 parents got involved on their own terms. Some could only commit to a few fairly evenly spaced meetings in the evening. Others were keen to keep diaries, make video recordings and work with staff on a daily basis. Our job was to use the time the parents were willing to spend with us to good effect.

We learnt not to make simplistic judgements about parents' commitment to the project on the basis of how often they showed up or the material that they brought with them. All the parents were deeply concerned about their children. We soon realised that we had to plan meetings very carefully around work shifts. Running meetings in the evenings with a crèche so that parents had no anxieties about childcare, and providing a meal to ensure energy and conviviality often worked best.

For one or two of the parents, this was the first time that they had become deeply involved in work at the centre. For example, Sardi, Zaki's mother, had spent enormous amounts of time with her son in the nursery and had become a regular parent/helper (she subsequently went on to train as a paid crèche worker). Abid, Zaki's father, was unable to spend much time in the nursery because of his work commitments. Abid had a deep interest in his son's learning and joined a group of fathers attending an evening course on early literacy issues. During the research project, Abid became very involved in attending evening meetings, sharing his views and using the camcorder at home. Some of the richest video clips that parents brought us were of Zaki and his father chatting in Urdu and English, and mixing up paste to decorate their kitchen (Figure 2.1). Abid clearly understood the importance of Zaki's 'rotation' schema (for an explanation of the concept of 'schema', see the Appendix) and was feeding his interest in stirring things with appropriate curriculum content (Athey, 1990, p. 203).

Figure 2.1 Zaki filmed at home

Sardi and Abid's video sequence shows Abid encouraging Zaki, then $3\frac{1}{2}$ years old, to rotate a screwdriver and attempt to repair a door hinge; he encourages Zaki to mix the paste (Zaki refers to this as making the dinner) and allows him to disassemble and then repair a trolley by unscrewing and then screwing back on all of its eight wheels. Each of the beautifully video-filmed learning sequences made by Sardi show Zaki on his own or, more often, deeply engaged in activities with his father.

When we completed this project, 9 out of 10 of the original families had sustained their involvement over the entire five months. Despite the fact that three marriages had broken down in this period, only one couple felt that they had to withdraw from the project as a result of this marital conflict.

Working in this way, parents developed strong relationships with nursery staff and gained new insights into their children's learning. Athey describes this as 'Parents participating with professionals with an articulated pedagogy' (Athey, 1990, p. 50).

The nursery curriculum also became much richer and more relevant because it increasingly acknowledged and built on the children's learning at home. Although we had previously made home visits, and knew a great deal about the children's social and emotional lives, for the first time the focus was on cognition. We began to know much more about what excited and interested the children and could then plan to support and extend their interests in the nursery to great effect.

The importance of video material

Videos of the children

Evening meetings were always well attended by parents, particularly when video clips of their own children were to be viewed and discussed. In Chapter 7, we look closely at the way in which parents developed insights into their children's learning and shared their understandings with staff through attending study groups and making and watching tapes.

Videos of the adults engaging with the children

Parents and nursery staff wanted clear boundaries set with regard to watching videos that had been made of adults interacting with children in the nursery and in home settings. Parents were clearly anxious that staff might watch the videos and make judgements or formulate opinions about the parents' interventions without having heard the parents' perspective. Nursery staff had the same kind of anxieties. They were very happy to agree that the analysis of the video should be a shared activity. However, once again, we had completely underestimated how much video footage the project would generate. During this period we made 24 hours of footage, and this included for the first time home video material.

The quality of these tapes was very high and they made rich and rewarding viewing. The children were almost always learning at a deep level. Parents seemed to have put to good use their training sessions on the Leuven involvement scale and made well-informed decisions about what was worth videoing. Subsequently, they made informed decisions about what kind of provision to make for their children in the home.

Since we were committed to offering training to all parents who expressed an interest in getting more involved in their children's learning we decided that it would be useful to produce a CD-ROM as a training tool. By carefully selecting video clips from home and nursery and matching them with a simple text, it was possible for us to communicate and share complex and dynamic ideas with parents (Whalley and Whalley, 1996). The CD-ROM demonstrated both the complexity and the intimacy of the relationships between parents, nursery staff and children, and the rich dialogue that had been established in a fairly short time between all the partners in this project. It is used in-house regularly by parents, particularly fathers, nursery staff and visitors.

One riveting sequence on the CD-ROM was made by staff who were allowed to film Sean, aged 3, and his father, John, at home. John first allowed staff to film, and then taught himself how to set up the camcorder. He made some gripping home movies of Sean learning to subdivide space by cutting up bread with a fairly sharp knife. Through John's tapes, we began to appreciate the extent to which parents were taking on their role as parent-educators. This helped us to put into perspective the relatively small contribution that we make to any child's life as early childhood educators.

When Sean was not in the nursery he was still learning all the time; his father took him on long walks each day with his dog. John carried Sean in a pannier and went on cycle rides to visit derelict manor houses, and to tea dances with the old folks at the home. He took Sean on trade union marches and down to the park as part of his daily routine. Challenged by other project parents as to how safe it really was to take his son to the park, which was full of 'winos', dog faeces and refuse, John responded that his son knew all the 'winos' by name and that he was bringing him up to be a socialist soldier.

Mainstreaming the work: extending the programme to the whole nursery, 1997–2000

We had learnt a great deal, and all the nursery staff were deeply committed to sustaining a dialogue with parents. We knew that it would be important to develop an approach that could become part of everyday nursery practice. Working with the parents, we negotiated the aims of the project.

Our aims for the children were to:

- value each child's individuality, enhance each child's self-esteem and identify the cognitive concerns of all the children in the nursery;
- generate stimulating curriculum content, particularly in areas that are sometimes neglected in the the early years, such as mathematics and science; and
- extend the impact of the research and development work to younger siblings in the home.

For the parents, our aims were to:

- encourage parents, to observe and understand how and what their children are learning at home;
- acknowledge the skills and competencies of parents and build on these to enhance our own pedagogical strategies;
- encourage parents to feel equal and active in their involvement, and to develop an information exchange as a two-way process; and
- provide accessible and relevant routes into involvement so that *all* families using the nursery feel informed about their children's development – fathers as well as mothers, isolated vulnerable parents, and parents who are traditionally 'hard to reach'.

For the nursery staff and other early childhood educators, our aims were to:

- make it possible for all the nursery staff to become 'practitioner researchers' able to debate issues among themselves, to articulate their understanding of theory and practice, and to develop a genuine dialogue with parents; and

- share the parents' and nursery staff's knowledge and experience with as wide an audience as possible.

The children's perspective

The philosophy of our nursery has always been that the curriculum should encourage children to have high self-esteem and a strong sense of self-efficacy, since 'children's expectations may be more influential in their learning than their ability' (Smiley and Dweck, 1994). Like Rutter (1997), we believe resilience should be seen as an outcome of education.

Children can become very effective decision-makers. They need to be able to plan and translate their plans into actions (Laevers, 1995). They also need to hypothesise and experiment. If we are to help them develop this sense of mastery, it is critically important that we take children's central cognitive concerns as a starting point for our nursery curriculum (Sylva, 1994). Children's thinking is characterised by their ability to 'conceptualise and consolidate' (Handy, quoted in Scott, 1997, p. 4).

Parents and nursery staff, who are important adults in young children's lives, need to be centrally concerned with the provision of a rich and challenging curriculum. 'The development of co-ordinating complexities of thinking must be cultivated and fleshed out from birth in the home and in the school' (Athey, 1990, p. 206).

Nursery staff worked hard to match their observations of the children with those of the parents. Each member of staff took responsibility for reading and reviewing the diary entries that parents brought in from home and the video vignettes that some parents offered us. All nursery staff met together each week and matched the parents' observations with those made in the nursery by the staff team. With both sets of information, curriculum planning in the nursery became much more focused, and we were able to respond quickly to individual children. Staff developed the workshop environments within the nursery so that children could 'service themselves' and access almost all the materials independently.

Autonomy

Nursery staff were convinced that developing a sense of autonomy was important for children. We worked closely with the parents and the children to develop a shared understanding of autonomy:

- an action that has been freely chosen;
- where the child willingly self-regulates;
- for which the child accepts full responsibility;
- which is based on personal conviction, and is not simply about obedience (Burk-Rodgers, 1998).

The Pen Green nursery team and the parents became 'autonomy supporting educators'. We shared the belief that offering children choices was critically important and that the choices 'should be geared to the children's level of involvement' (Burk-Rodgers, 1998, p. 77). We knew different members of the nursery staff encouraged children to be autonomous in different ways and to different degrees (Bertram, 1995). We also knew that there were big differences between rules, boundaries and the level of choice offered to children at home and at nursery (Nucci and Smetana, 1996). Staff set up groups to establish parents' views on autonomy and to find ways to encourage children to make decisions and choices in nursery. These focused discussions provided rich material for debate in staff meetings.

Boys being boys

Over a number of years nursery staff had noticed that from January to March, a small group of four-year-old boys would emerge who appeared to be less engaged and tended to behave problematically. This was often the case even when the boys concerned had previously shown consistently high levels of involvement. Each year, staff tried different strategies to engage these boys but without much success, and their behaviour had been interpreted by nursery staff as some kind of 'rite of transition', a need to be assertive before entry into primary school.

In January 1998, at the end of the first year of the 'mainstreamed' project, for the first time, staff noticed that this pattern of behaviour did not occur. The group of four-year-old boys due to move on to primary school in September remained deeply involved. We speculated that this was because we were matching their cognitive needs with a much richer curriculum content heavily weighted, probably for the first time, toward mathematics and science.

Becoming scientists and mathematicians

Over the five years of the project, the children's hypothesising became increasingly complex. We became aware that as early years educators we needed further in-service training in the areas of mathematics and science; relatively few of us had qualifications, extensive experience or confidence in these curriculum areas. As our understanding of children's home concerns and nursery concerns has developed, we have continued to make greater provision for science and mathematics in the nursery. We set up in-service training days in 1998 which focused on these aspects of the curriculum so that staff felt better able to respond to children's fascination with levers, pulleys, gravity, rotation, spheres and trajectories. In Chapter 8, we see the impact this had on girls as well as boys.

Pen Green discovery area

By 1999, nursery staff were working with architects, designers, manufacturers and educational consultants to develop a new science discovery area.

This was funded in part by the DfEE and through our own fund-raising efforts. Our decision-making process was heavily informed by watching the nursery children in a number of different settings. Initially, we took them, with their parents, to the Science Museum in London, where they investigated water channels and wheat chutes, and used conveyor belts. Subsequently, we gave the children opportunities to experiment with a range of equipment in schools and parks. For example, we took a small group of children to Chatsworth Park to experiment with a range of outdoor play equipment. Our children found the Archimedean screw too hard to turn, and staff discovered that the flow of water from the local stream fed insufficient water into the system for it to present any challenge to children. Time was well spent in reconnaissance.

Perhaps the most important part of this planning stage was time spent in discussion with each other as a nursery team. We knew from our extensive observations of children in nursery that what was needed was a stimulating and challenging environment, where, through effective interactions with staff and their peers, children's thinking and hypothesising could be supported and extended. Initially, we focused on concepts that the children were already exploring in the nursery and identified aspects of the new provision that might enhance their learning. We wanted the children to feel that they were in control of the new equipment and that they could make independent decisions about how it was used. 'Returning to the bedrock education principles, children need to actively learn, physically through movement. If they can't make equipment work by themselves, they become frustrated and the curriculum becomes one of "can't do". Self motivation is damaged. Autonomy turns to dependency on adults for help' (Bruce, 1999).

The physical environment was designed in such a way that through sound, light, texture and colour, children's aesthetic, kinesthetic and emotional needs were satisfied (Ceppi and Zini, 1998). In this way we celebrated our pedagogy and our understanding of children's learning styles through the architecture (Figure 2.2). This discovery area offered children a much enhanced provision, including a very deep and large sandpit with a conveyor belt, and horizontal and vertical pulleys with visible workings. It also contained a complex system of water chutes that could be dammed and flooded, and the water flow could be directed by the children. With additional support from the DfEE, we invested in closed-circuit television (CCTV) cameras so that we could record the use of this equipment, study the way that this new provision supported and extended children's learning, and consolidate and reflect on our pedagogical approaches (Pen Green/DfEE, 1999).

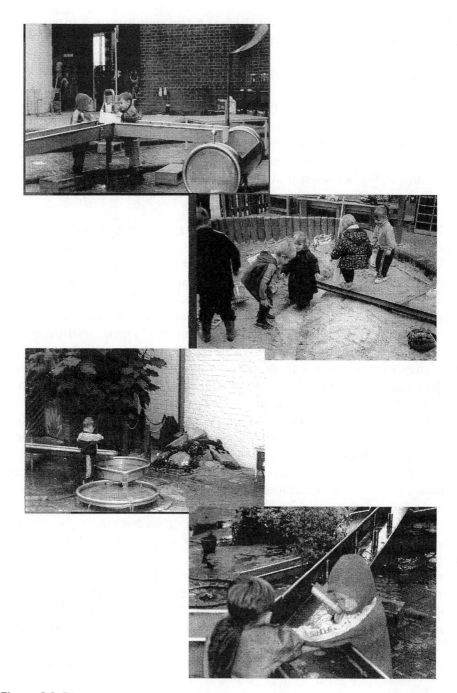

Figure 2.2 Discovery area

Supporting siblings

In 1996 and 1997, the project parents noted that the insights they had gained from child development theory and sharing ideas with other parents, and their own nursery children's learning, had a direct impact on younger siblings in the family. This impact on siblings was a strong feature of the Froebel Early Education Project (Athey, 1990, p. 56). As a staff group, we knew that 'rich experiences really do produce rich brains' (Nash, 1997, p. 37; Blakemore, 1998), and that is why it seemed critical to us that we should be making direct links with children from birth to 3 years old as well as with nursery-aged children: 'The early months, never mind the early years of a child's life, are critical to their life chances' (Barber, 1996, p. 244).

In 1998, by popular demand, two baby and toddler study groups were set up, and they were co-led by parents and staff who had been involved in the nursery parents' study groups. Both groups were called 'Growing Together' groups and were always full. Unlike the nursery parent study groups, parents attended the Growing Together groups *with* their babies and toddlers. These parents were offered the same training sessions in child development concepts as the nursery parents, and an additional training session on using the video camera.

Within each session, parents were encouraged to observe and support their children's learning. The provision included treasure baskets (Goldschmied, 1991) and heuristic play materials as well as water, sand and playdough.

Parents became increasingly confident in using the video to record important learning moments at home, and they brought these video vignettes to the session. Within the sessions, staff videoed interesting learning sequences and printed them out through the computer so that parents could take them home to show to partners or grandparents (see Figure 2.3). In Chapter 9, there is a full account of the work undertaken in Growing Together groups.

The parents' perspective

Parents using the nursery had demonstrated a deep commitment to supporting and nurturing their children in the pilot project. They had shown us that it was possible for parents who had everything stacked against them in terms of socio-economic status, lack of educational achievement and low levels of family support to become very effective advocates for their children. Since 'Parents' expectations are the most powerful predictor of children's later school success' (Bredekamp and Shephard, 1989, p. 22), we knew that it would be important to sustain and extend the programme.

Different parents: different approaches

Since parents are all very different, we were aware that we needed to offer them a range of 'ways in' to the project. Some parents had time during the day and valued the opportunities we offered to share problems and anxieties with other parents in study groups that ran for a year or more. In these groups they would discuss their children's cognitive concerns and share problems and perceptions regarding their child's social and emotional

Figure 2.3 Lucy's learning sequence

needs. Parents' diary entries, nursery observations and video vignettes of the children in nursery were used to inform these sessions. Sometimes parents would bring in the videotapes they had made at home. By 1999, 33 per cent of parents had borrowed the video camera and brought in vignettes of their children playing and learning at home, and nursery staff had made 10 videotapes and sent them out to parents when parents or partners could not come into the nursery.

Other parents attended a monthly evening meeting. We tried to make each of these evening sessions a self-contained discussion group. During the day, parents were asked to fill in a reply slip to say whether they would be attending that night or not. If we knew they were coming, then video vignettes of their children were made in the nursery. These short video clips formed the basis for sharing information in the evening session about their child's learning needs.

In Chapter 3, Colette Tait describes the many strategies we developed to encourage parents to take part. Nursery staff made no assumptions about commitment on the basis of attendance at meetings. We observed parents who, after attending only one training session, managed to maintain high levels of involvement, keeping home diaries, sharing this information with nursery staff, and video filming at home even when they could not physically attend meetings at the nursery on a regular basis. The issue of attrition was critically important to us, and we wanted to encourage parents to sustain their involvement over time. However, we knew that pressures of parenting, tiredness, anxiety, work commitments, and practical difficulties like access and babysitting would often create problems for parents.

Involving fathers

Getting in touch with fathers was sometimes a problem. We have always had a policy of regular home visiting before the child starts nursery, and then three times a year as a general rule. However, many of the nursery children were living in reconstituted families, and in several cases fathers had no contact with their biological children. In other cases, when parents had separated acrimoniously, fathers were not informed about what was happening in their children's lives at nursery. Often staff did not have fathers' addresses, and all contact was through the child's mother. Additionally, even where mothers and fathers were living together, some mothers told us that they censored information coming from the nursery because they thought it would not be important, or appropriate, for the child's father to be involved. We clearly could not afford to be gender neutral in developing this project.

Involving fathers or male carers is, however, a complex issue. Staff at Pen Green have had some degree of success in engaging fathers in practical ways in the past (Whalley, 1998). Encouraging fathers to sustain their involvement over time has been more problematic (Chandler, 1997). In Chapter 5, we consider in more detail the new ways in which staff have worked to consistently engage fathers.

Direct work with parents who are isolated, vulnerable or distrustful of 'the system'

We were aware in the early stages of the pilot project that some women attending sessions had an overwhelming need to talk about themselves and what was going on in their lives even when the group had as its focus children's learning and development. Since there are many groups at the centre which offer support to isolated, depressed and vulnerable families, these parents sometimes simply 'dropped out' of the research project and joined a therapeutic or support group where the focus was, more appropriately, on their adult needs (Whalley, 1997b). There was also a small number of mothers who did not appear to benefit from the experience of meeting and sharing with others information about their children's development. These women, although initially enthusiastic, tended to withdraw after two or three sessions. Most of these women had been excluded from school and had left school before the age of 16.

We sensed that it might be particularly important to engage both these groups of women, since they often had older children who were struggling and failing in the primary or secondary phase. However, if these parents were to accept any form of intervention, it had to be offered on an individual basis. Some of these women were experiencing extremes of poverty or social isolation because of drug usage, or because there were professional concerns about child protection issues. Others were suffering from depression, perhaps as a result of emotional or sexual abuse in childhood. Janet Shaw (1991) describes in detail the effectiveness of individual work with such parents and the importance of sustained home visiting. Shaw's work makes it clear that it is possible, and indeed essential, to encourage parents in these circumstances to become involved in their children's learning. In Chapter 6, Cath Arnold describes at some length interventions that worked with women who were fairly distrustful of the 'system'.

The impact on parents

All the parents involved in this project were asked to fill in a questionnaire concerned with the impact of the project on their relationship with their child. *Most* parents reported significant changes in the way that they responded to their child. *All* the parents commented on their increased understanding of the learning potential there was in everyday experiences. *Most* reported that being involved in the project had changed the way that they selected books, toys, and Christmas and birthday presents for their children.

The following account is an extract from one parents' feedback on the impact of the project.

Louise C:

At home Philip is very demanding. I have to be no more than a few inches away from him most of the time, and when I do get to be in a different room from him, he checks on me every few minutes. Since taking part in the research project, I try to find things that interest him, so that when I'm washing up or making the beds or just cooking dinner, he has things to do that hold his interest long enough for me to do what I've got to do.

Since the project started, I've learnt to be a bit more tolerant about the mess they make (most of the time). They have learnt that there are places where they can paint and draw (in the dining room), and that as long as they keep to the few rules that I try to make them keep, I allow them a bit more leeway; i.e. I won't tidy up the table if they are halfway through colouring or drawing a picture. I'll leave it until they get home from school.

When Allan and I were trying to work out what they would get for Christmas, we did try to link with what Philip did in nursery – we bought him a fishing game (which he plays with most days), playdough, lots of cutters. He also got a small parcel with stickers, Sellotape, glue, scissors and paper shapes. Allan wasn't sure about these, but they were a big hit. We also bought things they had particularly asked for but these haven't been played with as much. It has also made me realise that toys are not always the most obvious things for him to play with. Philip will often empty the drawer with all the plastic dishes, and play with them for a long time. One of the 'toys' he likes best, is the egg timer he wanted me to buy. He has had a lot of fun with that and it is never far away from his favourite toys.

Having the videos has helped to keep family and friends up to date. His grandma feels she misses such a lot since he started full-time nursery, it's nice to show her videos of what he's doing.

For me, it is good to know that Philip is no better or worse behaved than many other children. It is nice to know that other people have the same problems, and to know that your child is developing normally. I hope that he will continue with these friendships he has already made.

It has made me think about the things I do with the boys – I would never have thought to take Philip to the Science Museum, but he had a great time, and took in more than I would have expected him to. Keeping his diary has helped to show me how he has developed and grown and changed – although it is only by going back and reading it that I can see it.

It just seems a shame that there will not be a similar project at school – it would be interesting to see how he develops, but I can appreciate that there are too many children and not enough teachers to tailor a child's education.

For me it has been good to know that other parents get cross, upset and annoyed at their children and all that any parent can do is love their child always – unconditionally.

A catalyst for training and adult learning

Many parents who have been involved in the research and development project have also gone on to undertake accredited training in childcare and other subjects. Some have gone on to become childcare workers. Having attended a research study group for one to two years, a number of project parents have gone on to undertake a City and Guilds crèche worker course at Pen Green Centre, or to qualify through the National Vocational Qualification (NVQ) route (Pen Green Centre is an assessment centre for the delivery of NVQs in education and childcare).

For example, there were 10 parents in the Tuesday afternoon study group; of these, the following seven parents have gone on to undertake training or to run childcare services in a voluntary or paid capacity:

Rosanna – works as a volunteer co-leading a weekly baby massage group, has undertaken paid work as a research worker for the Sure Start project, and is now running groups for the Sure Start Project.

Dave – works voluntarily in the Pen Green nursery and has embarked on his NVQ level 3 in childcare. He also works full-time at night.

Lesley – has completed the NVQ level 3 in childcare and is now employed 15 hours a week in Pen Green nursery, working with children with special needs. Lesley also has paid work in the local primary school.

Carole – has gained an A grade in A-level English, has undertaken four weeks' supply work in nursery, and now has paid work in a local primary school.

Louise – works as a childcare worker at a local sports centre, having previously undertaken home study in childcare. She is a paid co-leader of one of the Growing Together study groups and completed her NVQ level 3 at Pen Green. She is now working full time as a member of the nursery team.

Eloise – works as a volunteer co-leading a weekly parent and toddler play session and has paid work as a member of the kitchen staff.

Tracey – has undertaken and passed A-level English and works part-time outside the centre.

The nursery staff perspective

Mainstreaming the work in the nursery

Our key concern as the research project developed was to see whether what we had achieved could be sustained and consolidated within Pen Green's early childhood setting. For example, by 1998, we had 84 per cent of nursery families involved in the programme. Not only were these parents involved, but their involvement had continued throughout the time their child was in nursery, and their commitment to their children's learning was sustained on transition into the infant school. Attrition, an acknowledged problem in many parent intervention programmes, was not a significant feature of this research and development project.

In the first year of the project, much of the research and development work had been undertaken by the research team and a small core of the nursery staff, although all staff were involved in a practitioner research training programme. From 1998–2000, we wanted to encourage *all* staff to become more deeply engaged in the project so that much of the research work could become 'mainstreamed'. We wanted the key concepts of training for parents, and the sharing of information on children's development from home and from nursery to become part of the everyday activity of the community nursery. Only in this way could we be sure that these important activities could be sustained beyond the lifetime of the research project.

At various stages in the project, staff needed to raise concerns over the increase in their workload as a result of the new ways of working. Sometimes they needed to discuss their anxieties when parents were hard to engage. It was also clear that certain staff were particularly excited by the project, and it was important that they had 'time out' to become more actively involved. Other members of staff, because of family commitments, pressures relating to other aspects of their work or personal inclination, were rather less engaged.

Having time to think and reflect on the work they do is critical if early childhood educators are to become increasingly rigorous and insightful in their practice. It is also important that the staff who work in the nursery know how to articulate their experiences (Drummond, 1989). When teachers do not have a clearly articulated pedagogical approach or a deep understanding of children's development, they may find it difficult to share information with parents and may perceive parents' questions as a challenge to their professionalism (Athey, 1990).

All nursery staff were allocated some additional time to make an extended home visit to interview the nursery child's parents, and to develop portfolios of the children's learning. Needless to say, the 'time out' allocation was never enough and was often at the end of an already very long day. When staff were involved in running study groups, they were replaced in nursery. Toward the end of the project, nursery staff who had also trained to work with adults were able to be paid to run the evening study groups through the local further education college.

All nursery staff were offered additional training in:

- video techniques;
- staff issues around being video recorded;
- ethical frameworks for interviewing;
- interview techniques;
- styles of engaging parents; and
- producing portfolios of children's learning.

The impact on staff

Members of the nursery staff who were asked to fill in questionnaires about what kind of an impact they felt the research project had made commented on the richer provision, the increasing in-depth nature of nursery planning sessions, and the greater relevance of the experiences we were offering to children.

Angela, a senior family worker (currently head of Pen Green nursery), reflected:

I feel that the research project has given a focus to some parents and helped them to understand their children's learning and it has given us an opportunity to extend their learning. Parents have been able to discuss and challenge our teaching styles and our practice in an open and non-threatening way. The families in my group who have kept diaries have recorded many of their children's interests and this information was invaluable to me when I returned to work after maternity leave. I feel most parents who have been involved are able to talk about their child's learning positively and with confidence. I feel that the children have gained and that they are having their needs addressed and catered for.

Trevor Chandler, the former head of centre, commented:

Through attending the weekly research group, parents have shown their deepening level of understanding of their children's learning at home and the nursery. Through sharing this knowledge and experience in the group they have provided play and learning opportunities for their children based upon their child's dominant schemas. One mother who has a child with special needs described their holiday where her daughter experienced so many different sensory experiences. Her mother proudly celebrated her child's learning. The knowledge shared within the group has been regularly fed back to the nursery staff and informed the nursery's planning which, in turn, has enriched the child's experience.

On the evening meetings, more fathers have been involved and they have felt included, and this has enriched their understanding of their child's play and learning opportunities. One father said, following an evening meeting, that it has had a profound effect on his understanding of his child's play and behaviour, and he sees his son very differently now.

The perspective of early childhood educators and the research community

As a centre we are committed to supporting and training early childhood educators from the public, private and voluntary sector both locally and nationally. For example, staff at Pen Green were involved in training over 5,000 practitioners in 1999 (Bertram and Pascal, 2000).

Setting up a dissemination project for this work has become increasingly important as the project has developed. Both parents and staff from Pen Green have been involved in offering training to others. For example, local playgroups asked for and received training in child development concepts with the CD-ROM that the research team developed for use with parents. Local teachers in primary schools in Corby have decided to set up small-scale projects, and staff and parents from Pen Green have worked alongside them. In Chapters 11 and 12, respectively, Cath Arnold and Kate Hayward describe the impact of some of this work in primary schools.

What we have established at Pen Green is a multifaceted intervention project with, as its principal focus, parents' involvement in their children's learning. Small-scale projects like this one rarely have the staff time or funding to establish and maintain a database, and record the research process. At a cross-departmental review of provision for young children (1990), Marjorie Smith from the Thomas Coram Research Unit and John Bright from the government's Social Exclusion Unit both made the point that it was essentially this kind of *process information* that was often not included in reports (Bright, 1998; Oliver, Smith and Barker, 1998). Yet this sort of information was of particular interest to organisations seeking to replicate good practice. This is why we decided to write up and publish the research and development project in an accessible format so that it could be used by a range of early years professionals. Through a series of national conferences and seminars, other educators have also been offered training so that they can set up similar programmes in diverse locations. In February 2000, a new Parents' Involvement in Their Children's Learning (PICL) video was completed. It contained vignettes of parents engaging with children in their own homes and parents and workers engaging with children in the nursery.

Over a period of six months, a team of practitioners, researchers and parents co-constructed professional development materials, which were designed and developed in house and then produced for dissemination across a range of settings. In 2001–7, the Pen Green research team began working with 25 local authorities in England and have disseminated this approach across the UK. Staff have also undertaken training and dissemination work in Ireland, Italy, Portugal, New Zealand, Australia and Brazil.

With the advent of the children centre initiative (2004–8), central government and local authorities are at last beginning to address the issues of transformation and change for children and families in our poorest communities: involving parents in their children's learning is seen as perhaps the most critical aspect of this work (Blanden, 2006). By 2010, we will have 3,500 children's centres – one in every community. If children's centres are to make a difference, staff in all these centres will need to be committed to developing the social and cultural capital within their local communities.

Staff at Pen Green are committed to a strengths-based approach, always valuing what people within the community offer, and building on it. Pen Green staff see parents as their child's best educators, and encourage parents to be passionate advocates on behalf of their children; from their first day in a parent and toddler group or when they start in the nursery, right the way through their primary, secondary and tertiary education.

In the 1980s, when we first opened the centre, professionals often talked about 'hard to reach families'. We failed to recognise the fact that in many cases it was services that were hard to access. In 2007, it is still hard for some parents to access services in children's centres. Mari, one of the parents that uses the services in Pen Green, lives on a New Age Travellers site. She recently undertook a study of the pedagogical impact of parents on the Travellers site on their children's learning; she celebrated the way that parents were working with their children in her own community. Mari had to draw our attention to the issues that sometimes made it difficult for other members of her community to use Pen Green's services. We had to change our professional practice.

If children's centres are to engage effectively with all parents, their staff will need to challenge traditional ways of working. Children's centres will need to become learning communities engaging with people respectfully and creating services that are so relevant and responsive that all families want to use them (Whalley, 2006).

Moving on

This research and development project has raised important issues for all of us. As we work hard to develop even more effective ways of working with children and parents, we need to recognise:

- the great untapped energy and ability of parents and their deep commitment to supporting their children's development;
- the importance of developing a mutual understanding based on shared experiences;
- the need to have a clearly articulated pedagogical approach – when we are clear about our own beliefs, we can share them with parents;
- the need to employ staff who are confident, articulate, well trained and excited about working with adults as well as working with children;
- that it takes time to establish an equal, active and responsible partnership where parents decide what interests them. Parents may write beautiful 'baby biographies' for a year at a time or just attend one session on understanding their children's educational needs. Parents need to get involved in their own time and in their own way;
- that working with adults in this way is always political; in Chris Pascal's words (1996, p. 2), 'we want to encourage parents to stop accepting their lot and start creating the world they'd like to be part of.' In the words of Paulo Freire, it is about opening up for parents a 'language of possibilities' (Freire, 1970, p. 68).

CHAPTER 3

Getting to Know the Families

Colette Tait

Our image of the child is rich in potential, strong, powerful, competent and, most of all, connected to adults and other children.

(Malaguzzi, 1993; quoted in Edwards, Gandini and Forman, 1998, p. 42)

In this chapter, I want to look at the many different ways we try to encourage parents to become involved in their children's learning. Over the life of the project we developed a range of 'models of engagement' to appeal to as many different nursery parents as possible. Firstly, I will share how we 'get to know' the families we are working with, and want to appeal to. I will describe the nine different 'models of engagement' we have set up, how we monitor the uptake of the service by parents, some of the problems we have encountered, and, finally, where involvement leads to for those parents who become deeply involved.

Family life in Corby

We recognise the fact that parents are not a homogeneous group – their lives vary greatly – and, therefore, the 'method of engagement' that works for one family will not necessarily work for another. For us to be effective in engaging as many parents as possible, we need really to 'get to know the families'. We also need to be prepared to adapt the ways we work in order to accommodate different families' needs, and also the continually changing needs of families. In one nursery year, the changes listed in Table 3.1 were experienced by the families using the nursery.

Obviously, a family experiencing marital breakdown and access issues will have very different needs from a family who have just moved home.

Table 3.1 Major life events in the family

Event	Number reported	% sample
Change of job	16	32.7
Major illness	15	30.6
Change of address	12	24.4
Separation	12	24.4
Divorce	6	12.2
Someone moving out	6	12.2
Access difficulties	7	14.3
Someone moving in	10	20.4
Birth	9	18.4
Recent unemployment	9	18.4
Serious accident/illness	4	8.2
Other major events	9	18.4

Coping with transition

At Pen Green we had a community nursery and a playgroup (Educare) on the same site. Over the three years of the project, we began to see increasing numbers of children 'sharing' places between the two provisions or combining a Pen Green nursery place with spending time with a childminder or a family carer. We suspected that children were having to cope with many different transitions on a weekly basis, and so we decided to find out where nursery children were spending their time each week. We asked parents to fill in a form (Figure 3.1) telling us where their child spent time each week, including sleepovers because of shift work. This proved to be a very useful data set.

It is important that we are aware of the varying working patterns of the families who use the centre. Table 3.2 shows the many different shift patterns worked by some of our families.

Trying to be responsive

When children are allocated nursery places at Pen Green, they are also allocated a family worker. A family worker would have 8–10 children in his or her family group, and would aim to work and get to know the whole family, and not just the child attending nursery. Before the child even begins nursery, the family worker would visit the family in their own home. The family worker would take with them a first visit/registration pack, which gives the family some written information about Pen Green. As well as form filling at this first visit, it is an ideal opportunity to start building up a good relationship with the whole family. During the nursery year, the family workers continue to regularly 'home visit' their own families (Arnold, 1997b).

Figure 3.1 Form to ascertain where a child spends time each *week*

Where and with whom does your child spend time on a regular weekly/fortnightly basis?						
Name of child						
Week I	a.m.	Lunch time	p.m.	Tea time	Evening	Overnight
Monday Tuesday Wednesday Thursday Friday Saturday Sunday						

On an occasional basis my child may spend time with: (e.g., staying at friends, grandparents etc.)

It is really important for us to know where and with whom our nursery children spend time. For example, some children spend every other weekend with their father or grandparents, and it is important for us to listen and understand who they are telling us about and the experiences they are having.

Table 3.2 Families' shift-work patterns

Shift pattern		Factories/workplaces
Three-shift pattern:	6 a.m.–2 p.m. 2 p.m.–10 p.m. 10 p.m.–6 a.m.	GoldenWonder Weetabix
Continental shifts (including weekends)	4 days on, 2 days off 8 days on, 4 days off	Oxford University Press Quebecor
Twilight shift	5 p.m.–10 p.m.	RS Components Finnegans Famous Cakes
School hours	10 a.m.–3 p.m.	CityFax Asda
Part-time	9 a.m.–2 p.m. 1 p.m.–6 p.m. 5 p.m.–10 p.m.	RS Components and many other local factories
Weekend shift	Friday night shift and Saturday night shift Saturday day shift and Sunday day shift	Solway Foods

At the beginning of the research project, we wanted to find out about the family context and the working patterns of both mothers and fathers. We set up a very basic database which would give us this information. This was done simply by a card index system.

Each card would show:

- the nursery child's name, date of birth, address and family worker's name;
- the mother's name, address and working hours; and
- the father's name, address and working hours.

This, of course, presented problems immediately, as many families did not easily fit into this template. What about families where there had been a divorce or separation? What if either mother or father had a new partner – whom do we try to engage? Should we concentrate our efforts on the child's biological mother or father, the child's step-parent, everybody – or nobody?

Figure 3.2 graphs the constitution of one family who currently use the centre. Once families separate, and become reconstituted families, it can become very complicated. Just who should we be sharing information with about the children's educational achievements and development? How do we define a family unit?

Parental responsibility: the Children Act definition

The issue of parental responsibility (PR) was one of our first stumbling blocks. We decided to find out where we stood legally. We arranged for a

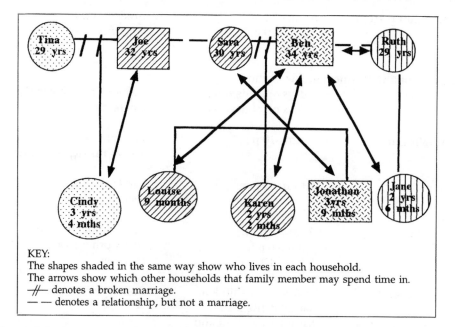

KEY:
The shapes shaded in the same way show who lives in each household.
The arrows show which other households that family member may spend time in.
—#— denotes a broken marriage.
— — denotes a relationship, but not a marriage.

Figure 3.2 How do we define a family unit?

local solicitor to come and hold a training session for staff about PR under the Children Act 1989 (Department of Health, 1991; updated December 2003). We needed to know if, by law, we were obligated to contact parents regarding their children; we also needed to know if, there were situations in which it would be inappropriate for us to contact particular parents. We felt very strongly that parents needed to know 'the facts' about PR. This training session was incredibly informative and enlightening, and lots of different examples of family constitution were discussed.

Establishing PR was a much bigger issue than we had anticipated. There were also added complications for the family workers – how would it be best to deal with the father who is known for his violent temper, and who, we now realise does not actually have PR? There have also been instances in the past where mothers, wanting to punish fathers, have told centre staff that they are no longer allowed access to their children, and cannot, for instance, collect them from nursery, when, in fact, they did still have PR. In these situations it was critical for us, as a staff group, to be clear about where we stood legally. We also realised that unless we were sure parents understood the relevance of PR, they would be likely to make the same assumptions that we, as a staff group, had made; for example, that the biological father of a child automatically has PR. We produced an information sheet for parents (Figure 3.3) telling them what PR is, who would automatically have PR, the consequences of not having PR, and, most importantly, how to obtain PR. Family workers then returned to families, armed with this information, to clarify the situation.

We added to the card index system a note about who had PR for each individual child. We still, on occasion, have to call the solicitor to clarify a situation, but, generally, all staff members and families using the centre are clearer about PR. This has made us more able to deal with difficult and sensitive situations, such as the biological father who does not realise he does not have PR.

So far, the database gave us some basic facts:

- who was in each household;
- the working hours of the adults; and
- which adults had PR.

What we then needed to do was use the database to monitor parents' involvement in the centre.

Using the database

We established this database early in the nursery year. We wanted to use it to find out how involved parents already were, and begin to look at ways of encouraging more families to become involved. We also wanted to develop other services or activities that might appeal to a wider range of parents. We needed to look at what was already happening within the centre and begin to build up a picture of the parents' involvement in their children's learning.

PARENTAL RESPONSIBILITY (PR)
Who has parental responsibility?

Parental responsibility (PR) was established in the Children Act 1989 and updated December 2003. Not all parents have parental responsibility.

These people have parental responsibility:

- The natural mother of the child.
- The natural father of the child **provided he was married to the mother when the child was born, or registers the birth of the child alongside the mother, or subsequently marries her.**
- Anyone who has a Residence Order which is currently in force in respect of the child.

These people do not automatically have PR:

- **The father of the child if he and the mother have not been married and he has not registered the birth alongside the mother.**
- Grandparents or other relatives.
- Step-fathers.
- Guardians of the child appointed by will.

What does this mean for my child in nursery?

- This means that at nursery consent forms can **only** be signed by parents with PR.
- That children can be collected by parents who do not have PR **but staff should have written consent** from the parents who has PR.

How do parents get parental responsibility?
Parental responsibility can be acquired by formal **written** agreement with the mother or by order of court. If you want to find out more, many solicitors offer a short consultation free of charge.

Figure 3.3 Parental responsibility (PR) information sheet

Building up a picture

When children start nursery at Pen Green, there is a requirement that they be 'settled in' for the first two weeks. This means that either a parent or an adult carer, perhaps a grandparent who does not have the same work commitments as many of our nursery parents, stays with the child in the nursery for this two-week period. As well as enabling the child to become accustomed to nursery, this also gives the parent or carer a chance to see how the centre works and what other groups and activities are going on that they may be interested in. We noted, on our database, who settled each child in. Of course, this two-week period also enables family workers to get to know families more closely and begin to build a deeper relationship with the parents.

Once all the children are settled in nursery, we hold four training sessions for parents on key child development concepts. These sessions are explained fully in Chapter 4.

These concepts underpin the practice in the nursery on a daily basis and help staff to look at how and what the children are learning. They help us to consider whether the nursery provision matches the interests of individual children. These key concepts have, over the last five or six years, become 'tools' that help us to understand and develop our pedagogy. They help to increase our awareness about how children learn and communicate to parents and the wider community information about teaching and learning. Each of these training sessions is offered morning, afternoon and evening, with a free crèche, to accommodate the working patterns of our nursery parents. Again, we monitor who attends the sessions and at what time of day.

At this point, reasonably early in the nursery year (October), we are beginning to build up a picture of the nursery families; we already know the working patterns of mothers and fathers. This enables us to hold groups or training sessions at times we know people are not working. We know whether adults in the nursery child's household have PR and we also know which parents have attended the key concept training sessions; but is this enough?

Parents' experience and aspirations

Although the database gave us basic information about each family's domestic constitution, it did not give us any information about the parents' own educational experiences or their aspirations for their children. Are our nursery children living with people who have had positive experiences of education themselves; do they have high expectations of their children – or not? We felt that we needed the answers to these types of questions, so we decided to produce a questionnaire that could be used as a guide during semi-structured interviews with parents. These would be interviews when we would hopefully find out the following kinds of information:

- at what age the parents left full-time education;
- whether they had undertaken further education (FE) or higher education (HE);
- what they wanted for their child from the nursery; and
- what they believed their child was getting from the nursery.

As we wanted parents to feel comfortable and able to chat freely while taking part in these interviews, we offered to do the interview either in their own homes or in the centre. We found that, almost without exception, parents asked for the interview to be carried out in their own home. We assume from this that the nursery parents are comfortable with the staff, and the relationships generally appear to be strong and non-judgemental. The questionnaire was produced by members of staff and parents with the help of Dr Colin Fletcher, then Professor of Educational Research at the University of Wolverhampton.

We held two training sessions for staff who would carry out these interviews. The training sessions looked at many issues. These ranged from the staff's concerns about potential child protection issues that might arise during an interview, to worries about how long to allow for each interview. There were, of course, many concerns and anxieties expressed by staff members about their ability to carry out the interview. Maureen, one of Pen Green's family workers, recalls, 'Initially, I felt quite anxious about the interviews, and therefore I really valued the training. When it came to carrying out the interviews, I really enjoyed them and still do.'

Therefore, quite a lot of time was allowed for staff to practise interviewing each other, in order to gain confidence. It was estimated that each interview would last approximately $1\frac{1}{2}$ hours. We also made the decision to buy in supply cover so that nursery staff were able to carry out their interviews without any added work pressure. Supply cover was 'bought in' for a series of whole days and half-days. It was then up to each interviewer to contact his or her families and book a time to carry out the interview, bearing in mind that only one member of the nursery staff could be released at any one time.

Mainstreaming the data collection

It became clear at a very early stage in the research project that the data we had collected were invaluable to the nursery staff. It is hard to remember how we managed without the data. If early childhood settings are really committed to engaging all the parents using their services, then this is essential information. Interviews were carried out three times – and some quite significant changes have been made to the interview schedule and the interview process:

1 The questionnaire has been refined and shortened. Some of the questions on the original questionnaire have been added to the registration/first home visit pack, such as the question regarding PR. This is because we feel it is critical for nursery staff to have this information at the beginning of the nursery year. We have also removed some of the questions which did not elicit any relevant information.
2 One particular question has been removed from the questionnaire and is now asked in family group meetings. This question was concerned with parents' attitudes to children displaying autonomous behaviour. We are particularly interested in this, as our nursery is set up as a self-servicing workshop where children are encouraged to make decisions and to be masterful. We want our nursery children to become 'the

manager of their own possibilities' (Laevers, 1995). This means that children as young as two are able to access materials with appropriate supervision and support, such as real saws, hammers and scissors when they need them. In order to gauge parents' attitudes at the beginning of the nursery year, we decided to show them, in a family group meeting, a short video clip of a young child using the workshop area in the nursery (Figure 3.4). Generally, once this has been shown, a rich and varied discussion ensues in which all parents and staff present get to air their views. This has proved much more successful than asking parents to rate activities on paper. Perhaps this is because it is far easier for people who are not confident with writing things down to become engaged in a verbal debate.

3 A major change has been in 'who carries out the interviews'. In the first year the interviews were carried out by family workers, the research team and the management team, but by the last year of the funded research project (1999), the family workers were very keen to carry out their own family interviews. This was almost a complete turnaround from the first year where the interviews were 'shared out fairly'. Family workers reported that, as well as being greatly enjoyable, the interview visits also helped them 'get to know' the interviewee's family more deeply. So, consequently, other members of staff only carried out their interviews if absolutely necessary, as, for example, if a member of the

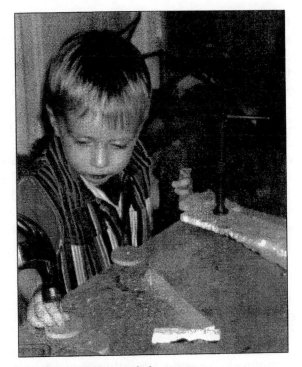

Figure 3.4 James in the nursery workshop area

nursery staff was on sick leave or maternity leave. This was a major piece of research and development work on the way to becoming mainstreamed nursery practice! This was very important to us, as it was our ambition to mainstream the project. We wanted to ensure that it would be practical for the centre to continue the work beyond the life-time of the funded project.

Using the interview information

Once all the semi-structured interviews were carried out, we needed to analyse the data. Each year, we have worked with a researcher experienced in analysing interview data with SPSS (a statistical computer package for social sciences). Initially, the data analysis proved to be a very frustrating process for us. The questions we had found most interesting and which had helped to enhance relationships between workers and parents tended to be qualitative, and, therefore, we were unable to analyse, with them this package. We were, however, very aware that we had gathered information which we did not want to lose, and so we had to find ways to incorporate the qualita-tive data effectively into the reports we produced. One of the ways we did this was by including direct quotations. This tended to give a real 'flavour' of our nursery parents' home lives, thoughts and aspirations for their children.

The quantitative data

From the quantitative data gathered during these interviews, we had a much clearer idea about the numbers of nursery parents who had experienced schooling as either a positive or negative experience. If parents have had negative experiences of schooling, they may find it hard even to enter the building. The centre is, after all, housed in the very school that many of our parents attended as children themselves. It is important, therefore, that staff are approachable and that the atmosphere is welcoming at all times. For example, we make a conscious effort to ensure that the rooms in which par-ents may attend groups or meetings are warm and comfortable. The chairs are usually arranged informally in a circle or semicircle, and there is always tea and coffee available for parents to help themselves to. To find out more about how we set up and run groups, please refer to Chapter 4.

One of the ways we try to 'make it OK' for parents to become involved, both in their children's learning and in the life of the centre, is by offering parents a range of different ways in which they can take part.

Models of engagement

I now want to describe some of the ways parents at Pen Green can become involved in their children's learning. We call these 'models of engagement'.

Attendance at initial key concept training sessions

As discussed earlier, these sessions are run at the beginning of the nursery year and look at the four key concepts workers use which inform the work within the nursery. These groups are open to all parents/carers of nursery children. They run in the morning, afternoon and evening with a free crèche. It is critical that groups are run three times in one day, as the varying shift patterns some of our parents' work often prevent them from attending some groups, such as those that happen only in the morning. If we only ran a group in the morning, some parents would only be able to attend the group every third or fourth week. The free crèche is also very important, as paying for childcare becomes prohibitive for parents on low incomes. This is sometimes a parent's 'first taster' of how groups are run at Pen Green.

Attendance at a long-term study group (Parents' Involvement in Their Children's Learning)

Parents have the opportunity to join a 'Parents' Involvement in Their Children's Learning' (PICL) research group. Parents are able to attend this group the whole of the time their child is in the nursery. This group is described in detail in Chapter 7, but, briefly, it runs every week in the morning and afternoon for parents/carers to attend and discuss with nursery workers their child's development both at home and at nursery. Parents are given a diary and are encouraged to make notes during the week about what their children are doing. They usually describe what their children are doing when they are deeply involved in play or when they are displaying schematic behaviour. This, of course, raises issues about levels of literacy – would being given a diary alienate a parent with very low literacy levels? We also need to consider the families we work with for whom English is a second language. Through knowing our families, we can hopefully pre-empt either of these problems – perhaps the parents for whom literacy is an issue, or those for whom English is a second language, could borrow the video camera, and bring a short video clip to the session. This is a method of information exchange that is always available to all families, whether they attend the research groups or not.

Family workers show the group short clips of video taken of the child playing in the nursery. This would be followed by discussion in some detail.

Attendance at an evening PICL research group

This group runs in the same way as the weekly long-term study groups but was originally only run once a month for those parents unable to access the daytime groups. It was initially set up to attract fathers, and it was advertised as a meeting rather than a group, which seemed to appeal to fathers.

We now run this group on a weekly basis, too, and have done so success-fully for the past six months. One of the fathers who regularly attends the evening research group comments, 'I wouldn't miss a Thursday. They usu-ally have a couple of minutes of video of him, and I like to see what he's getting up to.'

Individual sessions combining personal support, key concept training and information exchange

This model, again, appeals to a different set of parents. We feel that it is important to offer individual sessions for those parents who prefer to work in a one-to-one situation. Not all parents will enjoy being a part of a group – perhaps they perceive parents who attend groups as 'Goody Two-shoes par-ents' and do not want to associate with them. Perhaps their life situation is currently overwhelming, and focusing directly on their child's development, without taking time to talk about their own issues, is impossible. This model of engagement gives parents time to talk about themselves and their own family situation, as well as addressing the development of their child, both at home and at nursery (Shaw, 1991).

Home/nursery books

This is another very simple way of exchanging information with parents. A home/school book may include photos of the child in nursery with notes added by the family worker explaining what is happening in the photos. The family worker may ask for comments from the parents about similar things the child is doing at home, and vice versa. This book is, of course, something the child can show to his or her grandparents, aunties and uncles, and friends, and is something for him or her to be proud of.

Home/school video

This is an ideal way for a working parent to become a 'fly on the wall' in their child's nursery (Epstein *et al.*, 1996). The family workers would video a child in the nursery, and would perhaps add some comments themselves to the film to initiate a dialogue with the parents about the nursery child. This could then be sent home for the family to watch. As video cameras are used a lot in the nursery, the children become accustomed to being filmed and see it as 'the norm'. There is also a video camera in the nursery that parents can borrow, so this can easily become a two-way exchange, with the nursery staff able to see the child playing at home. For example, when Chelsea's par-ents sent in some home video of Chelsea enveloping (see Appendix) at home, the nursery staff were able to support and extend Chelsea's schema in the nursery, and support Chelsea with language about her activities at home.

Issue-specific evenings

Parents are able to attend one-off events. These events may focus on, for instance, mathematics or technology, and they tend to be run as interactive workshops, so they are quite a 'hands-on' experience for parents. Interestingly, these events have proven very popular with fathers/male carers. We need to find out whether this is because of the subject (for example, science and technology) or because they are one-off meetings, which have previously proven popular with male carers.

Trips to the Science Museum

Parents whose children are in their final year at nursery (some children attend the nursery for four to six terms) are offered the chance to go on a trip to the Science Museum. A group of parents, children and nursery workers would travel to London by train and spend the day at the museum, particularly using the science discovery area. This has attracted many fathers and male carers who perhaps, in previous years, would not otherwise have become involved in their child's nursery life.

Family group meetings

Family group meetings are held each term; this has been custom and practice at Pen Green over many years. They are meetings run by each family worker to which all their nursery parents are invited. This is a chance for parents/carers to chat, not only to their family worker, but also to other parents whose children share the same family worker. When arranging a time for this meeting, the family worker would look at the working patterns of his or her parents and would try to ensure the meeting was held at a time convenient to the greatest proportion of parents. These meetings tend to be very well attended and provide an opportunity for sharing information about the research project, chatting informally about child development, and, again, reiterating the key concepts used on a daily basis in the nursery.

The range of models currently used to engage parents is clearly very varied, and, as well as these nine models of engagement, there are always informal chats when children are dropped off and picked up from nursery. There is always ample time for this, as children are brought to nursery at any time from 8.15 to 10.00 a.m. There is no rigid start time. We are trying in this way to create space for as many parents as possible to become involved.

How do we know what's working?

It is all very well to offer all these different models, but how do we know what's actually working? This is where we have to go back to the database.

As explained earlier, each time an event occurs (for example, a family group meeting), a record is made of who attended, and this is recorded on the card index system. As well as recording attendance at events, we also note down when home/school books or videos are exchanged. From this card index system, we then set up a monitoring spreadsheet for each family group. This is updated on a weekly basis, so that we can see at a glance who is accessing services and which services are proving most popular.

During the first year we carried out this monitoring exercise, we realised, almost immediately, that there were not many fathers/male carers becoming directly involved. We decided that rather than second-guessing the reason for this, the best thing to do would be to ask some of those men why they were not becoming involved.

It appeared, given the conversations we had, that the fathers we wanted to involve needed a reason to come. All the fathers we spoke to said that, of course, they would attend their children's open evening once they were attending mainstream school 'because it's important for their education', but saw nursery as something different. The fathers did not want to 'share ideas about their child's learning' or have a chat and a coffee, which is the way in which we would generally advertise our groups. *These fathers wanted to know that they could make a difference to their child's education.*

Up until now, when we were advertising any groups or activities, we would send a letter or poster home with whoever collected the child from nursery. We decided to send out two letters/posters per family – one we would mail directly to the father/male carer, providing he had PR, and the other would be handed to the person collecting the child from nursery – this person was generally the mother.

What we also decided to do was to differentiate between the posters which we wanted to appeal to mothers and those which would hopefully attract men/fathers. On posters for women, we were generally more informal – inviting women to 'have a chat and a coffee' and 'share ideas'. On the posters for men, we included more factual 'achievement-oriented' information, which would hopefully reflect more traditional male values (Marshall, 1994). For instance, we included things like 'boys are under-achieving – how you can make a difference'. Figure 3.5 offers one example of two posters advertising the same event.

This approach has been successful, and we now always differentiate in the way that we advertise events and also always send information directly to fathers who have PR.

Developing our understanding of parental involvement

During each year, we have monitored the percentage of families of nursery children involved in some way. This has, of course, raised many questions for us; for example:

- How do we define the nature of involvement?
- Do we distinguish between those parents who regularly attend one of the study groups and those parents who make use of a home/school book?
- What about those families we are still unable to engage?

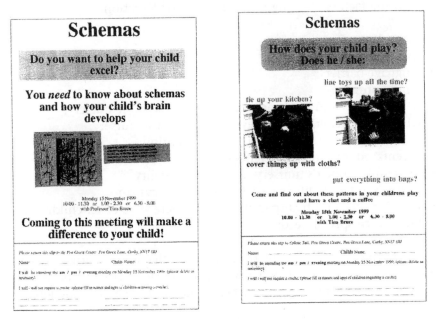

Figure 3.5 An example of two posters advertising the same event. The poster on the left is aimed at men.

We have used the same criteria each year whilst monitoring parental involvement in the project:

- Involvement, for us, is sustained use of any of the models of engagement. This would include the parent who, for example, only attends groups sporadically, but who keeps his or her diary on a regular basis, and discusses the child's learning with members of the nursery staff.
- We do not feel it would be very fair to distinguish between types of involvement – as we said earlier, not every method/model will suit every family. Even within one family, one adult may come to a study group, but the other adult may not be at all interested in that type of commitment. The other adult, however, may be very interested in technology and may enjoy sending and receiving videos of his or her child, or coming to issue-specific evenings.
- We have struggled with the fact that we have not been able to engage some families. This has been a relatively small percentage, approximately 16 per cent each year (approximately nine families per nursery year).

Parents who do not get involved

With hindsight, we now think that we had an unrealistic expectation when the PICL research project began. We hoped that we would engage 100 per cent of families, and were concerned when we did not achieve this. We suggested the following factors that might impinge on participation:

- marital status;
- the parents' employment;
- language barriers;
- family pressures;
- whether the child has been one or two years in the nursery;
- whether the parent had a previous child in the nursery;
- parents' apparent hostility to any intervention;
- parents' educational experiences;
- the family worker's (nursery nurse's) personality;
- changes in family life (e.g. sickness/pregnancy); and
- whether the child had special needs or there were other children in the home with special needs.

We returned once again to the interview schedules that we had carried out – it was apparent that many of the families were experiencing particular pressures and constraints. The emerging patterns that came out of the data were as follows:

- In two families, both parents were working intensively to create a 'better' future for their children. In both cases, this involved a culture change, that is, sending their children to village schools outside Corby.
- In one family, the father was working as a long-distance lorry driver; in four families, parents worked very anti-social shifts (one father was doing three jobs).
- Five out of nine of these other families had children who were only in the nursery for one year.
- Three out of nine of these families started nursery late and missed the critical two-week settling in the nursery period in September/October.
- Family pressures were very high in several families. These family pressures included caring for a sick mother, three families with special needs children, two families living in violent houses, one where a mother had just got married, one family who had moved house, and one family with a child with a severe health problem. In one family, both mother and father were learning disabled.
- In four families, the nursery key worker changed during the year because of maternity leave or long-term sick leave.

We have always been clear that parents need to get involved in their own time and their own way; nevertheless, we decided to discuss the issues of non-engagement with our advisory group. After lengthy debate, we have realised that there are some families who do not wish to become deeply involved. If we have been responsive, flexible and persistent in offering these families different ways and they still do not wish to be more involved, then we have to respect their wishes. We would, of course, continue to have informal chats with these carers, and share information about their children's learning in the nursery as well as ensuring all staff have access to training to enable them to work effectively with parents.

Different strengths of staff

As well as looking at numbers of families engaged (averaging 84 per cent each year), we have also looked at which model of engagement was most successful and which family worker had the greatest number of families involved in one way or another. This was not done in order to compare family workers pejoratively, but rather to identify training needs and individual strengths, and to celebrate family workers' achievements.

This data analysis was very interesting; it appeared, each year, that if a family worker was directly involved in the research project, perhaps as a leader of one of the study groups, then there were high levels of involvement from most of the parents in their family group in the research project. While all family workers spend one nursery session per week out of the nursery and working with adults in a group situation, not all nursery staff are involved in running the research study groups. (The range of groups run at the centre varies greatly from toddlers' messy play sessions to therapeutic support groups.) This was also backed up by the fact that the model of engagement which appealed consistently to the highest percentage of parents was the family group meetings.

From this, we could assume that if a worker has a 'vested interest' in a certain project or meeting, he or she will be more effective in engaging families. Although we are sure that 'vested interest' is a significant factor in a family worker's effectiveness in engaging parents, there have to be many other factors. For instance, some family workers' strengths may lie in one-to-one work. If this is the case, then they may not be enthusiastic about group work in the way that a worker who really enjoys working in groups will be, and will therefore be less effective in 'selling' these groups to parents.

This has training implications for nursery staff that need to be addressed. Although some family workers are good 'all-rounders', perhaps others would like to take up some specialised training. For instance, those members of staff who are very good in a one-to-one situation could do counselling training, and those that enjoy group work could take up more advanced group work training.

Looking at levels of involvement in this way also showed, as expected, that the members of staff least experienced in working with adults were least effective in engaging families within the centre. Again, this raises issues about staff training. We must ensure that all new members of staff are offered the same training opportunities as staff who have been at the centre for some time. It is important that training is reviewed annually.

The impact of 'getting involved'

For parents who do become involved in their children's learning, there are many benefits, relating to both their understanding of their children and their own raised self-esteem.

Over the last three years, we have found that parents who have been involved in their children's learning are keen to share their experiences with other parents. Louise comments, 'After learning about schemas and Leuven Involvement I became a lot more tolerant ... I began to understand why he was doing the things he was doing.' Louise and her family have obviously gained enormously through Louise's greater understanding of her son's development. Louise's husband, Scott, has recently become a school governor, and so will have a strong voice in his son's education in primary school.

Other parents appear to grow in confidence and feel more able to become advocates for their children. For example, Lesley said, 'I do feel more confident about going into Alice's school and asking questions.'

Many parents go on to deliver services, both within and outside the centre. As one father, Dave, commented: 'Due to my involvement with the PICL group I have been helping in the nursery on a voluntary basis. I have also been encouraged to pursue some formal qualifications in this field with a view to a career change in the future.'

Louise, who previously attended the nursery PICL group with her eldest son, who is now 6, currently attends the PICL group to investigate her three-year-old's learning. She also co-leads a Growing Together group for parents with children under 3, 'I now co-run a PICL group called "Growing Together" which is aimed at 0–nursery age children, and I find this very enjoyable and exciting – I love being able to share the experiences I had with my children with these parents, and also enjoying watching their children developing.'

Finally

Over the three years of the project, we have learnt that we must try to:

- address staff training needs as they arise;
- ensure that there is gender differentiation, both in the way groups are run and advertised, and in the types of trips and outings offered to parents;
- work flexibly and responsively, giving parents what they want and need; and
- ensure that there are 'different ways in' for parents.

It is important to continually reflect on our practice, looking at what is working, and what is not, and responding accordingly. Happily, the project has confirmed our very strong belief that parents are committed to, interested in and excited by their children's learning.

CHAPTER 4

Sharing Ideas with Parents about Key Child Development Concepts

Cath Arnold

This chapter considers ways in which parents can become involved in curriculum issues, describes the sorts of language and concepts the staff at Pen Green have been sharing with parents over a period of years, and looks at how to run group sessions and at what happens during those sessions.

Sharing ideas with parents

In 1990, Athey suggested, 'Legislation cannot decree that parents and professionals should work together to increase knowledge of child development or to work out ways of how an offered curriculum might more effectively become a received curriculum' (1990, p. 20). The notion of parents and professionals working together as equals on curriculum issues seemed a fairly radical idea when the Froebel Early Education Project was conceptualised during the early 1970s. The very idea that professionals do not have all the knowledge about the curriculum ready to pass on to children, and about which they can inform parents, was threatening to some professionals. For example, when my daughter started school in 1973, I was told on no account to allow her to do any writing at home, as she was going to school to learn how to do it the teacher's way. Even though I was a knowledgeable parent, who had participated in some teacher training, I accepted that the school knew best. However, Chris Athey and her team demonstrated in the Froebel Early Education Project (1973–8) that when professionals share information about the curriculum, it is helpful to the parents, the children and their siblings (Athey, 1990).

Professionals also gain confidence from discussing and articulating their practice in an open way with parents. Athey says, 'The greatest benefit to

teachers in working with parents is the spur toward making their own pedagogy more conscious and explicit' (1990, p. 66). It is this process of sharing
ideas about child development theories and also listening to parents'
detailed information about their own children that helps us to articulate our
pedagogy more clearly. As professionals, we are sharing our specialised
knowledge with parents and trying not to feel threatened by the fact that
the parent will often see what is happening more quickly and clearly than
we do. The recognition that the parents' specialised knowledge of their own
child can stimulate our thinking is part of our professional development.
The Froebel Early Education Project has been an inspiration to the staff at
Pen Green Centre and has greatly influenced our work with parents.

At the beginning of the twenty-first century, we have a government that
values the contribution of parents to their children's education. However,
parents are still viewed by many practitioners as 'helpers' rather than as
'equal and active partners' (Whalley, 1997b) engaged in the process of education. Unless practitioners truly value the contribution made by parents,
parents will continue to take on this less powerful role. If parents are listened to, their children receive the powerful message that their family, its
culture and values are worth something in the wider world.

What follows is an example of the sort of dialogue that is possible
between workers and parents:

Example of a parent being involved in the curriculum at the Pen Green nursery

> For several weeks now, a small group of children and workers have been trying to
> make waterwheels to use in our new water run. The water is quite shallow at its
> source, so we have been experimenting with making our wheels work at the narrow
> trough toward the end of the run. One very simple idea we have been using is to push
> lolly sticks into some florist's oasis. Jack (aged $3\frac{1}{2}$) is interested in objects that rotate.
> He has been involved in making and trying out various wheels. His family worker
> videos Jack involved in trying out the 'lolly stick and oasis' wheel and sends the tape
> home. Jack's mum, Donna, attends one of the weekly study groups, but we rarely see
> his dad, Tony, who works long hours. After watching the tape at home, Tony sends a
> message back to nursery: 'Why don't you try attaching little paddles to the ends of
> the lolly sticks? That would help the wheel to turn more easily.'

Tony, the father in this example, had obviously looked closely at the video
and felt able to offer an idea about how to extend and improve our experiment. Although we rarely see Tony, we are involved in solving a problem
together, which contributes to the curriculum we are offering the children
(including Jack) at nursery.

Practitioners are looking for practical ways forward. Many parents are
waiting to be invited to participate.

Ways of becoming involved

> Since parents are not a homogeneous group they all have different needs
> and different starting points. They will want to get involved in their chil-
> dren's early years settings in very different ways.
>
> (Whalley, 1997b, p. 17)

We have just heard how Tony is becoming involved in Jack's education at
nursery. Tony has already been present for a home visit from Jack's family
worker. He has also attended an open evening at the nursery. For the open
evening, the nursery was set up for parents and children to explore what is
available each day and to chat informally with workers. What the example
in the last section illustrates is a dialogue between practitioners and parents
about curriculum issues.

Parents are currently involved in their children's education at Pen Green
in the following ways:

- through daily chats with their child's family worker and other nursery
  staff;
- by attending sessions about key child development concepts (these sessions will be fully explored later in this chapter);
- by attending a nursery open evening;
- by keeping a diary of what their children do at home;
- by borrowing a nursery video camera to film their child at home;
- by receiving some video of their child filmed at nursery (like Jack's
  family);
- by attending a weekly study group during the day;
- by attending a weekly study group in the evening;
- by attending a family group meeting;
- by going on a trip to the Science Museum in London with their own
  child, two members of staff, and other parents with their children;
- by attending issue-specific workshops, such as science and technology;
- by attending individual sessions; and
- by contributing to a home/school book.

Sharing a language about the curriculum

In Chapter 2, we talked about the need for an honest exchange of ideas with
parents in a shared language. Any field of knowledge has its own language
or jargon. A specialist language may be a barrier to communicating with
parents. If we want power to be shared with parents, the first step is to share
any specialised language we are using. At Pen Green, we have been exchanging information with parents about 'schemas' or 'patterns of behaviour' for
about 20 years now (Athey, 1990; Bruce, 1997). Parents usually pick up this

technical language very quickly and apply it to what their own children are doing. We have numerous examples of parents understanding and using 'schematic language'. For example,

---

Sean's dad (about Sean's arrangement of his cars): 'Youse would call it infilling.'
Sean's mum (about Sean throwing a piece of lego that hits Margy's head): 'He's targetting a trajectory.'
Matthew's mum (about Matthew): 'It's all become so clear, just like curtains opening – now I know he's into trajectories, I can understand him much better.' (and about Matthew's sister, Amy): 'She's a transporter – I find different ways that she can carry things to nursery – a sling for her doll, a bike for her to ride on.'
William's mum (about William): 'He envelops his cars and trains with mud, then puts them under running water and washes the mud off.'
Levie's mum (about Levie): 'She likes transporting books – she irons them with her toy iron.'

When we share this technical language with parents, we also share our knowledge about how their children learn. It gives us a clear focus. So, as workers, rather than just saying to a parent, 'William has had a lovely time playing today' (which, in fact, tells them very little about what William has actually been doing at nursery), we can say, 'William really enjoyed building a vertical tower with hollow blocks today' (a more specific statement about what William has actually been doing).

We could choose to simplify our language, but parents might find that patronising. We can hardly claim a wish to be equal partners if we arbitrarily decide that the language is too difficult for parents to understand. Of course, we might explain that it was a 'very tall tower' and that William called it 'Notre Dame'.

As soon as we begin to share language about the curriculum, usually on the initial home visit, we are making our pedagogy more explicit (Drummond, 1993). Each explanation we offer helps us to understand the concepts more fully.

An example of making pedagogy more explicit

After working in the nursery for four months, Michele volunteered to show some students around. She was nervous at first but found that she enjoyed explaining about how individual children learn through 'schemas' or 'patterns of behaviour'. After the students' visit, Michele realised that, in helping the students to understand children she knew well, she had gained a greater understanding of how children learn and also that she felt a little more confident about her knowledge of schemas.

Although the dialogue with parents begins with the initial home visit (before a child starts nursery) and continues throughout each child's time at nursery, we do not expect parents just to pick up ideas in a haphazard way We plan and devote time to giving every parent the opportunity to learn about the key child development concepts we are using in the nursery. Some of these key concepts were described in Chapter 2. There are four concepts that we find particularly helpful:

- involvement (Laevers, 1994a, 1997);
- well-being (Laevers, 1997);
- adult style (Rogers, 1983; Pascal and Bertram, 1997; Whalley and Arnold, 1997a); and
- schemas (Athey, 1990; Bruce, 1997).

Using a group work model to share ideas with parents

Early childhood educators are in the unique position of coming into contact with children and their parents or carers on a daily basis. Because of this daily contact and a shared interest in the children, they are well placed to work with those adults as well as with their children. However, initial training, whether it is National Nursery Examination Board (NNEB), NVQ, social work, nursing or teacher training, does not usually prepare early educators for working with adults. Therefore, workers do need to undertake some group work training. This kind of training is offered to all staff at Pen Green on a regular basis.

When planning the curriculum for young children, educators use a constructivist approach to consider what each child brings to the learning situation (Athey, 1990, p. 43). In a similar way, we need to consider the rich experiences that adults bring to any learning situation and to adopt a 'person-centred' approach to adult education (Whitaker, 1986, p. 277). Whitaker says, 'Experience of small group work had led me to the belief in the power of groups to provide a particularly rich and creative learning environment for human growth' (*ibid.*, p. 276). He goes on to describe ways in which adults can 'share and draw on the considerable knowledge, experience and expertise present in the group' (*ibid.*, p. 278).

The Open University course team, in its notes to group leaders, refers to 'learner-centred study groups' (Whalley, 1996b, p. 7): 'This way of working acknowledges the fact that adult learners are not simply empty vessels waiting passively to be filled; they are highly motivated mature learners who bring an enormous amount of life experiences to each study group.' The study groups we have set up at Pen Green, as part of the Parents' Involvement in their Children's Learning (PICL) project, are discussion groups during which parents 'compare notes with nursery staff and watch video tapes of their children playing in nursery and at home' (Whalley, 1997b, p. 17). We are trying to create an environment in which 'adults reflect on their own past experiences, relate their present to their past experiences and access new information' (Whalley, 1996b, p. 7). Within this type of environment, there are 'tangible gains' for the leaders as well as for the group members.

Creating an environment and planning a session

We have several important practical issues to consider when planning to run sessions for parents on key concepts.

Timing

Parents are most keen to know about their children's development when the children have just started nursery (Arnold, 1997a). Therefore, it is crucial to arrange to run our training sessions during the first month or six weeks. These initial sessions are an important foundation on which to base our ongoing dialogue with the parents.

Time of day is also important. In order to give each parent an opportunity to attend each session, we run each session three times a day, that is, morning, afternoon or evening. (Parents have been known to attend more than one session on schemas in a day; they found it so enlightening they came back for more!)

Crèche

We always offer parents a crèche for their children. This enables them to participate in the sessions without distractions. We are also flexible about having children in with us during the sessions if they do not settle in crèche. (One little boy, James, clearly revealed his strong 'rotation' schema during an evening session in which we were using the carousel projector. He peered at the projector from every angle and was mesmerised by it each time it moved. This, along with the information his mum shared with the group about his interests at home, confirmed his strong interest in 'rotation'.)

Invitations to attend

We gather information about parental responsibility and send out two invitations, one to the child's mother and one to the child's father. Word of mouth is important, because parents usually want to know more than is on the initial letter or poster. This also helps us to make sure we include everyone, whatever their level of literacy. Each family worker talks to the parents of the children in their family group about the sessions. We might also have a large poster in the nursery so that parents can sign up and book crèche facilities.

Setting up the room

Comfortable armchairs arranged in a circle help parents to relax. (If armchairs are not available, adult-sized chairs will do.) We try to make the room more like a living room than a classroom. It is important to have tea and coffee available and to make drinks for parents as they arrive.

Planning the sessions

We have found that groups ran more smoothly if two workers run each session. The content delivery needs to be planned well in advance. However detailed and meticulous the planning, it is very important to be flexible and to allow plenty of time for parents to express their views. This is often the first time the parents have returned to an 'educational environment' since they left school, and strong feelings about school often emerge in the group. Although parents may themselves have had poor experience of the education system, most are clear that they want their children to succeed. If, as workers, we do not allow parents to express their views freely, they may continue to experience the system as letting them down in some way. This is particularly relevant in Corby, where very few adults have experienced further or higher education.

The group leaders can consider in advance what is likely to happen during the initial meeting of the group. Like any small group, to be effective, the group has to work on at least two levels:

- group task – tackling the business of the group; and
- group process – satisfying social needs and meeting people's needs for acceptance, recognition, belonging, etc. (Whalley, 1996b, p. 11).

Training in group work prepares us to think about what to do if a group member completely dominates the session or seems not to participate at all. The two workers can agree beforehand to take on different roles during the session. One can lead and try to keep the group on task, while the other can support individual parents and make sure that quieter parents are heard. Rather than the two workers sitting together, it can be more enabling for group members if the two leaders are part of the group. Sitting alongside a parent, who might be vulnerable, is a helpful strategy.

However well we have planned the content of the group in advance, each group takes on a dynamic of its own which no one can anticipate. This makes each session exciting and interesting for everyone involved.

A typical session

Each of the initial key concept sessions begins with one of the group leaders introducing himself or herself and trying to put parents at their ease. Humour might be appropriate; for example, if everything has gone wrong for the leader that day, she might share that with the group. If anyone in the room is worried about leaving their child in the crèche, they will be offered reassurance. Children are always brought back to parents within five minutes if they do not settle. This sets the tone for the group. The leaders can demonstrate that whatever is important to the group members is important to the whole group.

One of the leaders then asks each parent to introduce themselves to the rest of the group and perhaps say something about their own child. Occasionally, parents are reluctant to do this, and we must accept their decision. If they agree to introduce themselves, then the ice is broken and they have spoken in the group for the first time. People can get quite anxious waiting for their turn.

For these initial key concept sessions, we try to engage as many parents as possible. The study groups work best with 8 to 10 members, as borne out by the research. According to Mullins (1989, p. 376), 'cohesiveness becomes more difficult to achieve when a group exceeds 10–12 members.' If the group is larger than the optimum number, it works better to ask each person to move around the room and introduce themselves individually to other group members. This is less threatening and can be fun, but may take longer. During each session, one of the group leaders introduces the theory underpinning the concept to be covered in that session.

Session 1: involvement

The involvement session begins with a brief introduction to the work of Professor Ferre Laevers and the theory underpinning the concept of 'involvement'. Laevers's work is well established and rigorous, and it is particularly accessible to early years workers. We have found that parents readily take on these ideas.

The important point to convey to parents is that Laevers has been looking at the processes of learning as well as the outcomes or products. He is interested in what is happening inside children as they learn. He has developed a scale and signals to describe how 'involved' each child is in what they are doing at any given moment (Laevers, 1997). Being deeply involved means that a child is developing and learning, and that fundamental changes are occurring.

At that point in the session, we show some of our own nursery video of a child deeply involved. A favourite clip is Lynsey mixing pasta, water and other materials at a table. As she moves her arm across the table, she knocks a metal pan to the floor. It clatters but she is not distracted from what she is doing. We then ask the parents to discuss Lynsey's level of involvement. We might contrast that clip with a piece of video where a child is less involved, as, for example, when an adult is taking too strong a lead and not noticing what the child really wants to do. Some discussion of the concept of 'involvement' would follow. This is often when parents begin to relate their experiences of their own child to more general child development theory.

Next we hand out sheets outlining signals and levels of involvement. Laevers (1997, p. 19) says,

We speak about involvement when children (or adults) are 'intensely engaged in an activity. They are in a special state. They are concentrating and are eager to continue with the activity. They feel intrinsically moti-vated to carry on, because the activity falls in with what they want to learn and know.' (Laevers, 1997)

The signs of involvement Laevers has identified are:

- concentration;
- energy;
- complexity and creativity;
- facial expression and composure;
- persistence;
- precision;
- reaction time;
- verbal expression; and
- satisfaction (*ibid.*, pp. 20–1).

Not all of the signals would necessarily be present at once, though four or five of the signals are usually apparent when a child (or adult) is deeply involved. The signals are considered alongside 'a continuum ranging from "no activity at all" (level 1) to "total implication in the activity" (level 5)' (Laevers, 1994b, p. 163). Further discussion with the parents would then follow. We emphasise the point that when we are rating a child's involve-ment, we are not judging the child, but we are judging the provision we offer them at nursery.

An example of providing for a child's needs and using his involvement as a gauge

When Geoffrey started nursery, he appeared to 'flit' from one area to another and was constantly 'on the move'. After observing him closely, we realised that he spent a great deal of his time 'checking out' what was on offer in each area of the nursery. He was rarely judged to be 'deeply involved'. We noticed, however, that he spent up to five min-utes and displayed some of the signals of involvement when playing in the sand. We used this information to collect resources and to set up a 'site office', with hard hats, vehicles, sand, gravel, spades, guttering, mobile phone, clipboard, tape measure and spirit level. We took Geoffrey and other children on a visit to a building site. Subsequently, Geoffrey began to play for longer periods of time and to become involved in more complex play, such as role-playing 'being a builder'. Eventually, he began to cooperate with other chil-dren and to extend his sustained play to other areas of the nursery.

We point out that when children are deeply involved (that is at levels 4–5,) they are really developing and learning. This is the perfect time to observe children and to capture on video or write down what they are doing. If children are deeply involved, then the learning experience is obviously important to them and therefore gives us a clue as to what to offer them next. Involvement comes in peaks and troughs. Each child has his or her own rhythm (Arnold, 1997a). While we would not expect children or adults to be deeply involved all the time, if we never see children deeply involved, we must look at how we are supporting their learning. Children do need to be challenged. 'Involvement only occurs somewhere between "being able to do something" and "not yet being able to do something"; "understanding something" and "being on the verge of understanding"' (Laevers, 1997, p. 20).

If there is time toward the end of the session, the group would practise rating levels of involvement using short video clips. This could be individually or in pairs. As a group, we could think about what we, as adults, become deeply involved in. If we can empathise with children, that will help us to understand and to encourage the children in what is important to them.

Session 2: well-being

Introductions are an important beginning to all of the sessions. Sometimes the group will consist of the same people; at other times, new people may arrive. Some parents work shifts and have to attend sessions at different times of day and so join different groups each week. Beginning in the same way each time establishes a kind of format, and the predictability of using a similar format is comforting for some parents and workers. It may be that parents who refused point-blank to say anything during the first session will feel more confident when they come to the second session purely because they know the sorts of things other people say.

After the introductions, we ask parents to think back to their own childhoods and to think about a time or times when they were happy. After a few minutes' reflecting on this, we ask each member of the group to share their memories with the person next to them. As workers, we participate in this exercise, being sensitive to particularly shy parents or to parents who may feel left out. If a parent is new to the Pen Green Centre or has a special need, the workers will watch to see whether another parent moves to include this new parent. If no other parent includes the new parent, usually because there is an odd number of people in the group, then one of the workers will pair with him or her. When the talking dies down (usually after 10 minutes or so), we ask people to share their memories with the large group. We are always clear that there is no requirement to share these memories with the large group. For some people, this exercise can be distressing. One parent, for example, could remember no happy times during her childhood. We were able to offer her an opportunity to explore her feelings further, if she wished to, with the counsellor who comes into the centre once a week to work with individual parents or workers.

Using ideas generated in the group, we jot down some key words and phrases on a flip chart, such as 'holidays', 'the fair', and 'playing out with my friends', and 'playing shops on my own'. (Sadly, few people mention school.) After sharing memories of the experiences, we try to remember and identify the feelings associated with those experiences, such as 'excitement', 'being in charge', 'exhilaration' and 'contentment'.

When members of the group have explored their own ideas about feelings associated with happy times, one of the workers introduces the work that Laevers has been carrying out on children's emotional 'well-being' (Laevers, 1997, p. 17). The workers at Pen Green have met Laevers and have been impressed with his value base. We have found that his theory of the concept of 'well-being' is one on which we can operate. The emotional well-being of their children is always a concern of parents and carers, especially when children are starting to attend nursery or any new setting.

Laevers is interested in what is going on inside children while they are learning. Many factors can stop children from being able to learn. The way that Laevers describes the inability to learn is through each child's 'level of well-being' (Laevers, 1997, 15). He says that 'the level of well-being in children indicates how they are doing emotionally' (ibid.). Once again, we are looking at how well we, in the nursery, are meeting the needs of individual children. 'The degree of well-being shows us how much the educational environment succeeds in helping the child to feel at home, to be her/himself, to remain in contact with her/himself and have her/his emotional needs (the need for attention, recognition, competence ...) fulfilled' (Laevers, 1994b, p. 5). Laevers comments that 'crying is not necessarily an indication of low well-being' (Laevers, 1995). Crying may mean that children are in touch with their own feelings.

Laevers has identified 'a number of characteristics in a child's behaviour' to which we might refer in order to assess each child's well-being. Not all of the characteristics need to be present for a child to be at a high level of well-being. At least half of the signals being present indicate a high level of well-being. These are the signals:

- openness and receptivity;
- flexibility;
- self-confidence and self-esteem;
- being able to defend oneself and self-esteem;
- vitality;
- relaxation and inner peace;
- enjoyment without restraints; and
- being in close contact with one's inner self (Laevers, 1997, pp. 18–19).

Some of the signals link closely with our own work on the programme 'Learning to be Strong: Assertiveness for Under-fives'. Whalley (1994, p. 78) says, 'Our concern with children's emotional needs also led us to watch the withdrawn, vulnerable children in the nursery more carefully. We became more and more aware that these children had few strategies for coping with anger or hostility from their peers.'

In 1986, we began working with children in small groups, using role-play to explore ideas about friendships, bullying, boundaries, strangers and feelings. Now we routinely offer children an opportunity to express their feelings and fears, to learn some new strategies, and to practise using these strategies in a safe environment with the support of adults.

At this point in the key concept session, we give parents a handout listing Laevers's signals for well-being. We discuss each one in more detail and compare them with the feelings the group had identified that day. We hope that parents will discuss well-being in relation to their own children. Again, this can be a tricky issue. It is often easier for parents to reflect on the fact that their child's well-being was low two months ago because the dog died, than it is to talk about a child whose well-being is low today because of a family row.

We hope that we are giving parents permission to express their feelings about their children or about themselves. We are certainly saying that each child's emotional well-being is the foundation on which their education is built.

We discuss strategies for helping young children to express their feelings. We have a good selection of storybooks in the nursery that deal with a range of feelings, and we can suggest suitable stories that parents might then use. A parent mentioned that her child was scared that Santa Claus would come into her bedroom. *Worried Arthur* by Joan Stimson (1995) deals with this issue and even describes a strategy, that is, leaving Santa a note saying, 'Please if it is at all possible, as my bedroom is a little untidy ... could you leave any presents just here?' This parent borrowed the book to read to her child and found it very helpful.

This session might also alert us to the fact that a parent has painful, unresolved feelings. We can acknowledge this afterward with the parent and make sure that this parent knows that professional help is available. We can recommend organisations or individual counsellors if the parent is ready to seek help.

Session 3: adult style

After the introductions, one of the group workers introduces the idea that the engagement style adopted by adults affects how children learn. We begin by introducing the descriptions of adult style used in the Effective Early Learning Project at University College Worcester (Pascal and Bertram, 1997).

Rogers drew attention to the 'facilitative attitudes' of some therapists as perceived by their clients: 'When clients in therapy perceived their therapists as rating high in genuineness, prizing and empathetic understanding, self-learning and therapeutic change were facilitated' (Rogers, 1983, p. 128).

The facilitative styles adopted by the Effective Early Learning Project are

- stimulation;
- sensitivity; and
- autonomy.

We offer brief descriptions, and then watch some of our own video clips and discuss the styles being used by different educators. Extremes are useful in order to illustrate the differences in style of individual members of staff. We have one clip, filmed on a visit to a European nursery, in which an adult leans over from behind a child and places the child's hands on its collage. It is obvious that the child has very little autonomy. One father compared this with his experience at Corby police station when he was arrested and had his fingerprints taken! We have generally found it less threatening to discuss the styles of people we do not know or are never likely to meet.

Another clip shows one of our own workers working in the block area with two two-year-olds. She works at the children's level (physically) and moves between the three styles with amazing skill, encouraging the two children to cooperate in some shared building, keeping them safe while encouraging them to move to the edge of their capabilities. The children's involvement in this joint venture is sustained for 20 minutes.

Usually, there is a great deal of discussion and sometimes disagreement about what individuals think is happening in the video clips. A wide range of opinions are usually expressed about autonomy. One parent recently commented, 'I can understand you not allowing children to operate technical equipment like videos in nursery because of the younger children, but Chloe operates the video on her own all of the time at home.' Sometimes children are allowed more autonomy at nursery than at home, as when using real tools, but in this instance Chloe is allowed to operate the video at home, but not at nursery.

During the session on adult style, we also give the parents a handout describing our own work on adult pedagogic strategies (these are discussed in full in Chapter 5). After sharing and discussing the pedagogic strategies, we watch some more video clips and try to analyse them in terms of the eight strategies that staff and parents at Pen Green have identified. This might stimulate more discussion of questions such as 'what is appropriate risk?' or 'how can we help children go beyond our own knowledge base?'

Session 4: schemas

Again, in session 4, we begin with introductions. One worker then introduces the idea of 'schemas' or 'repeated patterns' through which young children learn. On the initial home visit, one of our questions is, 'What does your child do that does your head in?' We might remind parents of that question, as often children's persistent behaviour is also schematic. As soon as we begin to give examples of 'lining up toys', 'carrying things about from

one place to another' (transporting), and 'enclosing or enveloping' everything in sight, parents begin to chip in with their own examples of what
they have observed.

We often consolidate what we were saying by showing a case study on
video of one child's explorations, demonstrating that children can be investigating a cluster of schemas and coordinating them with each other. We
often use William on the 'Involving Parents' video to illustrate a child with
a cluster of schemas. If we have managed to gather video clips of the children whose parents are attending the session, we would then show each clip
and have a short discussion of what each child might be exploring afterward. Parents can always contribute evidence from home to confirm our
point or to take our thinking in another direction.

Working with the sceptics

Occasionally, parents express the view that schemas are 'a load of tosh'. Even
these sceptical parents can become intrigued or interested after watching or
videoing their own children at home. Sometimes parents will come back when
a second or third child starts attending nursery. At this point, with more time to
watch their child, they begin to understand the significance of schemas.

Parents are always given *A Schema Booklet for Parents* (Mairs, 1990) on
their initial home visit. They can use this to refer to initially, and they often
ask for more information on schemas. We would recommend various book-
lets and articles and we would also say,

- watch your child;
- talk to your family worker; and
- attend one of the study groups.

We invite parents both to attend and to speak at conferences held at the Pen
Green Centre. By talking about their own children to a wide range of workers,
the parents contribute a great deal to current knowledge about young children. Nothing is more impressive than hearing parents speak with passion and
confidence about their own child. The experience of speaking to an audience
of 150-200 people can have a huge impact not only on the audience, but on
the parents themselves and on other parents who use the centre.

Although there is some direct teaching of theory during each session, the
emphasis is on involving each member of the group in discussion. It is helpful to acknowledge that people learn in different ways (Dryden and Vos,
1994; Whalley, 1999a). Each session contains some auditory information
and some information that is presented visually; however, most information
is shared through interpersonal discussion. There is usually a handout.
Whenever possible, participants draw on their own first-hand experiences or
observations. We are trying to involve the participants in whichever way
suits them best. If parents are too shy to contribute to the group discussion,
we can offer them an individual session at another time.

Sustaining interest in the key concepts

The sessions introducing key concepts to parents described in this chapter are only part of the story. It is not simply a case of sharing the concepts with the parents, who then go away with a full understanding, able to operate on them effectively. Unless the parents become involved in discussing and making use of these concepts, they will have very little impact. However, if parents take a diary and, as we suggest, write down what their children do when they are 'deeply involved' (Laevers, 1997), this leads to further discussion and analysis. The concepts are not something we add on or use as a token salute to theory. They are very useful concepts that help us to understand and to discuss children's development and learning with parents and colleagues on a daily basis.

One way we have 'managed' to hold those daily conversations with parents is to focus on one or two children for observation each day. We have then targeted these children's parents or carers at the end of the session, so that we are also gathering information about what the children are currently doing at home. We have found that these conversations help to enrich our summative assessment of each child's development and learning. Parents' evenings are much more relevant when they are continuations of a dialogue engaged in during the school or nursery year.

Many of us are struggling with record-keeping, and we can lighten our load by involving parents. Working with parents makes our workload more manageable. Parents are definitely interested – they are only waiting for an invitation from us.

A very real constraint for all early childhood settings is lack of money and resources. Conversation is valuable and costs us only the effort. Notebooks can be bought for about 10 pence each, one notebook is all that parents need to start keeping a diary. We are finding that each child's record of nursery or school is much more relevant when it includes information from the parents.

When sharing ideas with parents in this way, we find it is important to remember that:

- parents are experts on the subject of their own children and can share their expertise with professionals;
- it can be helpful if professionals share specialised language and concepts with parents;
- professionals can use a group work model to share information with parents about key child development concepts; and
- practitioners need to be open and honest with parents and to see them as allies in collecting information about children's development and learning.

CHAPTER 5

Parents and Staff as Co-educators – 'Parents' Means Fathers Too

Margy Whalley and Trevor Chandler

This chapter explores the importance of the adult role in supporting and extending children's learning within early years settings. Parents and early years professionals need to work closely together if we are to provide the optimum opportunities for children to learn and develop. 'Parents and teachers can help children separately or they can work together to the greater benefit of the children' (Athey, 1990, p. 66). We have used two pieces of action research to highlight the importance of recognising mothers' and fathers' role as their children's first and most consistent educators.

Parents and staff as co-educators

The approach that we use in working with parents is rooted in the philosophy and ethos of our centre. Traditionally, parent education programmes have been based on a deficit model, targeting the families perceived to be most in need. For example, workers in the Head Start programme in the USA assumed that 'parents would benefit from the intervention of professionals, organised the relationship on professionals' terms, and tended to see children as needing to be rescued from inadequate backgrounds' (Ball, 1994, p. 44). Pugh *et al.* critique this kind of approach, as 'programmes that rely on professionalism disempower parents' (Pugh, De'Ath and Smith, 1994, p. 88). In Chapter 1, we describe the community development approach to working with parents, and it is this way of working that underpins our approach to developing a deeper understanding of the adult's role in extending children's learning.

Constructivists: interactionists

The importance of the adult in supporting and extending children's learning is well documented. The way in which the adult supports the child depends upon the adult's belief in how children learn. The relationship between the professional and the parent or carer is also influenced by our beliefs, as early years workers, about what working together in partnership really means. Malaguzzi, the philosopher and pedagogue who worked in partnership with parents and educators in Reggio Emilia, describes this process as

> understanding the child as a co-constructor an active participant, wanting and responding to a wide range of relationships, in the home and outside, with other children and adults. ... We can open up the possibility of a childhood of many relationships and opportunities, in which both the home and the early childhood institution have important, complementary but different parts to play.

> (Malaguzzi, cited in Dahlberg *et al.*, 1999, p. 52)

The timing and level of intervention by the adult are crucial in helping or hindering a child's learning. To require children to work within an adult-imposed framework is not helpful. If what is being offered to children bears no relation to their own interests, then they will not become deeply engaged. On the other hand, if children are left to 'just get on with it', they may become frustrated. It seems that the natural instinct of many adults is to do things for children, especially if they are in a hurry or if they cannot bear to see the child struggling.

At Pen Green, we subscribed to a constructivist approach. Athey describes constructivists as 'child-centred teachers who are trying to become more conscious and more theoretically aware of what is involved in the process of "coming to know". Constructivists are interested in the processes by which children construct their own knowledge' (Athey, 1990, p. 30). Bruce (1997, p. 10) calls this way of working an interactionist approach. It seemed to us that parents and staff needed to share their understanding of this way of working. We needed to know more about the strategies that parents and nursery staff adopt when interacting with children in the home setting and the nursery setting. We wanted to look more closely at the ways in which all the important adults in children's lives support their learning and development so that we could identify strengths and avoid inconsistencies in our various approaches.

Adult engagement styles

In Chapter 4, we describe the concept of the adult engagement style and how this concept is shared with parents. It was from the start a far more problematic concept for parents and staff than involvement, well-being and schemas. Pascal and Bertram (1997) apply three main descriptors to the adult styles of engagement:

- autonomy;
- sensitivity; and
- stimulation.

Nursery staff and parents struggled with these definitions and examples when we first encountered them through the Effective Early Learning (EEL) project (Pascal and Bertram, 1997). We were well aware that the adult's ability to engage the child was a critical factor in terms of the child's ability to become deeply involved in learning. However, we found it hard to achieve any consensus as to the degree of autonomy that was optimal to children's learning or what behaviour on the part of the adult constituted 'sensitive engagement'. Some of the nursery staff had used the EEL measures with groups of teachers and had found that, even in professional groups, it was often difficult to achieve a consensus on the basis of these classifications. Early years practitioners tended, in the first instance, to make judgements from their own value base (Drummond, 1993). During the training programmes that are a core part of the EEL project, early childhood educators are given time and training to work through these issues so that the judgements they make are moderated against those of others.

When we watched videos of adults providing stimulating 'materials' for children, it often seemed to us that the interventions were too adult directed to encourage real participation. Although we used Pascal and Bertram's descriptors in the pilot phase of our research, it seemed to us that this was a critical area for development in our own study. We were not simply concerned with defining appropriate adult engagement styles in terms of the role of the early childhood educator. We were also concerned with the adult engagement styles in terms of how parents, as the child's first educator, could most effectively engage with their children in the home setting.

Developing our own categories of effective teaching strategies

Instead of focusing, as so often seems to happen, on what parents were not doing well, we decided it would be salutary to build on what parents were doing really well. The parents involved in the project agreed that nursery staff could video them interacting with their children in the nursery early in the morning during the settling-in period. Subsequently, nursery staff were also videoed working with the same children.

Obstacles to progress

We were aware that during the first phase of the project nursery staff were often reluctant to be filmed. In fact, we had many hours of videotape in which the nursery resembled the *Marie Celeste* with all the adults having abandoned ship! It was clear that staff consistently avoided being in front of the camera.

At this point we came across the work in New Zealand of Maggie Haggerty (1996), who had produced, for her MA dissertation, evidence relating to the same problem. (Maggie Haggerty had worked with student teachers in New Zealand, who experienced many of the same anxieties expressed by our staff group.) At Pen Green, we decided to run a training day with an external consultant to discuss and debate all the issues nursery staff had about being filmed, and about filming other people. Working together with the parents, staff acknowledged their fears and anxieties, which included:

- their feelings about being judged by others;
- their issues about power, particularly the power of the person holding the camera;
- their issues about personal shyness; and
- their issues about how their performance was affected by the pressure of being videoed.

A plan was drawn up for the rest of the research programme, and all the nursery staff agreed that they would be filmed working with at least one of the research project children over an eight-week period. They decided to set up a 'buddy' system so that they filmed and were filmed by a colleague in whom they had a high degree of confidence. Each member of the nursery staff was filmed with a project child, and then they (or a colleague) filmed the child with his or her parent at the beginning of each nursery session. At the end of this period we had made 16 video vignettes of nursery staff and parents working with individual project children. Staff then agreed to continue to use the 'buddy' system we had developed so that they could make videos of all the other project children during the spring term.

The parents did not, in the main, express the same kind of reservations as the nursery staff about being videoed. Since all new parents settle their children into nursery for a two-week period, they were accustomed to the nursery routine at the beginning of the day. Most parents regularly spend time at the beginning of each day settling the children in and because of the flexible start (parents can bring children in from 8.15 a.m. onward) this was a relatively relaxed and unpressured time in nursery. It seemed that the reservations and anxieties parents would naturally feel on interacting with their children had been regularly worked through on these occasions and they had a high degree of confidence in the staff. They did not feel that staff were making negative judgements about their parenting styles. Accordingly, the pressure of the camera's presence did not seem to have the same impact on parents.

Video analysis session

On the last day of the autumn term, we held an informal video analysis session for both nursery staff and project parents. On this occasion, we wanted the nursery staff and parents to view the video clips as empirical data that needed to be closely observed and then analysed. We decided to try out a new approach (Jordan and Henderson, 1995) to watching and analysing the tapes. Staff and parents shared a meal together, and then sat down in front of the video screen. We set aside a $2\frac{1}{2}$ hour session, with $1\frac{1}{2}$ hours of video clips to view. The agreement between staff and parents was that we would watch the clips and anyone could ask for the tape to be stopped if:

- they wanted to discuss what they had observed; or
- they wanted clarification about what individual staff or parents were doing on the tape.

The only caveat was that the ensuing discussion could be sustained for only five minutes, after which we had once again to focus on the videotaped evidence. We could either go back over a controversial clip or move on to look at a new clip. In this way, we could make sure that the dialogical process (Freire, 1970) was grounded in the evidence base of the tapes, rather than on preconceived assumptions.

The video analysis group comprised the children's parents and their key workers. We watched the videos in sequence so that we saw particular children interacting first with their parents and then with their key worker. Staff were intrigued by the fact that they sometimes appeared to unconsciously mimic parental patterns of behaviour when they were trying to engage particular children within their key worker group. Some staff expressed anxieties about this and were concerned that parents might feel they were usurping the parental role; the parents, however, reassured them and affirmed how much they valued staff developing warm, responsive relationships with their children. The parents began to comment on their own styles of interacting with their children and were keen to explain why they had behaved in certain ways at certain times.

We hoped that through this discussion we would be able to identify consistent behaviour and differences in behaviour. We hoped to identify strengths in both parents' and staff's interventions. We wanted to consider how we could build on best practice to enhance the children's learning at home and in nursery.

Inevitably, even though we had allowed $2\frac{1}{2}$ hours, we were only able to review approximately 20 minutes of the tape in the first session! The level of debate and discussion was very high. Over the next two to three weeks, we completed three extended video analysis sessions. At the end of these discussions, we were able to identify some key features in the behaviour parents exhibited when interacting with their children in nursery:

- anticipation – parents seemed intuitively to know what to do next when a child needed something physically or emotionally;
- recall – the parents could share past experiences and relate them to what the children were doing or saying now while they played;
- mirroring experience through language – parents would verbally reflect back to the children what they were doing;
- extending experiences and accompanying the child – parents were quick to think about and show children new ways to approach things. They were also willing to allow their children's interest and give them the time and space to explore things;
- asking the child's view – parents seemed interested in what their children were thinking and feeling about things;
- encouraging autonomy – parents encouraged their children to make choices and decisions;
- boundary-setting/encouraging risk-taking – parents seemed to know when to step in and how to encourage their children to have a go; and
- judicious use of experience of failure/making mistakes – parents supported their children's right to experiment, to make mistakes and occasionally experience failure.

Developing the pedagogical strategies

A small group of nursery staff working with our pedagogical consultant, Professor Tina Bruce, spent many hours trying to identify underlying processes and the overt and conscious teaching strategies that both parents and nursery staff had used. Our aim was to develop a framework for effective teaching strategies. We wanted to develop categories that would help us to identify different pedagogical approaches and assess their effectiveness.

The categories needed to illustrate the complexity of the adult interventions. At the same time, the framework for observation needed to be a relatively simple tool, one that could be used regularly in our observations of each other, and of the parents. After a great deal of struggle with different forms of conceptual mapping, we did establish a set of fairly simple descriptors which illustrated complex interactions. The eight pedagogic strategies that follow are drawn from our observations of the different kinds of behaviour demonstrated by parents and nursery staff:

Effective pedagogical strategies

1 Subtle intervention
2 Knowledge of the child's embedded context, and ability to recall the child's previous experience
3 Affirmation of the child through facial expression and physical closeness
4 Encouraging children to make choices and decisions
5 The adult supports the child in taking appropriate risks
6 The adult encourages the child to go beyond the adult's own knowledge base and accompany them into new experiences
7 The adult has an awareness of the impact of their own attitudes and beliefs and how these might affect the child's learning
8 The adult demonstrates learning as a partnership; the adult is committed to their own learning and generates a spirit of enquiry.

(Whalley and Arnold, 1997a)

Subtle intervention

Staff and parents were all very aware of the danger of a 'hands-on' approach where the adult's 'hands on' inhibits the children's learning. We had all watched video clips in which inappropriate actions on the part of adults clearly took the initiative away from the child. Sometimes children's physical space was imposed on, and they were hurried along from activity to activity within an adult-determined timescale.

There were some subtle differences in the way that parents and staff intervened. Some parents seemed, at times, to be able to anticipate the next step that would keep their child engaged that little bit longer. Other parents knew just when to gently divert children's attention so that their emotional needs were met and at the same time they could continue to learn.

For the nursery staff, subtle intervention was often about waiting and watching before intervening. It involved the adult maintaining a respectful distance until children were clearly signalling that they needed help. It was about supporting and encouraging children to the point at which they were excited by the struggle and the intensity of the challenge, and then moving in gently to extend the learning.

Staff at staff meetings extended their understanding of subtle intervention through discussions of Bruner's concept of 'scaffolding learning' (Bruner, 1977), Vygotsky's zone of proximal development (Vygotsky, 1978), and Bruce's concept of 'match plus one' (Bruce, 1997).

We shared the view with parents that an overzealous focus on teaching could inhibit the children's learning. What worked best for children was an approach that combined observation, subtle intervention and reflection.

Knowledge of the child's embedded context and ability to recall the child's previous experience

From our observations of parents and nursery workers, it seemed that parents had a decided advantage in terms of their in-depth knowledge of their child's recent and relevant experiences. Often 2- and 3-year-olds would try hard to communicate important contextual information to staff about things they had done last night or at 'nanna's', and they were not always able to make themselves understood. Parents, however, were able to recognise what the children wanted to say and help them to articulate their experience, gently prompting them, at times, to assist them when they were trying to recall experiences over an extended period of time.

Since Pen Green nursery staff regularly make home visits to the children in their key worker groups, they do have some understanding of the child's home environment, and will probably know many of the important adults in the child's life. However, this was something that staff had to work at, whereas for parents it came quite naturally. Staff sometimes needed to make life books, with photographs of family members or home to nursery link books, to keep in touch with the important people and events in the children's life. Once again, this kind of information was not as subtle, or as intimate, as the knowledge held by parents, knowledge that could be built on to support and extend the children's learning. For example, Chelsea had gone to visit relatives in Scotland and had taken a much-loved bag full of her favourite toys and her make-up box. She saw it disappear down the conveyor belt, which carried the baggage out to the plane, and had been wild with excitement when she came back to nursery to share the experience. With support from her father, Warren, she was able to share the formative experience of seeing her baggage disappear and then reclaiming it, and her fascination with the conveyor belt that had carried it away. Staff and her parents were able to build on this information and extend her learning by visiting a much more complex conveyor belt in the Science Museum.

Affirmation of the child through facial expression and physical closeness

There were striking differences in the way that key workers and parents physically related to the children. Kristen, Naomi's mother, settled Naomi into nursery by encouraging her to play with the blocks, a favourite occupation. Naomi became absorbed quite quickly, and Kristen sat very close by but to one side of Naomi. Kristen gave Naomi all her attention and quietly played alongside until it was time for her to leave. A taped sequence of Naomi with her family worker (key worker) showed a very different scenario. Karen, Naomi's key worker, sits, physically, very close to Naomi while she is playing in a sandpit; other children move in and out, and Naomi repeatedly goes up to Karen to make sure that she has her full attention. At one point, Naomi touches Karen's face to redirect her gaze. It seemed that in many of the video clips family workers had to work physically closer to the children to reassure them and affirm that contact between adult and child.

The children seemed to be fairly confident that their parents were there for them and at times were rather less confident that they had the undivided attention of the nursery worker. Perhaps reasonably so, in that, at least for the duration of the settling-in period, the parents were very much focusing on one child, whereas nursery workers had to constantly respond to a minimum of four other children, and often many more. Parents often demonstrated a physical closeness to the children, but, to be effective, staff almost always had to engage closely with the children if the play was to develop and be sustained.

Encouraging children to make choices and decisions

Staff and parents avoided overdirecting the children. At the start of the day, the children were gently introduced to different areas within the nursery by their parents; both staff and parents were willing to follow the children's lead and accommodate their interests. It was obvious that for some children a side-by-side approach with the key worker gradually taking over the support role as the child's parents withdrew was the best way to accomplish a smooth transition into nursery. With other children, it was important to immediately establish peer support and assist them in finding their best friend before they could accept their parent's departure.

Some children came to nursery knowing exactly how they wanted to spend their time, and the adults would encourage them in that decision-making process. For example, Harry sometimes hid a favourite piece of Brio underneath a cupboard; while accepting that he could not take toys out of nursery, he was determined not to be thwarted in his extended play with the track and trains. Alice *needed* to sit on the rocking horse where she could watch her mother leave. From this secure vantage point, she could, with the support of her family worker, identify in which workshop area of the nursery she wanted to start her day. Zaki, knowing that the minibus would go out most days, would take responsibility for the clipboard and identify whose turn it was to go out and negotiate the destination.

Encouraging decision-making is a key feature of the nursery philosophy, and it became obvious from this shared piece of work that parents were, on the whole, prepared to give the children time to learn how to make good choices.

The adult supports the child in taking appropriate risks

In our analysis of the parents' interactions that we had on video, we noticed a huge strength in the parents' ability to encourage and support the children in experimentation. The parents were able to support their children's right to experiment, make mistakes and occasionally experience failure, and we needed to be equally aware, in the nursery, of the value of a 'judicious' measure of risk-taking and making mistakes. Parents seemed accustomed to diverting children when the experience of failure was overwhelming and were very committed to allowing children several 'shots' at a task before they gave up. Sometimes nursery staff were overanxious and overprotective, perhaps because their ability to comfort the child, if things went wrong, was not as great as that of most of the parents. On some occasions, however, the parents were more anxious than the nursery staff – for example, over the use of scissors in the nursery or when children were pouring drinks. Children who are overwatched and assessed to be incompetent will inevitably spill their juice and drop the tray of cups they are carrying even when they do have the competence to carry out these tasks.

Risk-taking at a deep level, such as permitting nursery age children to stay away overnight at a well-organised farm holiday, was something that daunted both parents and staff but the 3- and 4-year-olds who participated gained enormously despite all our shared anxieties.

The adult encourages the child to go beyond the adult's own knowledge base and accompany them into new experiences

At times, both staff and parents struggled to understand the children's persistent concerns. On many video clips, the adults watched the children deeply engaged in activities that were hard to define, as for instance, when children were intent on Sellotaping around the door handles and then connecting doors up and down the corridor with Sellotape and then with string. However, parents and staff were able to watch respectfully and follow up the observations with dialogue and adult-level investigation. Both staff and parents drew on their knowledge about the Leuven involvement levels, and, watching children who were clearly deeply involved, they were prepared to suspend 'disbelief' and encourage the children to develop their cognitive concerns, even when what they were doing was, at times, challenging. Children with beetle brows and tongues sticking out between their teeth, intent on making some new discovery, were generally supported in their task. The adults supporting them often had to dialogue at length, study key texts, and go with hunches to accompany the children into new experiences.

On one memorable occasion, Alice became deeply involved in conveyor belts (see Chapter 8 for Alice's portfolio). She had been taken to see a conveyor belt at the Science Museum and was keen to understand how it worked. Staff improvised a conveyor belt in the nursery by securing paper around a tabletop, and she spent hours intently learning how to manoeuvre the belt and watching objects move along it and drop into the metal container. Having experimented with many solid objects, she finally experimented with a ball, and she (and the nursery staff) stood by perplexed when, unlike all the other solid objects, the ball failed to drop off the conveyor belt. At $3\frac{1}{2}$ years, Alice had a 'false hypothesis' (Harlen, 1982) that all objects would follow the same laws and move forward and drop off the end of the conveyor belt, and most of the staff shared her view! Other staff had a very vague awareness of the forces, gravity and the laws of motion that were, indeed, in operation, and much discussion was needed before we could successfully extend Alice's learning opportunities appropriately.

Adults have an awareness of the impact of their own attitudes and beliefs and how these might affect the child's learning

Staff and parents had to work hard to develop understanding of how their own values, beliefs and attitudes were impacting on, and sometimes inhibiting, the child's right to learn. We all became aware that overanxiety was a common feature of staff and parent behaviour. The overwatched child who was always offered assistance when climbing the trees in the nursery garden or when experimenting on the climbing frame could not develop a sense of competence and confidence as a climber. Girls dressed in skirts and dresses were almost always at a disadvantage and were often offered assistance by our largely female staff group. In Loris Malaguzzi's words, 'every child has the right to be away from the ever watchful eye of the adult' (Malaguzzi, 1992, personal communication).

Sometimes our debates and struggle over values and beliefs went even deeper. One parent experiencing an overwhelmingly painful separation from a partner had chosen to tell her nursery child that his daddy was 'dead'. In fact, his father was well known in the community, passed the nursery every day, but had no contact with the child. Another parent, who was pregnant, was not permitted, within her own religion and culture, to share with her son information about how the baby was progressing, information which nursery staff would have considered to be appropriate. Paradoxically, her son's nursery worker was also pregnant, and all the other children in his key worker group would pat their nursery worker's tummy and eagerly ask questions about what was going on. Faced with these value-based dilemmas, staff and parents shared their views and feelings respectfully. While, in many cases, there was no easy reconciliation of different view points, the issue of children's rights was at least aired, and the best possible practice was ensured.

Adults demonstrate learning as a partnership; adults are committed to their own learning and generate a spirit of enquiry

Despite the fact that many of the parents were juggling with bringing up a family, part-time or full-time work, and coping on a low income, it was clear that, without exception, they had aspirations for their children and were anxious to support them in any way that they could. They responded to the challenge of videoing their children and thinking about their learning with as much enthusiasm as the nursery staff. Many of them were stimulated by their involvement in the project, and in the nursery generally, to go back to study or to pick up a half-completed course.

Staff became aware of huge gaps in their own learning, particularly in the area of science and mathematics, and much of our in-service training over the last three years has focused on these areas of the curriculum. In Chapter 2, we described how nursery staff had been deeply concerned about a disengaged group of four-year-old boys who always seemed to be 'roaming in gangs' around the nursery in February or March each year. It cannot be coincidental that when staff became highly in tune with the children's need to develop their understanding of scientific and mathematical concepts, and increased their own skills and competences in these areas, these kinds of negative behaviours diminished. Most staff undertook further- or higher-education courses, and training was given a high priority at Pen Green. Wherever possible, staff who undertook training in their own time were financially supported, given some time back, and offered 'time out' to complete assignments.

Involving fathers and male carers

At Pen Green, we have worked hard for a number of years to tackle issues of gender stereotyping (Ghedini *et al.*, 1995, p. 36). In a review of our work with fathers in 1990, we found that local fathers often failed to get involved in services and were either excluded by other parents or excluded themselves. For example, when the staff at the centre decided to positively encourage fathers to settle their children in nursery and worked hard to engage the fathers during the two-week settling-in period, 87 per cent of fathers turned up. In our discussions with parents, mothers initially assumed that their partners did not want to be involved, and the fathers assumed that their partners did not want them to be involved. In the vast majority of cases, these assumptions were not well founded.

Pen Green Centre's work to include fathers has met with some success. Fathers particularly enjoy attending meetings that focus on science and technology. One father spent 40 minutes exploring our key concepts CD-ROM at a parents' evening and said, the next day, that the information he had acquired had revolutionised the way that he saw his son's play.

The establishment of the research base in the centre has led to a further increase in the involvement of fathers. It was clear from the beginning that, if the research to study parents' involvement in their children's learning was to be successful, it was vital to involve fathers and other primary male carers in the work.

Extending the research to explore fathers'/male carers' engagement styles

Although there were two fathers involved in the original pilot project and a significant number of fathers involved in the second year, the video observations that informed our framework for pedagogical strategies only included one father. We had not, at that time, considered the particular qualities that fathers might bring to their role. It seemed to us important to replicate our work with a group of fathers.

Using the framework we had already developed on effective pedagogical strategies, we looked at the interactions between fathers and children in the nursery. The fathers who were invited to be part of this project had already demonstrated an interest in knowing more about their children's play in nursery and were happy to let us video them settling their children into nursery.

Six fathers got involved. It was interesting to note that all these fathers had been present at their children's birth and felt that this experience had had a strong emotional impact on their lives. Two of the fathers had two sons and found interesting parallels between their children. Both had older sons whom they described as typical boys, that is, loud, noisy and needing to run about a lot and play rough and tumble games. Their younger sons were quieter, and enjoyed drawing and stories. Those fathers that had more than one child often struggled with sharing their time between their two children.

The fathers who became involved (Figure 5.1) were:

- Alex, who is married with one daughter, Chloe. Alex and his partner are both in full-time employment;
- Rory, who is married with a daughter, Lindsey. Rory and his partner both work;
- Lewis, who is separated, has two sons, is unemployed and shares the care of the children;
- Dave, who is married with one son and one daughter, is in full-time employment, and his partner also works away from the home;
- Marcus, who has three children, lives with his partner and is employed in the nursery full-time; and
- Nick, who is married with two children, and both parents are employed.

Three of the fathers, Alex, Rory and Lewis, were recorded as they settled their children into the nursery before going to work. Alex stayed with his daughter Chloe for 30 minutes while she was deeply engaged in block play; Rory chatted to his daughter Lindsey, and Lewis helped his son Aaron on the nursery computer and encouraged another boy to join him. Dave was video-filmed as he sat with two children and read them a story while sitting on a sofa. Dave already works in the nursery on a sessional basis to gain experience of working in an early years setting, as he is planning to make a career change and study for an NVQ in education and childcare. His own child also attends the nursery. Marcus, a family worker in the nursery, sat with two nursery children playing with dough, cooking utensils and cones. Marcus is a full-time member of the nursery staff and his own child attended the nursery. Nick was filmed as he helped the children empty and clean out the fish tank.

Analysing the videotapes

Two of the centre staff met with four out of the six fathers to analyse the video recordings that we made (two of the fathers were unable to meet because of work commitments). The purpose of the meeting with the

Figure 5.1 Fathers who were involved in the project

fathers was to look at the nature of their interactions with their children. We also wanted to see if our framework of pedagogical strategies was as relevant to men working with children as it was for women working with children. In other words, were the pedagogical strategies gender neutral or were there were gender-specific differences?

David (1994) reflects on this issue when she notes that research on mothers and fathers concentrates too much on what fathers do in comparison with mothers, rather than on the quality of their time with children. 'What may be more important is their sensitivity (or not) to their child during such interactions' (David, 1994, p. 6).

From our shared analysis session, we made the following observations and identified some key issues.

Subtle intervention – fathers interacting with children gently and respectfully

All six fathers demonstrated this quality, and it was particularly strong in four of the six observations that were made. The first two examples illustrate what is meant by subtle intervention when fathers are interacting with their children or, indeed, with other children in the nursery.

Example 1 Dave, who was sitting on the sofa in the nursery is reading a story to Jessica. She is sitting on his lap in a very relaxed way. They are both involved in the story when Christopher walks up to them and sits beside Dave on the sofa. Dave invites Christopher to join them in the story and notices that Christopher has a plastic apron on, which is uncomfortable now that he is sitting down. He offers to help Christopher take off the apron and with his agreement does so. Christopher now chooses to sit by Dave and involve himself in the story. During this important interaction with Christopher, Dave maintains eye contact with Jessica and talks to her. He shows awareness of both children's needs and is able to engage and maintain their interest in the story.

Example 2 Alex is with his daughter in the block-play area. Chloe is very involved in building with the blocks. Alex maintains a discreet distance from her when she is using the blocks in a competent way. He is very quick to intervene when she gets stuck and she asks for help. Her request for help is both verbal and through eye contact. They are very much in tune with each other's signals. She asks for help when she could not get a block out of the shelf because they were too tightly packed, and Alex intervenes when he sees that the task is too difficult for her. When she tries to stand on a round block and she finds it difficult to keep her balance, Alex very quickly moves in to hold her hand and allow her to experiment safely.

Fathers demonstrate knowledge of their children's previous experiences and interests and/or current concerns

This strategy was demonstrated in all the observations, whether it was with the father's own children or other children in the nursery.

Example 3 When we are looking at the video together, Alex picks out the way that his daughter Chloe is walking with a long block in the block area. She is banging it up and down and walking with a stoop. He remarks that both Chloe's grandmothers use walking sticks, and she seems to be incorporating this into her block play.

Example 4 Rory fixes the button on Lindsey's dungarees. In doing so, he celebrates with Lindsey the fact that she dresses herself in the morning and does it very well. He plays a counting game with her by asking her how many names she, her mum and her dad have. She then goes through everyone's names.

Fathers show that they appreciate children's efforts and want to support them by getting physically close, working physically alongside, and through positive, reassuring facial expressions

Fathers in many of the video sequences clearly enjoyed being physically close to their children and were physically responsive and sensitive to their children's need for truth and reassurance.

Example 5 Nick moved in and out of being physically close. This may have been due to the activity that he was involved in, emptying the fish tank. It is interesting to note that when Nick was standing at the sink and involved in a conversation with another adult for a brief time, the children's level of involvement dropped quite noticeably. Nick was, however, quick to pick this up and squatted down to talk to the children. The children's level of involvement in the activity increased when he was actively engaging them.

Example 6 Rory remained physically distant from his daughter. He remained standing throughout their time together often with his arms folded. He was, however, able to engage his daughter in conversation even at a distance and sustained good eye contact with her with a lot of smiles and laughter exchanged between them. As he was about to leave Lindsey, he touched her face and they kissed goodbye.

Example 7 Lewis is with his son Aaron and another boy, Samuel, on the computer. Both Lewis and Aaron are sitting in chairs of their own while Samuel stands beside Lewis. They are all three very focused on the computer screen, and Lewis is sharing the mouse with the children. There is little eye contact between them while they are focused on the computer. However, there is one point where Lewis takes over the mouse from Aaron to achieve a task that they are sharing. Aaron appears to lose interest in the activity at this point, and he makes a move to walk away. Lewis disengages himself from the computer and gently touches Aaron on the arm to gain his attention. Aaron then returns to the computer task at Lewis's invitation. Lewis also invites Samuel to sit on his knee so that he can reach the mouse and see the computer screen more easily.

Fathers respect their children's right to make choices and decisions

The video recordings showed many instances of the fathers showing sensitivity to the children in terms of when to intervene and when to leave the children to carry on independently.

The fathers discussed this particular strategy at length. All the fathers believed in respecting children's rights to make their own choices and decisions. They did, however, say that this was hard to achieve. For example, when they had to go to work, they would do tasks for their children in order to get them to nursery on time. They felt that the times when they were with their children without having to be anywhere at a particular moment were very precious.

Example 8 Nick moves in and out of supporting the children to siphon the water off. He explains the importance of keeping the tube submerged in the water. The children experiment with taking the tube out to see what happens. The children are experimenting through direct experience and are in control of what they are doing in this complex task.

Example 9 Marcus always checks with the children when he intervenes to help them and never takes any intervention for granted. He offers the children different materials to use in their play, which they accept or reject. They usually accept what he offers, and his interventions are always in keeping with what the children are doing. His interventions extend the children's play and do not disrupt the flow of their play.

Example 10 When reading the story to Christopher and Jessica, Dave responds to their questions and requests. When Christopher first joins in the story, he wants to turn the pages very quickly before hearing the story in detail. Dave allows him to do this rather than telling him to wait and listen to the story. Dave remains child focused rather than task focused.

Fathers encourage and support their children to take risks appropriately

There were very few obvious examples of risk-taking in the video observations. As a staff group and with the fathers, we discussed the concept of 'risk-taking'. What may seem like an ordinary, safe, day-to-day activity to the casual observer, can, for an individual, be a huge personal risk. For Christopher, aged 3, to interrupt the storytelling between Dave and Jessica may have been a big risk.

Chloe took risks in building a tower with the blocks until they collapsed. She looked over to her dad when this happened and was reassured by his response that it was okay.

Some fathers felt that they were at times overprotective of their children. It was not always easy in practice to know when intervention was helpful and when it was either controlling or disempowering for the child. Fathers said that they felt as protective of their sons as their daughters, and they were also aware of their children's different emotional needs.

Fathers encourage the children to get involved in deep-level learning that goes beyond what the adult already knows; fathers support/accompany them in their play/learning

This strategy was the one that gave rise to most discussion. Most of the fathers said they had not experienced their children raising any questions that they did not know the answers to! They had a range of strategies for explaining things to their children. One father said that he would make up stories to answer his children's questions. These stories were used to explain what the child wanted to know in terms that the father thought he would understand. Another father said that he responded by giving the facts in as straightforward a way as possible; if he felt that the explanation would be problematic, he would change the subject.

The fathers in the group who attended the key concept training days on the curriculum had found them very useful, as they felt that it helped them understood more clearly how their children were involved in learning through their play.

Example 11 Christopher is pretending to make cakes with the dough. Marcus, his nursery worker joins in with the play through pretending to eat the cake when Christopher gives him a bit. He extends Christopher's learning by introducing a rolling pin and showing him how to flatten the dough. Christopher is deeply involved in the play, which reflects his interest and level of learning. Marcus also shows Christopher that one side of the pastry cutter is sharper than the other and that it is easier to cut the dough with the sharp edge. Christopher continues to use the pastry cutter in a more appropriate way with considerable satisfaction.

Fathers appear to be aware that what they say and how they behave reflects their own attitudes and beliefs, and that this has an effect on what the child is able to learn from them and share with them

Through their interactions with the children, all the fathers showed a high degree of sensitivity. This was reflected in the degree of non-verbal communication that was put into practice; for example, getting down physically to the child's level, good eye contact and using a tone of voice that was soft and animated. The language they used was clearly pitched at a level the children could understand and was concerned with the children's interests. Alex, in Example 1, was very concerned that his daughter Chloe had the right to take the lead in her play, although, in fact, what she wanted was an equal and active partnership. Sometimes she took the lead, sometimes she watched her dad, and sometimes they both played together.

Example 12 Alex decided to allow himself to be observed through the video recording because he understood that his daughter Chloe was deeply involved in block play when he brought her into nursery. Throughout her play, he maintains a distance and is respectful of his daughter's personal space so that she can develop her play.

Chloe is confident and playful in her block play. She pushes her building to the limit and celebrates her achievements with her dad and members of staff. She is not discouraged when her building collapses. She works and plays with confidence knowing that her dad is there to support her and she has his complete attention. When he tells her that he has to leave and go to work, she protests and then accepts that he needs to go. After he has gone, Chloe returns to her block play and continues to build.

Fathers work alongside children as resourceful friends and partners in their learning; adults enjoy learning in their own right and are curious and want to know more

The fathers involved in this research were very much in agreement with the idea of the adult as a resourceful friend; however, they struggled with the idea that they needed to develop their own learning. They wanted to develop their understanding of how children learn and wanted to know how they could help their children learn. The fathers did not feel that their children challenged in any way their understanding of the world around them.

Fathers communicating with their children

An analysis of the fathers' use of language showed that the amount of language used varied considerably. Two fathers talked with their children much of the time in their interactions, one of them using very little physical contact. Another father used very little language but was physically very close to the children and involved in the activity alongside them. All the fathers used language to explain things and extend children's learning. One father was very good at using language to reflect back to the child what the child was doing. Two of the fathers were fairly task centred in the activity they were involved in and used language to encourage the children to complete the task.

There was also a lot of eye contact between all the fathers and the children they were working with. The children showed themselves to be very comfortable with physical contact with the fathers. The fathers responded sensitively to the children, who set their own boundaries in terms of proximity and touch.

Issues that arose

The range of adult pedagogical strategies the fathers used were very similar to those we had noted in mothers at an earlier stage in the project. Differences often seemed to be more closely linked to personality than to gender. However, there *was* a difference in the fathers' perceptions of how far their own knowledge and understanding might be challenged by the child. It seemed that these fathers accepted their roles and responsibilities as teachers or first educators but did not see themselves as 'learners'.

The process of involving fathers in their children's learning is one that has to be constantly reviewed and negotiated. The fathers' response to this and other work has been very positive and demonstrates that fathers, as well as mothers, care passionately about their children's emotional and cognitive needs. The work at Pen Green Centre and, in particular, the research base has shown that parents, regardless of gender, class and ethnicity, have a genuine desire to be involved in their children's development and want to work in a genuine partnership with early years professionals.

There are enormous benefits to identifying a close working partnership between parents and early years workers:

- Parents benefit from increasing their knowledge and understanding of their children through group discussion with other parents and staff.
- Staff benefit through increasing their knowledge and understanding of the children's learning opportunities at home; their ability to provide continuity and new experiences for the child within the nursery is then extended.
- Children benefit because the significant adults in their lives are able to provide richer learning opportunities.
- Children also experience their parents and carers working closely together. This gives them a sense of continuity and of being cared for, and creates a trusting and secure environment in which they can learn and grow.

Our work on effective pedagogical strategies is a work in progress. We constantly review the evidence from our observations of interactions between workers and children and parents and children. We revised our framework in 2005 and included some additional strategies, as set out in the following box:

Adult pedagogical strategies (Checklist for observations)
1 The adult watches and listens to what children are doing before intervening.
2 The adult knows about children's family experiences and links what they have done previously to what they are doing now.
3 Adults show children they are interested by their facial expression, by being physically close to them, by mirroring children's facial expressions and verbal intonation, and therefore by empathising with children's expression of emotions.
4 The adult encourages the child to make choices and decisions and to take appropriate risks.
5 The adult encourages the child to go beyond what the adult knows about and is open to learning new things alongside the child.
6 The adult is aware of the impact of his or her own attitudes and beliefs and how these might affect the child's learning.
7 The adult plays and learns alongside the child. The adult is committed to his or her own learning and encourages the child's curiosity.
8 The adult checks the child's meaning and gives the child time to respond or to question.
9 The adult offers language to support the child's actions and offers new information to the child.
10 The adult acknowledges both the child's feelings and the child's competence and capability.

(Chandler, 2005; Pen Green, 2005)

CHAPTER 6

Persistence Pays Off: Working with Parents Who Find Our Services 'Hard to Reach'

Cath Arnold

This chapter looks at why we want to engage all parents of nursery children and how we adapt our methods to ensure that we are giving all the parents equal opportunities to be involved in their children's learning. The chapter draws on two parents' stories of their own educational experience as children and adults.

The background

As part of the Parents' Involvement in Their Children's Learning (PICL) project, we carry out a semi-structured interview with each of our nursery parents each year. We are aware that Corby has among its total population very few adults who go on to further or higher education (Corby Sure Start Bid, internal document produced for the DfEE Sure Start Unit in 1999). We feel that this is likely to have a significant effect on the parents' aspirations for their children. Therefore, we ask the parents about their own experiences of education during the interview. Often parents will expand on this by telling us more about their educational experiences during the interview or, informally, afterward. A substantial number of parents interviewed (about 30 per cent) have expressed their dissatisfaction particularly with the secondary phase of their schooling. A small number (6 per cent) were frequently excluded, were suspended from school, or were habitual truants. Either way, this small group of parents missed a substantial amount of schooling and, consequently, had very little experience of achievement as children.

In the past, the anti-social acts that led to exclusions have sometimes been viewed as the fault of the children or their families. The educational under-achievement of children from working-class families was seen by sociologists in the 1960s as 'their inability to defer gratification' or as 'a lower priority placed upon educational success' by families (Abbott, 1998, p. 65). Abbott, however, argues, 'It might be the case that working class parents were unconfident in their ability to deal adequately with the norms and values of schools and teachers' (*ibid.*). There was a feeling that schools and teachers knew best and only by conforming to their rules and values would pupils succeed.

What was not always acknowledged was that the expectations that teachers and schools have of their pupils and their families affect how those pupils feel and act (Faulkner, 1995). In a case study of a day nursery and nursery unit, Whalley (1992, p. 199) observed, 'Day nursery staff and nursery unit staff viewed their parents as somewhere on a range with abusive and neglectful at one extreme and poor and disadvantaged at the other. It becomes clear why the amount of parental involvement in this and other studies correlates with staff attitudes towards parents.' The judgements made by staff of parents affect how the family feels about school and, possibly, create a barrier to becoming more involved with school or education in general.

Why we want to engage all parents

Having an Equal Opportunities Policy does not necessarily mean that we offer equal opportunities to all families. We realise that we are working toward offering each child and family an equal opportunity to education and care. Parents are all different, and, therefore, to make the provision accessible to all families means that we are constantly questioning our ways of engaging parents (Whalley, 1997b). Each child is entitled to have his or her parents involved in his or her education, and we have a duty to provide the means by which parents are able to be involved. We have found that offering different ways to become involved, at different times of day and with a crèche, helps (see Chapter 4).

Longitudinal research studies give strong evidence that involving parents in their children's education benefits the children, their families and society (Athey, 1990; Rutter and Rutter, 1992; Easen, Kendall and Shaw, 1992; Fuerst and Fuerst, 1993; Weinberger, 1996). From a purely financial viewpoint, it is claimed that for every $1 spent on early education, $7 is saved because students are well adjusted citizens and have a better quality of life (Sylva, 1999). A similar claim was made (*TES*, 2000, p. 11) about Early Excellence Centres in the UK: 'Preliminary research by University College Worcester shows for every £1 invested in early excellence centres, £8 is saved on alternative services such as foster care and counselling.'

Sylva was concerned with assessing the 'quality' of early education on offer to the child. The Early Excellence evaluation programme was concerned with the quality of services to the whole family. Projects which involve parents and local communities in decision-making seem to have the most long-term impact on children and their families. Community projects from as far afield as Venezuela, India and South Africa confirm that involving parents and the local community is the key to helping children to achieve their potential both educationally and socially (Atmore, 1999; Sood, 1999; Yanez, 1999).

The Effective Provision of Pre-School Education (EPPE) Project has recently shown that 'what parents do, rather than who they are' is what makes a difference to children. What happens in the home is even more important than what happens in settings, as far as children's long-term development and learning, is concerned. Parents that are involved and know how to support their children, have higher aspirations, and their children do better within the education system (Sylva *et al.*, 2004).

Athey (1990, p. 20) makes the point, 'Most research in the 1960s and 70s was designed to assist the inadequate parent.' Parents were taught 'parenting skills' by experts. It was believed that child-rearing skills could be transmitted to parents by telling them what to do and encouraging them to practise it. The rich experience of bringing up their own children from birth, which parents brought to the learning situation, was not acknowledged as important. In the Froebel Early Education Project (Athey, 1990), the agenda was still set by the educators. However, the parents' contribution to professional knowledge about each child was acknowledged. During the 1980s and 1990s, there has been some shift in thinking in the sense that parents are recognised, at least in government rhetoric, as 'experts on their own children' (Athey, 1990, p. 61). Many parenting programmes still work from the premise that there are a lot of parenting skills that should be taught to 'less effective' parents.

Shaw (1991), working in the tradition of Athey and Bruce, set up a home-visiting project in the north-east of England. The six families that Shaw worked with were described as 'vulnerable'. They all lived in the 'inner city', were 'unemployed and had limited resources available to them, materially and in terms of their own previous education' (Shaw, 1991, p. 105). In addition, all of the families were living in 'highly stressful circumstances' (*ibid.*). Despite their individual needs, 'The agenda for discussion was negotiated between the parents and researcher' (Easen, Kendall and Shaw, 1992, pp. 282–96).

Shaw offered the parents a schematic interpretation of their children's actions, which enabled the parents to have an alternative way of understanding their children's actions. This led to the parents reflecting on their own education and upbringing. Shaw discovered that,

> Unremarkably, the parents' learning process appears to be similar to the child's learning process as described by Athey; that is, both children and parents have developed cognitive structures which have built up from experience and which underpin behaviour. First hand experience is therefore central to the learning process for children and parents.
>
> (Easen *et al.*, 1992, p. 287)

As a result of watching their own children and discussing what might be happening with the researcher, the parents and the researcher gained knowledge and saw things 'in new ways' (Easen *et al.*, 1992, p. 288). Mezirow (1977) calls this process 'perspective transformation'. Because perspectives have 'dimensions of thought, feelings and will', people begin to see things differently and to behave differently (Mezirow, 1977, p. 158).

In a similar way, our evidence shows that parents who become involved in the PICL project see their children's development and learning in a new 'light'. Our aim is to give all our nursery parents opportunities to become involved in the ways that suit them best.

Early in the project, it became apparent that *all* of our parents are potential participants. The respect we show for the parents' prior knowledge and experience can make a difference to how they feel about themselves and about their children. Easen *et al.* (1992, p. 294) comment, 'Through the validation of their experience, parents' self-esteem and confidence in their role as a parent and as an individual is enhanced.' Whalley (1997b, p. 92) makes a similar point: 'Parents need to know that staff care about them as well as their children.'

We were aware of parents using the centre facilities who had had poor experiences of education and schooling during their own childhoods, and we very much wanted to improve opportunities for them and their children.

This small group of parents attending the Pen Green Centre who were excluded from school or were habitual truants can give us an insight into what happened from their perspective. Two mothers, who were regular users of the centre, agreed to tell the stories of their own education, and they also agreed to share their views about what they wanted from the education system for their children. Both parents checked the full transcript of their own story.

These two parents had been involved in the PICL project, but only in a peripheral way. One of the parents attended a study group for six months and came to various other meetings and events. The other parent became involved on a one-to-one basis but did not sustain involvement with the group over time.

Jack (1987, p. 102) says, 'The oral interview not only allows women to articulate their own experiences but also to reflect upon the meaning of those experiences to them.' Rather than make speculations, as educators, about the reasons for exclusions and truanting, we wanted to be able to listen to their actual experiences and to 'construct our theories out of the actual experiences' (Wittner, 1987, p. 105).

These two stories are individual representations of the experiences of two parents and may help us to gain further insights about how we, as educators, can adapt our organisations and behaviour to accommodate the needs of a wider range of children and parents. Tracey and Kate represent a minority group. Laevers (1995) refers to children who 'fall out of the boat', and this description seems to fit their childhood experiences.

What is different or special about these parents

The two parents interviewed are parents who have been regular users of some of the centre's facilities for some years. One has attended the youth club in the centre and then had a child in the nursery for two years. The other parent has frequently used the family room (a room where parents can drop in and chat to other parents) over a number of years, and has had two children attend the nursery. We feel that we know both of these parents quite well. Neither is afraid to ask us for what they want for their child. Both have engaged in adult community education during the last couple of years and are therefore in a position to compare this model of education with their own earlier experience of schooling. Both parents would be perceived by their child's school as outspoken. Miller (2000, p. 140) says, 'the respondent will slant their account to fit with what they see as being the interviewer's area of interest and tell their story in a way that they believe will be sensible for the interviewer.' My role as interviewer was to listen to the parents' stories and to try to discover whether, in their opinions, the PICL project had had an impact on them or on their children.

It became obvious during the interviews that each parent had a huge personal agenda about their own schooling. The interview process itself gave each an opportunity to reflect on these experiences. Anderson (1987, p. 100) says, 'If we want to know how women feel about their lives, then we have to allow them to talk about their feelings as well as their activities.' The feelings about school that each parent expressed during the interview indicated the kinds of feelings that entering school buildings might still evoke for each of them today. Until each has some fresh 'first-hand experience' of school or education, that earlier experience continues to be the basis of thoughts, feelings and actions (Easen *et al.*, 1992).

Tracy's story about her education (a brief summary)

Tracy enjoyed junior school but was repeatedly excluded from senior school for disruptive behaviour. She was not allowed to sit any GCSEs, although she says she was 'good at maths and English'. Tracy feels she has done well, compared with many of her peers, who are 'junkies, alcys [alcoholics] and shoplifters'. She mentions 'a guy who was in my class all the time up the town. It used to be him I used to mess about with – he's an alcy, a junkie – he's a shoplifter'.

Tracy now has a partner, Tommy, and a son, David. She wants David 'to be himself and want to learn', 'to go to college if he wants to so that he gets a better start in life'. She acknowledges that 'if he doesn't want to learn, then nobody is going to force him to.'

Tracy was invited to record what David was doing at home, and she began to keep a diary when he first started nursery. She says that is what 'made me want to go back to learning'. She appreciated understanding what and how David was learning, 'whereas before I wouldn't probably think of ... well, he's throwing things, now I think "scattering".' She recognises his schema.

As an adult, Tracy has begun studying GCSE maths and English, but has found it diffiicult along with housework and a part-time job. She got a distinction on a computer course but says she 'is not really interested in computers'.

Recently, Tracy decided that she really wants to work with 'problem children'. She began a college course in the next town, but was told she had missed too much time after the first three weeks (both she and David had been ill). She still feels that things are stacked against her – she is juggling housework, money and caring for David.

Strauss and Corbin (1990, p. 63) say, 'One can count "raw" data, but one can't relate or talk about them easily.' The full transcript of Tracy's story can be analysed by 'conceptualising the data', that is, 'taking apart' each sentence and coding 'each discrete incident, idea or event'. When each incident has been coded in this way, we can compare phenomena with each other and examine any emerging themes.

After the initial 'open coding' of Tracy's story, a pattern began to emerge. Central to that pattern were Tracy's feelings (Table 6.1).

Tracy's story – childhood, lived experience

Table 6.1 Tracy's childhood experience

What was said or done	Feeling invoked	Consequences
Being blamed by teacher for brother's bad behaviour 'They knew where I came from.'	Anger	Wanting revenge/ disrupt lessons 'I start messing about.'
Being treated as less important than other children 'I wanted to take exams. I wasn't allowed.'	Feeling like an 'outcast'	Disrupting lessons and exclusion
A couple of teachers 'all right'	Not specified	
Getting caught or being blamed 'I was either kicked out or on the report card.'	Numbness	Accepting exclusion as norm
Fighting with teacher over jacket 'She's pulling it and I'm pulling it.'	Loss of control – going crazy/anger 'I started kicking – I don't know what I done.'	Being kicked out
Exaggerating and lying about school events at home 'I'm going to get done if I go home with this little rip.'	Fear of getting into trouble	Excluded/'bored at home' 'It's a loser's game.'
Community placement 'You could get privileges.'	Excitement/ enthusiasm	Enjoyment

There seems to have been a chain of events (Table 6.1) that were repeated during Tracy's secondary education:

1 (conditions) being treated unfairly
2 (phenomenon) feeling angry
3 (context) teachers don't help
4 (action) being disruptive
5 (consequences) being excluded (Strauss and Corbin, 1990, p. 124).

This happened over and over again. Repressed anger, which spilled out when Tracy lost control, seemed justified when we consider what happened from her perspective. Goleman (1996, p. 60) says

> Given the roots of anger in the fight wing of the fight-or-flight response, it is no surprise that Zillman finds that a universal trigger for anger is the sense of being endangered. Endangerment can be signaled not just by an outright physical threat but also, as is more often the case, by a symbolic threat to self-esteem or dignity: being treated unjustly or rudely, being insulted or demeaned, being frustrated in pursuing an important goal.

Tracy's mum would always go down to the school 'with the pram' and 'argue' with the teachers. Tracy and her mum are alike. When her dad became involved, he would only say one word, 'Bed!' Mostly, Tracy was 'grounded' by her parents for her behaviour.

Once, she remembers, she and her mum had to go in front of the governors. 'Me and my mum on two seats in front of about 15 governors.' On this occasion, Tracy felt that her mum was 'made to feel small', and Tracy 'felt bad' about that. Tracy was asked to leave the room so that her mum could defend her behaviour.

Deep down, Tracy knew that she was capable of studying and passing exams. Sadly, she became resigned to not fulfilling her potential. In the context of the classroom, where she felt 'an outcast', the only way in which she could feel powerful was by disrupting lessons.

According to Robin Hobbs, a psychotherapist running a Pen Green staff training session, one of our basic psychological needs is for excitement or drama (Hobbs, 1998), and school, to Tracy, was generally boring. Children and young people who primarily learn kinaesthetically need first-hand experiences and to experiment in a practical way with various resources in order to sustain interest and to learn (Gardner, 1991). Tracy opted for the '14–16 Curriculum Project' so that she did not have to sit still and listen in school all day and every day, and could participate in some practical and vocational experiences. This indicates that she recognised that her own learning style required variety.

Recent research on how our brains work shows that, broadly speaking, men are 'less likely to endure routine patiently', that 'boys are harder to teach', and that 'disruptive behaviour is not voluntary' (Moir and Moir, 1999, p. 134). The type of behaviour Tracy displayed is more typical of the 'macho culture' of boys (Epstein et al., 1998, p. 82). Often there is a 'class dynamic' to this type of challenging behaviour. The stereotype is that middle-class, neat children work hard and prize academic achievement (Epstein *et al.*, 1998, p. 100). In contrast, working-class children are sporty and can do well but only without appearing to do any work (*ibid.*).

What follows is Tracy's experience of education, as an adult.

Tracy's story – adulthood, lived experience

Table 6.2 Tracy's adulthood experience

What was said or done	Feeling invoked	Consequences
Having to grow up/pregnant 'Shock! I didn't speak to anyone for six months.'	Fear/uncertainty	Isolation 'I'd walk to the shop for something to do.'
Finding out what was available 'I didn't know all this was here.'	Hope/enthusiasm	Start keeping diary '. . . . back into writing and understanding what he's doing.'
Start studying mathematics and English	Hopeful	Confidence
Took on too much 'I couldn't keep the two going.'	Had a 'downfall'/ despondent	Gave up English
Became too hard 'I started getting stuck on it.'	Despondent	Gave up mathematics 'I know it's there.'
Went on computer course 'Looked through Tresham leaflet – I was stuck in limbo.'	Able	Achieved distinction
Began college course 'I wanted to work with kids in children's homes.'	Hopeful	Setting long-term goal
Being treated like a child 'They forget all them young girls have got no family. We're changing it to this day, that time.'	Powerless/disheartened	Gave up
Being capable/looking after house 'I'll cook the dinners, clean the house.'	Proud	Self-respect
Caring what son thinks 'I hope I'm not a down and out.'	Pride	Dignity/ responsibility

As an adult learner, Tracy has had varied experiences (Table 6.2). Clearly, she is keen to learn, but when things become too difficult to sustain, she does not have earlier positive experiences to remind her that she can succeed.

Tracy experiences the system and people within it as 'unfair'. Several times she has begun studying and has not gone as far as she hoped. It seems that her expectation of herself is that she will not succeed. Each time she has to give something up or the obstacles become too great, she says that she is 'disheartened', that she 'knew it would come'. She says, 'school disheartened me'.

This is an analysis of a chain of events that has occurred more than once for Tracy, as an adult:

1 (conditions) being treated unfairly
2 (phenomenon) feeling despondent
3 (context) being treated like a child/feeling powerless
4 (action) giving up
5 (consequences) not achieving goal.

This chain of events does not mean that Tracy has not made progress. It means that she has not yet achieved all the goals she has set herself.

Ironically, Tracy did well on a computer course, which, she says, 'is not really what I want to do'. She described herself as 'being in limbo' after giving up mathematics and English, and looking for something else to do. She sees using computers as a useful skill, but she would not want to make a career of it.

As time goes on and Tracy gains experience of various courses, she is becoming much clearer about what she wants to do and why she wants to do it. She sees herself working with disadvantaged children in this area of the town, mainly because she has a social conscience and cares about facilities for young people like herself. She feels that there is even less provision for teenagers now than when she was a teenager. She has some good memories of attending a youth club at Pen Green Centre when the building was much larger. She says that the youth workers 'treated us like adults'.

Tracy says that using the centre has been significant for her, that she 'started to learn from' when she discovered what was on offer for adults in the centre.

Tracy's belief in her own ability is still tenuous. With a few more small successes, she might gain confidence and be prepared to fight for her right to an education, which suits her pocket and family commitments.

The second story is Kate's.

Kate's story about her education (a brief summary)

Kate hated school from the day she started. She would run away from school when she was very young, and this continued into her secondary schooling. At first she did not want to be separated from her mum. She says,' 'I clung on to my mum.' Later on, she was scared that her dad would come in and 'hit a teacher,' or embarrass her because he was drunk. She thought, 'I've got to get out.' She felt that the teachers would compare her behaviour with his. She thought people would say, 'She's just like her dad.'

One teacher was nice to Kate. She felt he was on her 'level'. He handled 'the bad children'. He was the only one to ask, 'Did you not like your dad?' Another teacher told Kate that she 'would go nowhere', that she would leave school and 'have a bundle of kids'. Kate thought that teachers were only interested in 'toffee-nosed children'. She says, 'They didn't want to listen to me.' She remembers feeling humiliated, 'For swimming, you had to walk the whole length of the school with your swimming costume on.'

Kate has a partner and five children, ranging in age from 5 to 15. When her eldest child began bringing homework home, Kate realised that she 'hadn't a clue what she was talking about'.

Kate decided that she had to do something about getting an education. Between trying various part-time and full-time factory jobs, she went to college, did a computer course and 'loved it'. She found that most people were there for the same reason and that the students were 'treated like adults'.

Kate has had different experiences with each of her children and is slowly learning to be assertive, rather than 'flying off the handle' when dealing with authority figures. She still does not attend parents' evenings or best work assemblies. She says that teachers still have not learnt to tell her anything good about her children.

Kate's full story can be analysed as shown in Table 6.3.

Kate's story – childhood, lived experience

Table 6.3 Kate's childhood experience

What was said or done	Feeling invoked	Consequences/ subsequent action
Started school 'I don't want to be here – I don't have to be here.'	Fear and anxiety	Ran away 'I'd run out.'
Brothers at home with mum 'Well, they're there with my mum.'	Jealousy	Ran away 'It's horrible.'
Being treated unfairly by teacher 'I got hit in the eye with a golf ball, and the teacher told me not to be stupid.'	Anger	Ran away

▶

What was said or done	Feeling invoked	Consequences/ subsequent action
Being put down by teacher 'You'll go nowhere.'	Anger	Ran away
Being ignored 'I needed someone to say "Why are you angry?"'	Anger	Ran away 'I didn't tell the teachers where I was going.'
Being cheeky to teacher 'I'd do things so they'd tell me off and then I'd go.'	Power/they could not stop me	Ran away
Being humiliated '... walking the length of the school with your swimming costume on.'	Anger	Ran away
One nice teacher 'I couldn't sit and listen – I might like this and it's too late.'	Fear of liking school	Ran away
Teachers are only interested in snobs 'So let's pay all our attention to them and get them through.'	Anger	Ran away
Step-dad listened 'You're not happy there, are you?'	Valued	Stuck it out

The repeated pattern in Kate's story (Table 6.3) can be analysed in this way:

1 (conditions) being ignored/humiliated
2 (phenomenon) feeling scared and angry
3 (context) not fitting in
4 (action) running away
5 (consequences) not becoming engaged and therefore no qualifications.

Analysing a repeated pattern in this way stops us from judging Kate's actions and helps us to understand why she developed this strategy. Kate says that the interview process has helped her 'to see things more clearly'.

In Kate's story, the overriding feeling she expressed was one of fear; therefore, although she was angry, she saw escape or 'flight' as her only possible response to 'endangerment' (Goleman, 1996, p. 60). She says that her mum listened to her and would sometimes go to the school, but that her mum was also scared of the teachers, as she could not read or write.

This response became such a fixed pattern that when Kate was tempted to stay and engage with the curriculum, she was fearful that it was too late and that she had missed too much schooling to catch up. She did develop other strategies, but they all involved avoidance of school and teachers. When she was older, she would phone the school and pretend to be her mum, saying, 'Kate won't be in today – she's got really bad period pains.' Sometimes she would 'hide in a cupboard at lunchtime'.

Some form of 'escaping' continued to be her only strategy. When her mother remarried and Kate had a step-father who listened and understood that she did not like school, his advice was to 'stick it out'.

Kate felt angry when she was a child but feels her anger was ignored. As an adult, Kate is more in touch with her anger and has a deep commitment to support all her children (Table 6.4). Her own experience as a child seems to have given her an insight into how things can be handled differently. Her eldest daughter did run away from school, but her teachers listened to her version of events and were able to sort out a bullying problem. Kate still feels sad that she herself was not listened to when she was a child. Being an advocate for her children has enabled Kate to learn to 'talk things through' and not 'fly off the handle'. Kate identifies closely with one of her children, who is currently excluded from primary school. She says, 'He's not a bad kid – he just seems to get the blame. He's well known for getting into trouble and now he is punished for really petty things.'

Kate's story – adulthood, lived experience

Table 6.4 Kate's adulthood experience

What was said/done	Feeling invoked	Consequences
Inability to help with homework 'I hadn't a clue.'	Inadequacy 'It was so simple.'	Tackle problem of no education
Goes to college 'Other people are like me – they haven't got a clue either.'	Confidence	Achieving goal
Child's teacher not listening to him 'He's got my nature – when he goes on one ...'	Anger 'I'd be straight down.'	Losing control
Coming to research – being contradicted 'People are brought up in different ways.'	Inadequacy/anger 'My upbringing was terrible.'	Stopped going

▶

What was said/done	Feeling invoked	Consequences
Child's teacher putting child down 'A teacher called her "stupid" in front of other pupils.'	Anger	Thinking things through 'I wrote down everything she told me and showed the head of the school.'
Being assertive 'I was calm on the outside.'	Powerful	Being listened to by authority figures
Child's photos displayed in research base '... they are watching what he's doing.'	Pride 'That's my boy – I'd tell people.'	Observing child and recognising his ability 'When he's built that circle thing, that's really nice.'

Kate's experience of going to college has been positive. Kate thinks that the reason for her more positive experience at college is that 'the people are the same as me. They haven't a clue either. There are no smart arses.' Also she appreciated 'having a laugh and joke with the tutors'.

Kate is planning to go back to college later this year to study for an NVQ in play work. Her decision to go back to college has been a difficult one to make. She still has ambivalent feelings about the system. She knows it will be a struggle but believes that she can succeed and says, 'It'll be great to stick my finger up to people who didn't think I could do it.'

The adults' learning processes

Tracy has learnt to control her anger but still feels that the system is unfair. She seems resigned to not yet achieving her personal goals.

Kate no longer runs away from education. Even though she was not listened to as a child, she is able to listen to her children and to ensure that their teachers know how they feel. Most of Kate's energy, up to now, has been directed toward sorting out interpersonal and behavioural issues at her children's schools. Recently, one of her children was called 'stupid' by a teacher in front of other pupils. Kate not only listened to her child, but wrote down everything that happened, including the child's feelings. Kate contacted the school and discussed the issue with the head, who wanted no further action on Kate's part. Kate was not satisfied with this and insisted on an interview with the head and the teacher concerned. Kate was able to confront the teacher with evidence of how he had made her child feel.

We hope that by engaging parents in the PICL project, and encouraging them to discuss their children's emotional and intellectual development, many of them will feel confident enough to discuss their children's all-round development with other professionals.

We want parents to be involved in discussing their children's education. Listening to Tracy's and Kate's stories can help us to be more aware of some of the barriers to coming into nursery or school for a minority of parents.

The barriers to becoming involved from the parents' perspectives

Personal and interpersonal barriers

What follows are the personal feelings expressed by Tracy and Kate that might be evoked whenever either of them enters a school environment and might therefore prevent them from feeling at ease in such an environment:

- anger, fear and anxiety;
- not fitting in;
- feeling undervalued;
- feeling numb;
- isolation;
- tendency to run away/avoid authority; and
- inadequacy.

Some of these feelings were evoked originally because of the way Tracy and Kate were treated by other people in the environment, usually teachers. Their feelings about teachers and other authority figures might also be reinforced by family attitudes. These attitudes to other people are described as interpersonal.

Teachers in school are often perceived by pupils as very powerful (Pollard, 1996). In the memories and experiences that Tracy and Kate describe, the majority of teachers appear as people who act unfairly, blame certain children for everything that goes wrong, only like and help 'snobs' or hard-working children, and humiliate and ignore other children. Both parents acknowledge that there are exceptions.

The slighted pupils react by telling lies, exaggerating, dramatising, running away from school and disrupting lessons. They feel justified in behaving in this way.

The role of Tracy and Kate's parents was crucial. Neither set of parents was able to convince their child that attending school and working hard have long-term benefits. Both sets of parents felt uncomfortable in the school environment. They did not view teachers as being like them and therefore they were 'unconfident' in dealing with them assertively.

Organisations are usually run by powerful people or people who have succeeded in attaining a position of authority. Often they are run to suit the majority, and this may exclude minorities. We are aware of 'institutional racism'; that is, organisations may have rules or structures that prevent minority ethnic groups from joining (Arnold, 1967). Schools sometimes have rules that prevent some children from having an equal opportunity to attend; for example, obliging pupils to buy an expensive uniform. These sorts of barriers are structural.

Structural barriers

The overstructuring of the curriculum seemed to be a barrier to Tracy's becoming engaged at school. Silly practices like 'walking the whole length of the school in your swimming costume' made Kate feel humiliated and therefore less motivated to participate.

There seemed to be a lack of information for pupils and their parents about courses. Tracy did not seem to realise that if she chose the 14–16 Curriculum Project, she could not sit her GCSEs. Tracy's and Kate's parents were not knowledgeable about curriculum issues. Were any efforts made by the schools to communicate with them about curriculum matters? Did they attend open evenings? If not, how would they know what was available for their children? Were open evenings easily accessible?

When Tracy's jacket was torn in a tussle with a teacher, that was a huge issue for her. She felt she had to exaggerate what had happened so that she was not blamed for spoiling her new jacket. In this instance, her mum went straight down to the school to complain. Replacing the jacket was a serious concern in Tracy's household. Money is often tight and prevents some children from taking part in extra-curricular activities that might engage them more than the regular curriculum.

Strategies we have used to engage Tracy and Kate and other parents at Pen Green

Bearing in mind the sorts of barriers that may have prevented parents from participating in education in the past, we have developed the following strategies.

To overcome barriers connected to personal feelings

Often parents are anxious and lack confidence. If we accept them and their children and genuinely like them, parents will begin to loosen up. We must always be scrupulously fair, and sometimes this involves explaining our decisions and policies to parents. They have a right to know how decisions are made. Whenever possible, we can involve them in the decision-making process. We always try to listen to complaints and apologise if we are in the wrong.

It is important to acknowledge feelings, the parents' and their child's. Often something quite small makes parents angry. If their child goes home in wet socks, they are entitled to feel cross with us for not noticing. We can apologise and make sure we check socks in future.

We offer one-to-one support if parents are shy or lack confidence in a group situation. Sometimes they might want to express an anxiety, or we can spend time discussing the key concepts and how they relate to their child's progress.

Sometimes parents need convincing that they and their child have potential. We closely observe children, and our observations are invaluable information to pass on to parents on a daily basis if possible. This can alert the parent to specific things to watch out for at home and to share with us.

We often reflect back to parents the major role we see them playing in their child's development and learning. For example, when Tracy kept a diary, David was seeing her writing each day and that increased his knowledge of communication. Soon after, he became interested in numbers and letters.

To overcome barriers connected to attitudes to other people

We want parents to get to know us as individuals and we want to get to know each of them as an individual. The only way to do this is to spend time together. During the two weeks that parents spend settling their children into nursery, we have a golden opportunity to chat informally with them and to get to know a bit about them. It is only fair to tell them about ourselves and our families, if they are interested.

Once we know something about their life, we can try to engage them in coming to a group. Some parents might be ready to study or meet with other parents to discuss their children. Others just want to get a job or have some time to themselves. We have high expectations of parents and we know that the majority want more information about how children learn and how they can help them.

As time goes on, there are many other ways that we can build our relationships with parents. We can invite them on a trip with their child or to a social event in the centre, or ask them to show visitors around the centre. This acknowledges that they are our equals, that we enjoy and value time spent together, and that they have gained knowledge as a user of the services, which they can share with visitors.

Although we are working hard to build relationships, we try not to patronise parents. Being honest with them is important. For example, Kate did not agree with her son playing with dolls in the nursery. We discussed this issue on several occasions, all airing our views freely. We agreed to differ on this point.

Parents who are not confident about writing often like using a video camera. Often fathers are interested in technology for themselves and for their children. Tracy's partner became very engaged in observing David when they borrowed the nursery video camera.

Overcoming barriers to do with the rules and structure of the organisation

When the organisation is inflexible and unresponsive, it is not helpful. We find it is a good rule of thumb to think through the reasons for having rules. Our family room at Pen Green used to be a room where parents could smoke. Ten years ago, after nearly two years of discussion and consultation between parents and staff, we made it a no-smoking area. This was agreed mainly because of the children's health. However, we still feel that it is important to have a smoking area, which is now out of doors, if we are to welcome all parents into the centre. Most of the study and support groups have a no-smoking policy, which is negotiated when a group begins. However, we can be flexible and have a 'smoke break' halfway through a meeting if that suits the parents.

Coming out of the organisation and making visits to children's homes on a routine basis is something that staff and parents seem to appreciate. Tracy says, 'When Lorna (family worker) came, David was taking her up to his bedroom. He thought everyone lived at nursery. I said, "Lorna's got a house. Lorna's got children."'

When we evaluate our work, it is important to ask parents how things have been for them. New ideas stimulate our thinking, and often these come from parents. We are constantly listening out for what parents want and trying to offer it. Recently, some Portuguese families moved into the area from the Algarve, and they now have classes in English as a second language with crèche facilities for their children at the centre.

How Tracy and Kate got involved in the research and development project

Tracy

- Tracy became involved in attending a session on schemas. This was when David would still not separate from her, so he came along too and one of the workers played with him during the session.
- Tracy kept a diary of what David became involved in at home for six months of David's two years at nursery. Over the same six months, Tracy attended a weekly study group.
- Tracy and Tommy borrowed the nursery video camera twice. Tracy says Tommy 'is right into technology'. Shortly after this, both parents came to a science and technology evening in the nursery. We had set up the television and video camera, computers and our CD-ROM, which illustrates how children learn through exploring schemas. Tommy found it fascinating.
- Again, both parents came to an evening study group, when the focus was on boys' achievement.

- Each year we run an assertiveness programme for the children who are due to start school. We call it 'Learning to be Strong'. We begin by having a parents' meeting to discuss the programme with parents. Tracy and Tommy attended this meeting.
- Tracy went on a day trip to the Science Museum in London with other parents and staff and also attended a family group meeting at nursery.

Both parents came to a meeting about reports for school. During the interview, Tracy said that the following ways of being involved were significant for her. Keeping a diary was a turning point for Tracy. She said that that was 'when she started to learn'. She was 'back into writing and understanding what he's doing'. She also enjoyed attending the study group. Sometimes she would say outrageous things, but we all knew and liked her, and there was a spirit of fun in the group. Tracy remembers borrowing the video camera, although it was Tommy who did most of the filming. 'David would carry on with what he was doing when Tommy filmed him.' The 'Learning to be Strong' parents' meeting was important and helpful to both parents. The discussion about bullying helped Tracy and Tommy to make a difficult decision about which school to choose for David. The 'Learning to be Strong' sessions for David were 'well worth doing'. When David first started nursery, the family had just moved back to the area, and he was quite insecure. His family worker and parents put together a book containing photographs of people who were important to him. This 'family' book was significant for David. It helped him to settle at nursery. Tracy says, 'He used to walk about carrying his book.'

Kate's involvement in the project

It was when Kate's youngest child started nursery that the PICL project began. Kate did not see herself as the type of parent who becomes involved in centre activities. She said, 'I'm not the type – Pen Greeny. I haven't been to baby massage or to this group or that group.' She also expressed her ambivalence about not having been involved when her older children were nursery age. 'Why should I do it for him when I didn't do it for Carl? I've never done things like that before.' Despite her resistance to involvement, Kate became involved in the following ways.

- Kate attended a study group in the evening twice. She said during the interview that she finally came 'to see what it was like' because we kept 'nagging and nagging,' and she thought 'they *do* want me to come'. She found the first meeting 'interesting' but the next one was 'rubbish'. Her main reason for not enjoying the second meeting was that 'whatever I said, somebody always contradicted me'. (Kate is referring to other parents and staff disagreeing with her.) Some contentious issues were discussed to do with smacking and telling children to hit back when other children hit them. Given her history of 'being ignored' and 'not being listened to', she possibly found mild disagreement quite threatening to her self-esteem.

- Kate also became involved in discussing her son's portfolio individually with Cath. She agreed to take some photos of her son playing at home, after describing to us the complex play that he became involved in with his cars and using the bottom of the wardrobe in his bedroom. The photos never materialised, and when asked why, Kate said she tore them up because her house looked messy.
- Kate attended a meeting about reports for school.

Kate said that the following things about nursery were significant for her. Having a full-time place in nursery for her little boy, Mark, who had been 'a poorly baby'. Kate became interested in what Mark could do 'at his age'. She said, 'I was shocked at what he could do. He was doing different things to what Carl was doing.' Kate was proud of Mark's photos displayed in the research base. She said, 'I didn't think I'd ever see my kids' photos up anywhere here.' She added, 'Oh my God, people are going to come in here and see my son on the wall.'

We can learn a great deal from listening to these parents. It is easy to sit back and judge parents without knowing very much about their passionate concerns. We can measure the effectiveness of our service by how persistently we work to reach the parents who are finding our services hard to reach. The final comment is from Kate (about her children): 'I'd want them to do something like stay on at school and to think, "I *can* do this."' What we need to remember is that:

- we want all parents to become involved in discussing their child's education; and
- we may need to develop very different strategies to engage parents who have had poor experiences of education and schooling.

CHAPTER 7

The Impact on Parents' Lives

Annette Cummings

This chapter gives an account of how Annette, formerly a parent at Pen Green and now a teacher in the nursery, initially got involved in the research project. It also describes three nursery parents' different experiences of being involved in a study group over a period of one to three years.

Annette's account

As a family worker at Pen Green, I am now in my second year of co-leading a research and development study group that focuses on parents' involvement in their children's learning. As a group leader, I have found the group absorbing, thought-provoking and enlightening. It has been wonderful to watch the parents grow in confidence and knowledge as the year progresses. It is also fascinating to listen to the parents' views and comments on how their children engage in play at home. Each parent brings to the group a wealth of knowledge of their own child, which helps to provide a more holistic approach to the child when it comes to planning provision for the nursery (see Chapter 8). Throughout the two years that I have run the group, I have become very interested in the way that the parents' involvement with their children's learning project has had a knock-on effect in relation to the parents' own personal growth and development.

Getting involved in my own children's learning

One of the reasons that I really enjoy co-leading the Parents' Involvement in Their Children's Learning (PICL) group is that it was getting involved with my own children's learning that pushed me to go back to university to do a postgraduate teachers' certificate in education. When my eldest child started at the Pen Green nursery in 1993, the research and development at the work at the centre was in its early days. Even then, all the nursery parents had a chance to go to a training session on schemas, which was led by

Tina Bruce, an education consultant and author of several books on early childhood education.

At this time, I knew nothing about schemas, but I did know that the things Alexandria was doing at home were driving me mad. Alexandria, who was aged three at the time, had a favourite game, hide-and-seek. She used to get inside the duvet cover and do the press studs up, or get inside the curtain lining. She always wanted to dress up and put make-up on. Meanwhile, my youngest child, Olivia, who was aged 16 months, used to empty tins out of the kitchen cupboard, put them into her pram and wheel them around the house. Between both children, I thought I would go crazy.

I went along to a child development session, at the Pen Green Centre, when Alexandria was attending the nursery, and I found the whole thing mind-blowing. Everything fell into place. Alexandria was displaying typical 'envelopment' behaviour and Olivia was a 'transporter'. I was hooked. It all seemed so simple. The schema training helped me to understand my children better and also helped me to make extra provision at home to help them extend their play.

When Olivia showed signs of 'envelopment' schema, I just took it in my stride. I knew exactly how to support her in her play and bought her Polly Pocket dolls, which would incorporate both schemas (envelopment and transporting). Alexandria is now nine years old and is still a strong enveloper. She still likes to dress up and put make-up on. When she entered a fancy dress competition recently, she transformed herself into the Statue of Liberty!

Olivia is still displaying her cluster of schemas that include envelopment and transporting. On a recent holiday to Minorca, Olivia wanted to pack her own hand luggage. When we reached our apartment, she disappeared into the bedroom and reappeared five minutes later. I though nothing of it until I went to hang the clothes up in the wardrobe. When I opened the wardrobe door, there were 37 teddy bears staring at me. Olivia could not stop laughing. She thought it was very funny that nobody knew she had transported them all the way to Minorca from her room at home.

The parents that I work with (Figure 7.1) in the research group have had similar experiences. For example:

- Louise has two children, Sean and James, and is married to Scott. Sean started nursery in 1996 and left to go to school in 1998 when James, his younger brother, started using the nursery. Both children have had the benefit of attending nursery for two full years, which seems to us, at Pen Green, to be ideal. Louise has been attending the PICL research group for four years.
- Eloise is married to Dave, and they have two children, Becky and Jessica. Eloise has been going to the PICL group every week for the last three years. Becky spent a year at the nursery and has now moved on to primary school, and Jessica is full-time in the nursery and will be there for two years in all.

Figure 7.1 Parents in the research group: Eloise and Dave with Becky and Jessica

- Dave is married to Tracey and they have two children, Lorin and Ross. Both parents attend the PICL group. Lorin has moved on to school and Ross is in the nursery. Dave has been going to the PICL group for 18 months.

Starting the group

All new parents, both mothers and fathers, are encouraged by their family worker to join a research study group when their child starts nursery. They are normally introduced to the programme on an initial home visit well before the child comes into the nursery. As a teacher in the nursery, I always talk to the parents to explain how valuable it is for us to have information on what their child is doing at home, and I explain how that information is used in the nursery. I also explain that learning about why your children do certain things can help in terms of what you provide for them in the home. It can also increase your understanding of the way that children think. Parents are very interested in what their children are learning, and most of our parents have some link with the research project through attending the PICL group, keeping a diary, or coming to the key concept training sessions in the first term, or, sometimes, attending a family group meeting.

Some parents find going to a group difficult to handle, and sometimes it is the thought of their own literacy skills that comes to the forefront. Their anxieties about writing often date back to their own experiences of schooling. This literacy issue is sensibly dealt with by the staff so that most parents can feel comfortable about attending. Staff explain that, although some parents in the group will want to keep diaries, there is no need to write anything down if parents are reluctant writers. All parents can discuss their children's interests and development orally in a supportive small group setting. Sometimes parents have low self-esteem, so gentle encouragement is needed to get them to attend the group. I always tell the parents that joining the group is also a good way to make new friends, because, as parents, they all have at least one thing in common, their children.

The parents' reactions on joining the group

The parents' reactions on joining the group were as follows.

Louise's feelings on starting the group

Sean was three and had started nursery, and I decided to become involved in the PICL group. I had already been at the centre doing lots of other parent groups and I really enjoyed the centre. It gave me something to do during the day and somewhere where I could learn. So I started the PICL group and I really enjoyed it. It just broadened my horizons as to what Sean was doing.

Sean was really boisterous as a toddler; he was very physical. He was always into climbing, running around, hiding and running away. I had to run a lot after him and be behind him a lot of the time, as he was always doing dangerous things. James, my other little one, does exactly the same. I found Sean quite hard. Being your first child, I always felt as if wherever I looked it was always Sean that was, you know, mucking about, as they say, or running about or throwing things. He used to throw everything. He used to be quite rough with other children, which was really hard. When Sean started nursery, and I had the opportunity to join the PICL group and learn something about why he was doing these things, I thought 'brilliant'. It was an ideal opportunity to give him everything I could, you know, from learning myself. The PICL group really opened my eyes as to why Sean was doing things.

Going to the group itself was about making new friendships and also just about being able to get things off your chest and being reassured as to why the children were doing things, rather than bottling everything up – talking to people who understood as well, you know. The nursery staff who run the group could help you out.

Eloise's feelings on joining the group

My family worker at the time was Annette. She talked me into going. She talked about these wonderful diaries that we would keep and videotapes and all sorts of things, but I wasn't that keen, I must admit. The thought of keeping a diary didn't appeal to me, and I just thought that my writing would not be as good as everybody else's. I was placing myself low down, I didn't have the confidence, but I went to the first meeting and that was it. The staff were wonderful, they made you feel as if you wanted to go back, they gave you the confidence. They didn't pull you down if you said something that was utterly stupid.

When I first thought about going, I was cringing inside, and the night before was like 'Oh God, I've got to go to this group and somebody might speak to me. What if I go red and what if I say the wrong thing?' I thought I just didn't want to go, but I went, because I thought that Annette might kill me if I hadn't gone! Nobody sort of laughed at you. Whatever you said was good, you know. It just gave me the confidence to go back. If I had hated it, I would never have gone back.

Dave's feelings about starting the group

I started with the PICL group a month after Ross started nursery. He has been coming to nursery for roughly 18 months and I have been doing the PICL group for much the same time. I went along mainly to get involved with knowing why Ross was doing certain things, because when our daughter was coming up to seven, she came through the nursery, and there were things she did, playing at home, that would drive me mad. My wife Tracey was involved with the nursery anyway, coming to baby groups and groups with Lauren before. She would say, 'She's doing this because of this and this is her schema,' and I didn't know anything about what she was going on about.

I was interested to come along when Ross came to nursery because I was now permanent night shift, whereas before I used to work a double day shift, 6–2 or 2–10, so I couldn't get involved. I wanted to come along and find out why Ross was doing certain things and how he could be encouraged. We found that Lauren was always encouraged, with drawing and painting and writing and even with simple maths, at nursery. Now, at school, she is in the top group in the class, she reads really well, better than some children I know who are a lot older, and she writes and spells words that my boss at work would struggle with. She's really doing very, very well, so I was encouraged to come along to these things, to the group, to find out how I could help Ross in the same way as Lauren had benefited.

Also, going to this group, I have managed to find out about things that my child does that I was not particularly pleased with or happy about. We used to be a bit wary of Ross bouncing around, jumping off the furniture. Now, rather than tell him off all the time, we realise the only thing we can do is make what he does safer, so my sister-in-law bought him a trampoline for his birthday. He used it a lot, rather than the furniture, which is encouraging. He bounced around on the trampoline until he became, not bored with it, but he'd bounced enough, and now it's in the playhouse in the garden, and if they're out in the garden in the summer, he'll bounce on it again.

Getting to know about patterns in children's play

All the parents using the groups have made huge discoveries about the patterns in their children's play. Because they had all attended introductory sessions on schemas, they began to use Piagetian language with confidence to describe and account for their children's behaviour.

Finding out about schemas

Louise

When I first went to the group, it was just brilliant knowing why he was doing things, especially the throwing, because he used to throw everything, and obviously that was his trajectory schema. They told me that he was going on to learn about areas and everything to do with mathematics and things, and I was thinking, 'Wow,' and it took a little while to sink in, really. But then, as I went to the group, I learnt more and more why he was doing things at nursery, and it was relatively easy to see what he was doing at home. Sean used to flood my bathroom; he liked to see the water overflowing. Before, I was getting really angry because it was, like, so-called naughty things he was doing. Obviously, it still is a bit naughty sometimes, because you don't want your bathroom soaked or whatever, but why he was doing it was because he was learning. I used to try and think of alternative things for him to do which wasn't wrecking my house and being dangerous. One thing he used to love was glass – he loved to see it smashed, which was really out of order. So I took him to the bottle bank, you know, hoping it would satisfy his need, but it wasn't enough; he still used to go on about glass. So at the PICL group, which was a lovely group, we talked about it. You felt as if you could go in and tell the group what they were doing, getting worries off your chest, and you'd be reassured why he was doing things. So then the staff at the PICL group suggested I get some ice cubes. So in the summer I used to freeze loads of ice, and let him go out in the garden with a big bucket and a hammer. He loved the banging and he used to smash all the ice everywhere, all along the path and that. It seemed to satisfy his need and then he sort of went on to something else.

 I found the group really helped me in finding ideas for things for Sean to do that were interesting and safe.

Eloise

I enjoyed coming to the group. It made me understand what Becky was doing. I mean, she was driving me nuts. She was filling nappy sacks, Jessica was a baby at the time, and Becky was leaving them all over the house. If we wanted anything, it was in a nappy sack somewhere knotted up. That sort of opened my eyes, and I found other things more suitable than the plastic nappy sacks she was using, like paper bags and envelopes, and it's just gone on from there.

Becky's envelopment schema was so strong, you could leave her and the house could have fell down, and she wouldn't have cared. I mean, with Becky what she was doing at nursery, she has taken with her to school, and she is doing very, very well with language and literacy. I mean her language is brilliant.

Dave

I'd spoken to Tina Bruce on a number of occasions on study days, and I've always found what she had to say really interesting, because you look at your children and you don't realise the hidden things, their ways of thinking. Before the schema training, I would have spent all this money on toys that he wouldn't play with, whereas now I know I would have saved myself a lot of money, and I've bought him boxes, some wooden boxes, anything to put things in and move them about because he's into this enclosure schema. We've learnt that you don't have to spend a lot of money on expensive toys that they're not going to play with. At Christmas this year, through the PICL group, knowing that Ross was into dressing up (envelopment schema), we bought him a dressing-up Buzz Lightyear wings, mask and helmet. A lot of our friends spent hundreds of pounds on their children, but, with Ross, he had nearly everything he wanted. He was really excited about everything he got, and he plays with everything. Not just like Christmas Day and Boxing Day and it's all forgotten, he's still playing with everything we bought him now, and I think we'd have struggled to spend £50 on him this Christmas. I've gained a lot of new learning talking with Tina and finding out how she gets her ideas and things, and I've borrowed a book by Tina, from Trevor the head of centre, and I've been taking it to work with me, and it's fascinating – it's really good.

Ross has been interested in Sellotaping things, connecting things together with Sellotape, tying things, making up parcels. He's forever bringing us things in paper stuck with Sellotape and saying, 'I've brought you a present', so one of the staff suggested we buy him a Sellotape dispenser. Because he's got little hands, he can't peel the Sellotape off the roll, and they've got one at nursery and he knows how to use it. So we bought him a big Sellotape dispenser, some paper, pens and bits for Christmas. It was the best present we could have bought him at the time, this Sellotape dispenser, and the Sellotape was all over the house. But whereas a lot of parents would have been annoyed at the Sellotape stuck to the doors and wrapped around the chair legs and things, we know why he does it. It's made our life a lot calmer.

The diaries

Although I was involved with a research group when my daughter Olivia was at nursery, the one thing I regret is not keeping a diary of her everyday play. I do feel sad about it, but I make sure that I tell all new parents about how I feel in the hope that it will encourage them to keep their diaries up. At that time there was no support group for parents at Pen Green, so I felt isolated and insecure about what to write, and I did not make the effort. Nowadays, the subject of what to write in the diary always crops up and is covered during the session when the co-leader and myself talk through the key concepts in child development, which parents have been introduced to in their initial training session. Parents learn to apply these key concepts to their children's play. For instance, parents soon realise it's worth writing things down or videoing their children when they are deeply involved, and knowing about the involvement scale really seems to help.

During these sessions, the question of poor literacy skills and low self-esteem often rears its ugly head. Horrible tales from school are told, and many parents report how cutting remarks from teachers have had a detrimental and lasting effect on their self-esteem and belief in themselves as learners. Again, reassurance is what is needed. I have always explained that when I read their diaries I'm not interested in checking their spelling or grammar: I'm just interested in the content, and I want to find out what the children have been doing at home so I can feed that information back into the nursery planning. Once all the initial problems have been sorted out, and the group settles into a routine, it is a privilege to listen to what the parents have to say about children, and how they have been playing with them at home. Parents love to write about their children even if they are not sure what their play has been about, and when they come into the group, they like to talk about what their child has been doing even if they find their children's behaviour challenging.

Louise on keeping diaries

It's brilliant, I really enjoy writing things down, and even now I go back sometimes to Sean's and flick through. You can't believe some of the things you said, you forget so quickly. It's really good looking back at what you've said, and at the group you use your diary to sort of help prompt you then as to what they've been up to and why they were doing things. This is what the group is all about, sharing what your children are doing.

Eloise on diaries

Well, I have and I haven't kept them. Becky's was pretty good, Jessica's, I've not been so good this year, I don't know why, I just can't get into it. Maybe it's because Jessica's schemas aren't so clear. Becky had one schema, and she was easy to write about, whereas Jessica has a cluster of schemas. One day she's got one schema and the next week she's doing something else, so I don't know. It is nice to have a diary and look back at it, and I wish I'd carried on with Becky when she went to school, and I haven't. With Jessica, I will. Now Becky's left nursery, she's got her diary up in her wardrobe, and she's really proud of it, and her portfolio, she loves it, she's just so proud of it, and I am too.

Feeling confident in a group

Once a group is up and running and the boundaries have been set, it is amazing how quickly the group feels at ease. Boundaries around confidentiality are very important to make it safe for parents to open up and share experiences. It is very rewarding to see the group help each other, not only in terms of their children's learning but also through developing friendships and gaining personal support. Last year, in the group that I ran, the parents supported each other through two marital separations, two births, a death in the family, and an older child leaving home. As the trust builds up within the group between parents and staff, there are certain personal issues that parents may feel the need to share. These needs must be addressed not only to ensure the well-being of parents but also because it gives the other group members an idea of where those parents and their child are 'coming from'. For example, a sudden change in a child's behaviour might be because his mum and dad have separated, and the child does not want to see his dad.

Once the scenario has been discussed within the group, it gives some context to what the parent has written about the child. More often than not, there is a group member who has been through a similar situation and who can offer help with different strategies to cope during this difficult time.

Parents openly discuss and celebrate their children's play but will also talk freely about things that they are not happy about, especially if it is a child's challenging behaviour. The staff and other parents provide a listening ear and sometimes offer advice on how to deal with particular issues. Parents become confident to speak out in these relatively small groups. They become better at listening to other parents and feel able to offer appropriate advice to each other.

Louise on being part of a group

I suppose the big thing I got out of the group was that what the boys were up to was OK. It boosted my confidence as a parent just knowing it was OK. I used to feel, a lot of the time, that Sean was the only one in the whole world that was doing these things, and I got to realise that he wasn't. Everybody else was able to share their anxieties as parents, and it made me feel a whole lot better. Because, a lot of the time outside of the group, I'm really honest about what they do, and sometimes I used to think that maybe I said too much. I sometimes felt as if other parents wouldn't say the things, I said, they only said all the good things, and that used to make me feel even worse. So going to the research group was about sharing, and everybody in the group is the same, they used to share their anxieties, and it just helped us to understand that it was OK.

Eloise's feelings about the group

I felt confident at the group. You knew that you weren't going to be judged for smacking them for really being naughty. Like when Jessica, who was going through a cutting-up stage, got all my letters off the doormat and sat and cut them all up. I was cross and I had to tell her off because there was my TV licence and everything else in that pile, so I had to say that this was not right. I mean, even though she was doing her trajectory schema, I had to tell her that that was wrong. You know, she couldn't do things like that, she had to ask before she cut important things like the mail up.

There are days when your children really wind you up, and I felt confident enough to say, 'Yes, I'm having a really bad day.' I felt OK about it because everything you say in the group is in confidence anyway. We covered *everything* in the group. I mean, a couple of times we just sat and talked – it's not every week it's about your diary. If there was something bothering somebody, staff would sense that, then we would discuss that, if the person felt comfortable about it, which I quite enjoyed as well. Sometimes it was nice to get something off your chest. I mean, there was one session we were talking about ourselves, and a couple of them were in tears, you know, they had got something off their chest.

Sometimes it was nice to hear other people were going through the same thing as you, and you didn't know or realise about it. I mean, I didn't get very far at school and I never liked school, and I want things to be different for my children. I could have died at school and nobody would have known if I was there. I sat at the back of the class, and I think the PICL group has helped me, not to push my children to where they don't want to do anything, but to go with them. If they're having a bad day, I say, 'Well, fine, tomorrow's another day,' and we can start again and we'll try again, and we'll go as far as we can. We can do the best we can. You know, I speak to Becky's teacher every single day whether she likes it or not, and if Becky comes out of school and there's something bothering her, I go back now, whereas before, if I hadn't gone to the PICL group, I would have put my head down and said, 'Never mind.' Now I go back up and whether Becky's got the story wrong or right, I go and discuss it there and then. I do not keep it or hold on to it anymore, I just go and get it sorted out, which I would never have done before. So it has given me the confidence to do that. Before I would have died rather than go up and speak to the teachers.

Dave on being part of the group

If there's something that we don't particularly like him doing at home or something I am worrying about, I felt I could talk about it in the group. For instance, Ross had a dummy, and I used to say, he was nearly four at the time, and he still had this dummy stuck in his mouth. I mean, I criticise people for saying, I don't like my son playing with prams or I don't like my son playing with dolls or dressing up and all this, and I criticise people for that, yet I could see myself doing much the same thing and saying the same things about his dummy. I used to talk about it at the PICL group, I used to come to it and say, 'Look, what am I going to do about it, this dummy?' and lots of the parents were saying, you know, that they had to leave it for Santa. One of them said that her son buried it in the garden and things like that. We went on holiday, and for the whole fortnight Ross had it stuck in his mouth. I used to get really worried, thinking, 'Oh, what's he gonna do, he's got all these dummies, and people are gonna think, look at the size of that kid with that dummy.' The week after we came home, I was at the point of thinking, 'Oh, no.' I was gonna hide them or throw them all out and just tell him they'd gone. But one night he was going to bed, he had his dummy, and he just said to me, 'I don't like the taste of this.' I said, 'Well, we've only got two or three, try this one. I'll run it under the tap.' He replied, 'No, I don't like the taste of that one.' I said, 'We haven't got any more.' He replied,   'I don't want one then.' He put these three dummies on his chest of drawers in the bedroom and went to bed. That was the end of it, he never had them again, and afterward I kept thinking all this fuss I've made, and people would have been thinking, 'Oh my God, here he goes again about this bloody dummy.' But all this fuss I'd made, at the end of the day, he was the one who instigated finishing it, and we've learnt, a lot of the time, from the group, a lot of the parents had said that he'll give it up when he wants to, and I was thinking, 'When will that be?' But I didn't mind going to the PICL group and saying, 'Look, I'm really concerned about this,' even though, in a way, I was being very similar to the ones who say, I don't like him playing with prams, or I don't like him doing this. I could see that I was along those lines, but I didn't mind saying it because I felt really strongly about it.

What do parents get from the group for themselves?

When I was involved with a research project as a parent, I found the whole experience enlightening. It made me feel that I understood my children a lot better, and I did not get cross with them so easily. It made me look at what they were interested in, and I knew that if I wanted half an hour of time for myself, the best thing was to go to the junk market and buy Alexandria some more dressing-up clothes (envelopment schema) and Olivia, Polly Pocket dolls (envelopment/transporting schema), and then I would have time to sit and read a book or do the crossword because they would be busy. Apart from helping me with my children, the research project helped me to find a sense of direction and make a career change – from working in the fashion business to teaching. So off I went to De Montfort University and took a postgraduate certificate of education course. I passed the course with a distinction, but the proudest moment for me was when I stood in front of my year group and explained to them what schemas were all about, using my own children's patterns of play as examples. From the conversations I have with the parents who attend the PICL group and the three parents I have interviewed for this chapter, the general consensus is that the group is definitely a confidence builder, and in some cases, mine included, it can lead to a major career change. The majority of parents who have been involved with the PICL group go on to other courses such as the City and Guilds accredited crèche worker course that is run at Pen Green. Others go on to take the NVQ in childcare at the centre (Pen Green is an NVQ assessment centre). Some parents co-lead groups at the centre, and these parents can become paid workers through the local further education college if they have a basic qualification in training adult learners (City and Guilds 9282).

The PICL group also helps parents feel strong enough to make decisions about their children and to challenge the people who have all the power, and control when their child is unhappy. I have found that parents who had negative school experience, who had no support from their own parents, really do want to make a difference to their own children's education and support them all the way through their school careers. They want to be advocates for their children. Parents feel less stress when they understand why their children are playing in certain ways. With knowledge about child development concepts, they can try to turn problematic situations around, so that they can become positive learning experiences. Coming to the group every week has helped the parents get to know their children better and has helped them to build a better relationship with each other. Parents become committed group members and friendships grow in the group.

Parents have also told me how their children love their coming to the group. The children see their parents write in their diaries, and this encourages the children to be interested in writing and early literacy. The children also love the fact that their parents spend time in the nursery talking to staff at the beginning and end of each day; finding out what the children do at nursery that is the same as at, or different from, home is critically important for parents. They are also very anxious to know whom their children are playing with.

Parents enjoy watching their children on video in the group. It is a good chance for them to see what their children are engaged in at nursery. Also parents like to show off the videoing skills they have gained by coming to the training session on videoing children that is offered to all parents. This session is led by a professional video maker, Penny Lawrence, who works on the non-fiction parts of the *Teletubbies* series.

Parents become schema spotters and look far the involvement signals. Parents genuinely feel respected as their child's first educator. They see staff keeping records and planning for individual children, and they know that staff are deeply concerned to support each child's learning.

Louise – what it's meant to be part of the group

Coming to the group really helped my confidence in wanting to learn more about the children, and now I've gone on to run a group myself to do with babies. It's called 'Growing Together,' and it focuses on under-nursery-age children where parents can come and learn, from a really early age, why children are doing things. I really enjoy doing it because it's sort of an extension of me being involved with the PICL group as a parent. Now I'm helping to run this one, and it's really gone well. I found being in the role of the teacher strange at first because you feel a bit – well, you've always been to groups as a parent, but I want them to learn what I've learnt through the group. I'm really enthusiastic about, you know, letting them see what I've learnt through the group, how it's opened my eyes as to why my children are doing the things they do, and, you know, just finding that understanding. The group's helped my confidence. My boys come first, and being their advocate, going to school, and being able to talk to their teacher has been important.

When Sean started school, there was a bit of a problem. I sort of had a word with the teacher about it, and I wouldn't let it go. It was to do with his baseline assessment. I knew exactly why Sean hadn't done very well in baseline, because it takes Sean a few months, the person he is, to settle into change, to feel comfortable, to do his best. So I went in and explained that to the teacher. Now, you know, after a couple of months, he's coming out with flying colours. So, you know, I've followed it through with Sean, and the group has made me a lot more confident to speak to teachers. Like I say, when I had Sean, I really wanted to learn about children's development because you have a baby and it's a whole new world. I didn't really know anything about how children learn. I wanted to do something for myself so I did my diploma in child day care by correspondence. Then I went on to do the Confident Parent, Confident Children Open University group at Pen Green. Then I went on to do the PICL group, and since then it's really taken off. I really enjoy working with children. I now work in a play group at the sports centre. James goes to school in September, so I think that's a turning point for myself. I always thought I'd like to be at home with the children when they're small, but when they do go to school, then it's time for me. I'm halfway-knowing what I'd like to do, and, you know, I was just thinking about whether to do my NVQ when James goes to school in September.

Eloise – what's it's meant to me and the future

I'm seriously thinking about the crèche workers' course at Pen Green once Jessica's in school, because once she's in school I haven't got any more excuses. I do want to do the crèche workers' course, but something deep down inside says, 'Oh God.' I'll have to write and do essays, and that's what's holding me back. I could have done it this year, but I used Jessica as an excuse. So next year, I'm not going to have Jessica, so I'll see how I go. I might need a good kick up the backside to make me do it. Hopefully, the group will springboard me on to something else. I'd say I feel more confident with people. I have to push myself more because my husband's away from home, but if David was at home all the time, I don't know how I would be. You know, there's only one person that can help you, and that's yourself, really, in the end. The group made me understand my children more. It's given me the confidence to give them a push if they need it, and yet not to push them too hard. I don't get cross so quickly with them now, because if they're doing something, like Jessica cutting up the mail, even though I had to tell her that that was wrong, I don't scream and shout like I would have done. I will miss the group. It's not a trudge, it's not like 'Oh God, it's Tuesday afternoon, and I've got to go to the PICL group.' I feel good that it's Tuesday, I'm going to miss it; it's part of my life now. It's been three years and I've made friends. I help now at the Messy Play Group and I am mixing with parents. I have to speak to other people – it's something I make myself do. I have to push myself and I'm going to start a mums and tots group over at the school, with Connie on a Monday morning, starting next month, so that will be meeting new parents. It's a shame, really, that there's not the same thing at school where you could carry it on, but, I suppose, with the limited resources they have, they're just not able to do it.

Dave – what the group's meant to me and the future

The group helped me as a parent. I think it's great because I work permanent night shifts, and it's horrible to say, but it's more like a social event. I mean, you come and chat with other parents, and it's always good to come. I love it, I love coming to the group. We have a chat and a laugh. I've learnt so much more about my children, and I've learnt how to encourage them to learn through playing and what they're getting out of what they do. Apart from my own children, I've never had that much experience with younger children, so I started helping at the nursery: through my involvement with the PICL group, I've become more involved with Pen Green than my wife is. She's done her A-Level English here, but I've also done parent interviews for the Sure Start project and I've interviewed to appoint new staff. I've personally gained a lot from it. I mean, I sort of found out now I've got other career opportunities, really, as well as developing various skills like visiting other people in their houses and doing interviews. I've had training. I've helped out with interviews for staff at Pen Green as well, which I never have been asked to do anywhere, really, other than at work, and I also found that, in my opinion, my input has been valued, and that's something that helps everybody's self-esteem and personal development. One of the senior members of staff asked if I'd ever considered working with children as a career, which I hadn't. I'd never really thought it was a viable career opportunity, really, until I sort of looked into it, and then I thought maybe I could do the NVQ through gaining experience working with the Pen Green nursery children.

What next?

Louise

After Louise left school at 16, she went straight into an office, carrying out general administrative duties, and was amazed that she lasted in the job for eight years! When Sean was born, it was time for Louise to move on. She did O-level psychology and typing at the local college and eventually got a job at the local sports centre, working at reception and then moving on to working in the crèche.

At this point in her life, Sean had started attending nursery at Pen Green. Louise with her new baby James continued to use the baby groups, at Pen Green and then embarked on the Open University group, Confident Parents, Confident Children. Attending all these groups and courses made Louise want to gain more knowledge and insights into her children's learning. It was at this point that she joined the PICL group. From there, her career has snow-balled. She has had paid employment from the centre, working in the kitchen and in the office. She is now a course leader of the 'Growing Together' group paid for by the local college. This group is a research group concerned with supporting parents with babies and toddlers who want to understand more about their infant's learning and development.

Since Sean has moved to primary school, Louise has been a volunteer in the classroom, and her husband Scott has recently become a school gover-nor. Louise completed her NVQ Level 3 and worked as a member of supply staff in the nursery for some time. Subsequently, she became a full-time member of the nursery team.

Eloise

After spending time in the school system, Eloise left school at the age of 16 with one O-level in religious studies and some CSEs. She had very low self-esteem and felt as though the system had 'let her down'. She was enrolled in a work experience programme in a clothes shop and absolutely hated it.

Moving on, she got a job at a local supermarket, and when the yearly review of all employees began, Eloise was taken by two senior members of staff into a room and was told that she had to practise speaking into a mirror to boost her self-confidence. At this point she left the firm!

She was offered a year's work on the Community Industry Programme for school leavers, and she was placed in a local infant school as a classroom assistant. Eloise loved this job but had to leave when the year was up.

For the next 11 years, she worked in two factories and was employed as a packer. She then left to have her first child, Becky. Eloise began going to a group called 'Messy Play' for children aged under 3, and then moved on to join the PICL group. She now has paid employment in the centre, working as a kitchen assistant and as a volunteer. She helps to run the Messy Play session, supporting other parents and their children.

Dave

Dave left school at 17 and went on to a building site. He then worked as a painter and decorator for two years before moving into warehouse management.

Dave is on the road to a new career through coming to the centre and joining different groups. He has now enrolled in the Wider Opportunities Programme, a European Social Fund employment scheme run by staff at the centre. He is attending a course called 'Introduction to Childcare', which is a preparation course for the NVQ in childcare.

Dave works as a volunteer in the Pen Green nursery on a Thursday afternoon and now has paid work supporting a child with additional needs in the nursery every afternoon at story time.

Dave got involved with the Sure Start programme's parent-led needs assessment (Pen Green Research Base Report, 2000), interviewing parents on a range of issues. This was paid work, and he has been approached to do follow-up interviews this summer. Although Dave still works night shifts as a warehouse manager, his new career in childcare could not be further from the career he planned when he left school.

Benefits for parents and children

As a teacher and as a parent, I have seen the benefits of being involved with the research programme. Returning to university had an impact on my whole family. When my children used to see me preparing work for the next day, they would say, 'It must be easy at university – all you have to do is write!' Both children have told me they want to go to university. Alexandria wants to be an architect and Olivia wants to be a children's writer.

The parents that I interviewed for this chapter, Louise, Eloise and Dave, have all told me how coming to the group has made a huge impact on their children's lives. Sean, after a difficult transition into school, has settled down and is doing well. Becky has told Eloise that she wants to be a teacher, and Lorin has a high reading age for her age.

Their younger children James, Jessica and Ross are all decision-makers at nursery, and all have strong clusters of schemas, which are supported at home by their parents and in nursery by the staff. All their children have a strong sense of security and a belief in themselves which makes them confident, autonomous learners, risk-takers, and likely to succeed in school.

Parents and carers of young children in whatever family configuration or circumstance thus have an absolutely vital role in education for they are the most significant reference point with regard to children's identity, learning stance, the scaffolding of understanding of learning outcomes.

(Pollard, 1996, p. 307)

CHAPTER 8

Dialogue and Documentation: Sharing Information and Developing a Rich Curriculum

Margy Whalley and Marcus Dennison

In this chapter, we describe:

- the conditions under which a *dialogue* can develop between parents and nursery staff, and nursery staff and other early childhood professionals;
- the way in which information about children's learning at home and at nursery can be shared, and common understandings negotiated through the *Pen Green Loop*; and
- the development of a range of *documentation* and its use as a critical tool for communication with parents, and for staff development.

Reflective practice

Practice needs theory and theory needs practice, just like a fish needs clean water. Practice apart from critical reflection, which illuminates the theory embedded in practice, cannot help our understanding. Revealing the theory embedded in practice undoubtedly helps the subject of practice to understand practice by reflecting and improving on it.

(Freire, 1996a, p. 108)

Staff at Pen Green are deeply concerned with *praxis*. Praxis means reflective practice or, in the language of early years, 'learning by doing', and then spending time thinking about what you have done and making links between theory and practice. In Colin Fletcher's words (1999, p. 159), praxis is about 'revising and refuting action on the basis of reflection'. What this means for us at Pen Green is that we have begun the process of converting our competence as early years practitioners into theory that can be understood and then discussed with parents and other early childhood educators.

Charles Handy, the management guru, describes those of us in the field of education as 'conceptually impoverished' (Handy, quoted in Scott, 1996, p. 4), without the conceptual skills to resolve the dilemmas we now face. He argues, 'It is no good doing things right – using technical and human skills – if they are not the right things to do.' Our view is that early years education is the one phase of education which is conceptually rich; child development concepts underpin all our day-to-day practice. What has been lacking in the past in the foundation stage is a *shared* language with which to articulate our shared understandings (Drummond, 1989; Whalley, 1994). We have made reference to this shared language in several chapters because it seems to us to be a central issue for early years educators.

Relatively few settings have appropriate levels of non-contact time for staff to reflect on their practice and learn to dialogue with each other, the children, the parents and the wider community. Staff at Pen Green, however, have always had non-contact time, and our practice is underpinned by a strong theoretical framework. Many of the Pen Green staff team, like early years educators in other settings, first became interested in working with young children because of a passion for social justice and commitment to children's rights. Staff were aware that critical reflection was the key to improving practice and that we had to constantly improve our own understanding if we were to honour the needs of the children. Korczak (writing in the 1940s) identifies the all-important emotional dimension to this learning process. 'Thanks to theory I know, thanks to practice, I feel. Theory enriches intellect, practice deepens feelings, trains the will' (Korczak, quoted in Bettleheim, 1990).

Developing a dialogue

Freire (1970, p. 71) tells us that there is a series of steps which have to be taken before participants, in this case staff and parents, can engage in critical thinking. What we need to do is to:

- perceive our own ignorance and give up the idea that we are the exclusive owners of truth and knowledge;
- identify with others and recognise the fact that 'naming the world' is not the task of an elite;
- value the contribution of others and listen to them with humility, respecting the particular view of the world held by different people;
- get in touch with how much we need other people and have no fear of being displaced; and
- be humble; have faith in others and believe in their strengths.

Throughout the 1990s, Pen Green nursery staff worked hard to develop this way of engaging in critical thinking in collaboration with parents and other professional colleagues.

Recognising our own ignorance

Some of the staff were parents themselves, but not all; some lived locally but others travelled in a distance of 25 miles; none of us knew enough about the context in which the children lived. Often the assumptions we made about children and families were wildly out of line with reality. Through regular home visiting on the parents' terms and at times that suited their family lifestyle, staff became more knowledgeable about the children and their families. With this information, we could celebrate the richness and diversity of the children's experiences and at the same time become more aware of the pressures children and families were experiencing.

Identifying with parents

Staff quickly learnt to 'start from where people were'; parents who were desperately trying to hold down two jobs and struggling with childcare did not want to be perceived as uncooperative if they could not turn up for daytime or evening meetings at the nursery. However, without exception, they valued the time staff spent in visiting them at home. When staff sent videotapes home of the children playing and learning in nursery, parents were willing to reciprocate in kind. Often these tapes would contain just a short video clip of a child deeply involved in an interesting learning experience; sometimes the child would be engaged in behaviour which staff did not understand. Staff would add to the vignette of the child's activity a small video clip of themselves asking the parents whether they had seen the child involved in this kind of play at home. Parents would almost always offer a response. While they accepted our desire to understand more about the children's cognitive concerns, they also reminded us that significant social events were also relevant and gave us information about the important life events that were taking place. When staff asked parents if they would be interviewed about their own educational experiences, they willingly shared their memories of struggling to make themselves heard in the school system. They made it clear to us that they wanted something more and better for their children.

Valuing parents' contribution

Many parents did attend meetings or get involved in study groups, and these were always run in a way that respected the different needs of families. Parents arriving at 7 p.m., having just come off a shift, needed a relaxed atmosphere and refreshments, but they often also wanted a well-prepared and focused discussion. In these groups, we had to establish a dialectic where contradictions could be tolerated, important problems could be posed, and important questions answered (Allman, 1983, p. 111). Parents were given opportunities to explore their own uncertainties; they were not force fed content and knowledge.

Mutual need

Nursery staff were very clear that they needed the information that parents held about the children's learning at home. Without this information, we could not provide the kind of supportive, stimulating and challenging curriculum that the nursery children deserved.

> The roles of professional experience and parents' everyday experience are seen as complementary but equally important. The former constitutes a 'public' (and generalised) form of theory about child development, whilst the latter represents a 'personal theory' about the development of a particular child. An interaction between the two 'theories' or ways of explaining a child's actions may produce an enriched understanding as a basis for both to act in relation to the child. *Only through the combination of both types of information could a broad and accurate picture be built up of a child's developmental process.*
>
> (Easen, Kendall and Shaw, 1992, p. 285; emphasis added)

Recognising parents' key role as the child's first and most consistent educators did not leave staff feeling deskilled or supplanted. Parents and staff began to see themselves as co-educators, co-constructing an appropriate curriculum to meet the cognitive and affective needs of every child.

Recognising parents' strengths

We were constantly having to revisit the theory and review our own practice in the light of information proffered by the parents and our detailed observations of the children. At times, we struggled to understand what a child was doing and were unable to support a child's deep interest in a particular learning experience. Then we were very dependent on parents for additional insights. Chris Athey describes the same process in the Froebel project: 'because the search was for fundamental patterns of thought, parents became increasingly involved, to the point of fascination in educational issues that, in the past, might have been thought to be the sole province of professionals' (Athey, 1990, p. 207).

The Pen Green Loop

In describing the Pen Green Loop (see Figure 8.1), we are trying to address what Chris Athey calls the three Ps of early childhood educators: 'parents, participating with professionals within an articulated pedagogical approach' (Athey, 1990, p. 56). The learning loop is a dynamic process whereby all the important adults in a child's life give each other feedback on what seems to be centrally important to the child, and how and what children are learning in the home and in the nursery.

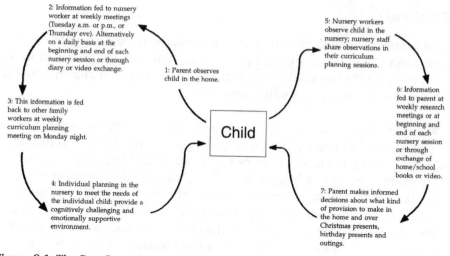

Figure 8.1 The Pen Green Loop

Parent-led observations and feedback to staff (see Figure 8.1, sequence 1–4)

Parents had, in the main, attended at least two training sessions on the key child development concepts that inform our practice in the nursery.

They were also offered a training session on how to use the camcorder and how to make effective video vignettes of their children playing and learning at a deep level. These parents went on to make detailed observations of their children at home and shared these observations with the nursery staff either verbally or in written form at the start of the nursery session, or during one of the study groups. In these study groups, parents were given time to reflect on what their children had been doing. They shared ideas with other parents and received information from staff about what was interesting the children in the nursery. Like Louise in Chapter 7, parents often relished the opportunity to share their anxiety about apparently naughty behaviour (Athey, 1990, p. 207). They were often reassured when their children's behaviour was reframed as consistent and predictable. Staff were able to relate the children's play to the child development concepts that parents had studied, and parents were also able to attribute new significance to what their children were doing (Athey, 1990).

Some of these parents borrowed the nursery camcorder or used their own, and made video vignettes of their children playing in the home setting. Nursery staff were given some additional time out of nursery to copy these diary entries so that the diaries could be retained by parents. Staff also jotted down verbal information offered by the parents directly on the nursery planning sheet, or recorded it in each child's 'celebration of achievement' file. The research staff and nursery staff who ran the study groups made it a priority to watch videos brought from home and to make notes on a special data sheet, which they subsequently entered into the child's file.

Alternatively, they might share the information brought from home with the child's key worker at a weekly curriculum-planning session which all the nursery staff attend. In these staff planning sessions, individual staff would present their observations of particular children; other staff would share any other observational evidence gathered from home or from nursery. The whole staff group would then begin to familiarise themselves with the children's interests and identify their cognitive constants and any emerging patterns in their play. Staff would also share their knowledge about the children's emotional well-being and developing social relationships within the nursery.

On the basis of informed observations in the nursery (Bruce, 1997, p. 67), which were fleshed out by observations in the home setting, staff could then begin to plan to meet the needs of individual children or groups of children.

Staff-led observations and feedback to parents (see Figure 8.1, sequence 5–7)

In the same way that parents observe their own particular children at home, staff have a system for observing the children in the nursery. Every day, two children are flagged up as 'focus children' (systematically, over a four- to six-week period, every child in the nursery is targeted), and all staff, students and parent helpers make sure that they fill in observational records on these children if they come into 'their areas' in the nursery. These observations provide the evidence base for planning for each child. It is the child's key worker's responsibility at the end of each session to collect all the observations that have been made that day. If staff are on leave, colleagues will put their observations in the children's files or wait and swap observations at the Monday evening nursery planning session, which lasts from 4.30 to 6.00 p.m. At this planning session, nursery staff are encouraged to challenge each other's thinking and begin to make links between theory and practice.

Nursery staff also receive regular supervision from a senior member of staff. They can use these supervision sessions to discuss issues about particular children in more depth. All the observations that staff make and the decisions they make about planning for the children in nursery are shared with the parents. Information can be passed on to parents in the following ways:

- through daily chats at the beginning or end of a session;
- through home-school books or videos that nursery staff have made; and
- through the research study group that runs in the morning, afternoon and evening each week.

Parents use the information that staff share with them to make informed decisions about how to extend the provision that is available at home to support their children's learning, what sort of outings they might go on, and what kinds of Christmas or birthday presents they might select.

Freire reflects on how knowledge emerges through just this kind of dialogue. In this way, we can 'reconsider through the considerations of others,
our own considerations' (Freire, 1970, p. 61).

To demonstrate how effective this sort of exchange of information can be,
we next consider a worked example of the learning loop.

Parents and staff as co-educators: the learning loop

Alice and the conveyor belt

Every week, we plan to support and extend children's learning in our nursery, and we often start with their questions. Alice's questions were all about
how conveyor belts work. However, we need to put her questions in some
kind of context.

Chelsea, Alice's friend, had travelled up to Scotland in December and saw
her luggage 'disappear' down a conveyor belt. She wanted to know where
her luggage went to. She came back to nursery and shared her experience
with her friends and the nursery staff. In January, the nursery staff made a
number of experimental conveyor belts to explain the concept to Chelsea,
although it was Alice, not Chelsea, who became deeply involved. At the end
of January, Alice and her mother went with a small group of parents and
children from the nursery to visit the Launch Pad at the Science Museum.
She found the complex conveyor belt particularly exciting. Chris Athey
(1990) comments on the importance of widening children's experience
beyond the school walls, to feed their schemas and to generate new learning.
Susan Greenfield also reflects the same viewpoint: 'Experience is a key factor
in shaping the micro-circuiting of the brain' (Greenfield, 1997, p. 122).

Home/nursery dialogue

Lesley, Alice's mother, is aware that, at 3 years, 10 months, Alice has a cluster of schemas. The schemas that have been particularly important to Alice
for several weeks are enclosure, envelopment and rotation.

> Enclosure is concerned with enclosing oneself, an object or space.
> Envelopment is concerned with covering or surrounding oneself, an object or a space.
> Rotation is concerned with turning, twisting, or rolling oneself or objects in the
> environment around (Arnold, 1997a).

Lesley regularly keeps a diary of what Alice does at home and brings it into
the research study group every Tuesday afternoon. These particular diary
entries show some interesting examples of envelopment:

16 Oct: Alice found a balloon in the drawer. After I had blown it up for
her, she spent a little while chasing it. I then caught her spreading

William's nappy cream all over the balloon! Aarrgh!

17 Oct: Alice was drawing on a little note pad. As she finished with each page, she ripped it off the pad and wrapped up a fridge magnet in each piece of paper.

20 Jan: I bought her a Sellotape dispenser for Christmas, and she now uses up rolls and rolls of Sellotape ... She wrapped sellotape around her little brother in his baby walker.

Lesley's family worker also runs the study group, so he makes copies of these diary entries and shares the information with other staff and puts her comments into Alice's file.

Problem-solving in nursery

Over several months, Alice spent time experimenting with the conveyor belt. She was actively engaged in problem-solving. It took her some time to understand that, by pulling the belt underneath, from right to left, she could make objects move from left to right, so that they fell with a satisfying clunk into a metal container.

Alice had a hypothesis that all the objects she put on the belt would move along the belt in the same way, and then drop off the end. When she put a ball on the conveyor belt, she was initially intrigued. However, after trying two or three times to make the ball behave in the same way as the flat objects, she rejected it. She chose to discard the ball because it presented her with contradictory evidence. She was excited by her own theory and she continued to experiment with other objects which behaved in a way that confirmed her hypothesis. Wynne Harlen (1982) writes of children's need to develop a 'false hypothesis'. Alice's false hypothesis was that all the objects she placed on the conveyor belt would behave in the same way. As she becomes more experienced, she will modify her hypothesis.

In the research study group, Alice's key worker, Marcus, showed Lesley what Alice had been doing in nursery (Figure 8.2). Both Lesley and her partner were fascinated by the conveyor belt experiment and impressed by Alice's concentration and disposition to learn. In both the study group and the staff meeting, we shared ideas about just what Alice is learning.

What is Alice learning?

It seemed to nursery staff that Alice was developing an understanding of some important mathematical and physical concepts: 'Learning mathematics or science is not so much learning facts as learning ways of thinking' (Lee and Das Gupta, 1995, p. 219). The concepts she was investigating are concerned with:
- forces and motion;
- friction and gravity; and
- surface area.

Figure 8.2 Alice and the conveyor belt learning sequence

At the research study group

Research Feedback Form
Name of Child: Alice
Name of Parent: Lesley
Group Attending: am / pm / evening 28th October

Issues Raised
Lesley has noticed that Alice is wrapping up the door handles with Sellotape. She is also wrapping up (enveloping) the television tuner in tea towels or tissues. Lesley says she will let her wrap up all the family xmas presents. Alice woke at 6am and tried to envelop her whole face with lipstick and blusher (she doesn't enjoy face paints). She also wrapped plasters round all her fingers.

Research Feedback Form
Name of Child: Alice
Name of Parent: Lesley
Group Attending: am / pm / evening 28th October

Issues Raised:
Lesley noticed that Alice was winding her lipstick out until it was fully distended and then put the top on it — squelching the lipstick inside. At this point Lesley banned further use of the lipstick. Alice also tried to cover her whole face with eye shadow but it didn't work (envelopment). Alice gave her mother a pretend 'feather' which was a straw enveloped with paper and Sellotape.

Figure 8.3 Examples of Alice's research feedback form

Lesley continues to attend the research study group, which is held on a Tuesday afternoon. Each week, she shares her diary entries with the staff who run the group and with other parents. The members of staff running the group keep a record of the group discussion that relates to Alice on a 'research feedback' form (Figure 8.3), which is then put into Alice's 'celebration of achievement' file for her family worker to read.

This particular study group spent some time discussing how parents could best support children's envelopment schema and when it was necessary to set some boundaries to inappropriate behaviour. Lesley's comment was that 'my relationship with Alice has become much more engaged – I feel I am on her level and much more in tune with her play. Finding out about schemas has helped to put me one step ahead!' Chris Athey (1990) does make the point that to 'identify a schema is not necessarily to love it'. Lesley was very clear that she had set an appropriate boundary to Alice's use of her make-up bag, and David, Alice's father, was happy to offer Alice an alternative, as we can see from the extracts from the research feedback in Figure 8.4.

Research Feedback Form
Name of Child: Alice
Name of Parent: Lesley
Group Attending: am / pm / evening 18th November

Issues Raised:
Alice had enveloped an egg box in paper and wound it round with Sellotape. and some raffle tickets all in one big parcel. She used up the rest of the roll of Sellotape. Lesley asked her to go to the loo before she went out and Alice came downstairs and commented, 'the loo roll looks just like the Sellotape.' Alice enveloped her dolls' faces with chalk like she had her own in nursery.

David, her dad, brought her two children's lipsticks and she put the purple one on top of the pink one and said she had made a new colour. Lesley let her use some tiny paint pallets at home and she mixed colours. Sometimes she envelops her little brother, William, in the beanbag!

Research Feedback Form
Name of Child: Alice
Name of Parent: Lesley
Group Attending: am / pm / evening 25th November

Issues Raised:
Lesley reported that Alice had run into nursery saying 'my daddy's really ustaful'. She wasn't sure is she meant beautiful or useless!

Alice had made a dog lead with links and attached it to William (18 months) and encouraged him to 'walk' like a dog. She sometimes says 'the dog done it' if she spills her drink. This morning Alice was cutting out a boat and a house and colouring them in and she had to stick them in Lesley's research diary.

Figure 8.4 Extracts from research feedback

Planning to support and extend Alice's learning

Nursery staff made plans to support and extend Alice's learning with a PLOD (possible lines of direction) chart. Central to the nursery planning were the narrative and video observations parents and staff had made of Alice's cognitive constants at home and at nursery.

Alice is learning at a deep level; at nursery, we want to build on what she *can* do and encourage her to develop an interest in what excites her. The PLOD chart we have developed (Bartholomew and Bruce, 1993, p. 45) helps us to integrate our observations of the children's interests and schemas, and at the same time make links with the early learning goals. At the centre of the PLOD (Figure 8.5) are the names of several children who all share Alice's

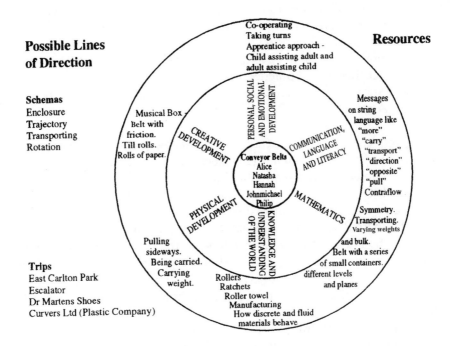

Figure 8.5 Extracts from research feedback

interests. Chris Athey (1990, p. 30) makes the point that 'unreflective child centredness has led to the false belief that every child needs a unique educational programme. Constructivist teachers know that many children share similar cognitive concerns.'

By 4 years of age, Alice was still experimenting with the conveyor belt, but by now the nursery provision not only included the improvised 'belts' that staff had made out of paper, but also a manufactured conveyor belt. This conveyor belt, when placed in the sandpit, offered Alice and other nursery children a new range of possible lines of direction. Alice's parents' deep commitment to her learning and their partnership with the nursery staff have made it possible for us to offer Alice a stimulating and challenging nursery environment.

Documentation

Pedagogical documentation as defined by Gunilla Dahlberg (Dahlberg, Moss and Pence, 1999) makes it possible for:

- the child to revisit and reflect on what she has done, and in this way to make her learning an active process;
- nursery staff to enter into a dialogue, and communicate in action with the child and her parents;

- the nursery staff group to open up the nursery, so that it becomes a public space, an arena for discussing critical questions and for reflection;
- the nursery staff to develop materials as a basis for reconstructing pedagogical practice; for reflective dialogue, negotiation and challenge; and to connect theory and practice; and
- nursery staff to problematise their practice and planning and open it to critical analysis.

Dahlberg reflects on the long tradition of pedagogical documentation in Sweden and in Italy. She differentiates between the reflexive problematising approach of Kohier in Sweden and Rinaldi in Reggio Emilia, and the approach of traditionalists who see observing children 'as being about mapping some universal and objective social reality' (Dahlberg, Moss and Pence, 1999, p. 145). Dahlberg defines pedagogical documentation as critically different from 'child observation'; 'as we understand it, the purpose of child observation is to assess children's psychological development in relation to already pre-determined categories produced from developmental psychology and which define what the normal child should be doing at a particular age' (ibid., p. 146).

Susan Isaacs at the Malting House School in the 1930s, who pioneered the use of observation and whose studies have influenced many early years practitioners in the UK, was concerned with building and substantiating generalisable theories about children's learning and development. However, she was also concerned with differences in the behaviour between children and in finding out more about the particular interests of individual children (Drummond, 1993, p. 49). She was also deeply interested in knowing more about children's rich emotional lives and showed a remarkable acceptance and understanding of children's negative feelings. There is nothing sanitised about Isaacs' descriptions of experimentation inside and outside the classroom (Isaacs, 1936). The children in her school were interested in life, death and bringing things back to life. Compare her notes in 1930 with those of the Pen Green nursery staff in 2000.

Susan Isaacs' observations in 1930

13.7.25: Some of the children called out that the rabbit was dying. They found it in the summerhouse, hardly able to move. They were very sorry and talked much about it. They shut it up in the hutch and gave it warm milk.

14.7.25: The rabbit had died in the night. Dan found it and said, 'It's dead – its tummy does not move up and down now.' Paul said, 'My daddy says that if we put it into water it will get alive again.' Mrs I said, 'Shall we do so and see? 'They put it into a bath of water. Some of them said, 'It's alive, because it's moving.' This was a circular movement, due to the currents in the water: Mrs I therefore put in a small stick which also moved round and round, and they agreed that the stick was not alive. They then suggested that they should bury the rabbit, and all helped to dig a hole and bury it.

15.7.25: Frank and Duncan talked of digging the rabbit up – but Frank said, 'It's not there – it's gone up to the sky.' They began to dig but tired of it and ran off to something else. Later they came back and dug again. Duncan, however, said, 'Don't bother – it's gone – it's up in the sky' and gave up digging. Mrs I therefore said, 'Shall we see if it's there?' and also dug. They found the rabbit, and were very interested to see it still there.

(Isaacs 1936, pp. 182–3)

Pen Green staff observations in 2000

5.2.2000: We are reading 'The Dog that Dug'. On one page, there is a picture of the skeleton of a dinosaur: James asks if the dinosaur have been eaten. I explain that it died a long time ago and that the skin and flesh have rotted away. James asks, 'When we are dead, why are we always dead?' I explain how things stop working inside us and don't start again. He says, 'My grandpa Alex is dead.' I ask him if he is sad. 'No,' he says, and then 'A little bit,' and then 'My Grandma is sad.' I say that she is probably missing his Grandpa's company. James asks, 'Who is going to sleep with her now?' I say that I don't know. He asks, 'When you get old you die', and 'Am I getting older?' He continues, 'When I'm big, I'll be old. Are you old?' he asks me. I say that we get older every day. James asks, 'Am I getting older?'

Drummond (1993, p. 50) makes the point that Isaacs' work, celebrating, as it does, children's individual emotional and intellectual lives, also provides a salutary warning for early childhood educators: 'If we choose to see only those aspects of learning of which we approve, we will lose the opportunity to see more of the picture, to learn more about learning ... there is always more to learn, and more to see' (*ibid.*). It would be very easy as adults to focus our observations on what interests us, on the aesthetically pleasing, for example, rather than on those things which are of deep concern to young children.

Penny Lawrence, in our video-training sessions for parents and staff, reminded us that while the camera provides a window into the child's world, we see that world through the lens of our values and beliefs, and we focus the camera on what we consider to be worth observing.

While there are some significant differences between the documentation that takes place in Sweden and in Reggio Emilia and that which takes place at Pen Green, there are also some similarities. The time-honoured tradition of observation which underpins the work at Pen Green derives from the studies undertaken by such baby biographers as Darwin, Piaget and Navarra (Bruce, 1997, p. 10) and the observational approach pioneered by Susan Isaacs in the 1930s. At Pen Green, we focus on the children's learning process. We observe what children are doing and saying, and we then interpret and analyse what we see, using currently available theory (Bruce, 1997, p. 67). Subsequently, we share ideas with colleagues and the children's parents, and develop plans to support and extend the children's learning. We document this whole process, working in collaboration with the children's primary carers.

James's interest in death, dying, beheading and whether executioners were 'bad men' was supported and extended by the nursery staff. He was offered storybooks that enhanced his understanding, such as *Grandfather Cherry Blossom and Kintaro, the Nature Boy*. His strong trajectory schema, which we had observed since he was two and three years old, had led to an interest and developing competence in using the saws on the workbench and in making swords. James was supported and extended by the introduction of a special kitchen saw so that he could behead a dead fish and examine its bone structure. He was fascinated by the concept of transformation of state and tried to make the decapitated fish come alive again in a bowl of water. He also reflected to his key worker that if we left the fish in water for a long time, it would come alive, and if that did not work, we could put the fish in the lake and it would come alive. Much of James's learning about cause and effect was through hypothesising, and verbal discussion, practical investigation and reflection. James showed little interest in representing his experience, although at one point he briefly wallowed in red paint. The formal record of the experience was through the documentation of the staff and his mother, that is, video clips and notes in James's file. However, the learning process was deep and sustained over several weeks, and we have included both home video of James and his mother, Louise, and nursery video in our new training pack.

Like Gunilla Dahlberg in Sweden and Carlina Rinaldi in Italy, staff at Pen Green have begun to see how making our observations, dialogue, analysis and planning more explicit can be useful for staff, parents, children and the wider community. 'Documentation offers the teacher a unique opportunity to listen again, see again, and therefore revisit indirectly and with others, the events and processes in which he or she was co-protagonist, directly or indirectly. This revisiting with colleagues helps create common meaning and values' (Edwards, Gandini and Forman, 1998, pp. 121–2).

Portfolios of children's learning

At Pen Green, we now produce *portfolios of the children's learning*. These portfolios are critical if we are to develop and improve our practice for the following reasons:

- The portfolios are useful for children because they can revisit and reflect on what they have done; we call this metacognition.
- They are useful for nursery staff because they form the basis for discussion between children and their parents; they also encourage reflection and make it possible for staff to reconstruct their pedagogical practice. Staff can dialogue with colleagues, problematise their practice, and make links between theory and practice.
- Documentation is also important for parents because when their children's work is opened up for discussion in this way, parents can ask critical questions and reflect on what their child is doing at nursery.
- These portfolios also honour the contribution that parents are making as their child's first educators. The dialogue we enter into with parents, children and the wider community is not cosy. We often need to share strong views and challenge each other's ways of thinking. Parents are passionately committed to supporting their children's learning, and nursery staff work with parents as equal, active and responsible partners.

All documentation at Pen Green is developed through a dialogue with the children's parents. Becky's portfolio shows how the information is collected, how observations are shared, and how parents and staff work together to support and extend Becky's learning. The final document is a celebration of Becky's achievements, which she takes home and which she can share with her teacher when she moves on to primary school.

Becky's portfolio

BECKY STARTS NURSERY

When Becky came into nursery in September 1997, her mum reported, 'Becky can spend hours hanging outdoor clothes, moving and folding them – then repeating the process all over again.'

After being in nursery for a couple of weeks, she is enveloping herself and others in stickers. Her mum reports, 'Plain white stickers are not good enough; they must be coloured ones ... she draws circles, cuts them out and puts them on top of each other.'

Becky seems to have an envelopment schema.

DEFINITION OF SCHEMA

'Schemas are patterns of linked behaviours which the child can generalise and use in a whole variety of different situations. It is best to think of schemas as being a cluster of pieces which fit together' (Bruce, 1997).

▶

Becky's cluster of schemas

Envelopment – covering or surrounding oneself, an object or a space.

Enclosure – enclosing oneself, an object or a space.

Going through – causing oneself or some material to go through a boundary and emerge at the other side.

Layering – placing materials in a layer combining envelopment and on top schemas.

SUPPORTING HER SCHEMA AT NURSERY

When we plan for children's learning, we use a chart called a PLOD (possible lines of direction).

The purpose of the PLOD is to ensure staff provide children with a broad, wide and deep curriculum. Other children benefit from this type of planning. Chris Athey (1990, p. 30) points out,

> Unreflective child centredness has led to the false belief that every child requires a unique educational programme. Constructivist teachers know that many children share similar cognitive concerns.

Becky's PLOD (Figure 8.6) relates to her interest in making parcels and envelopes. When we have planned effectively for the children's learning in this way, they are able to play and learn at a deep level. Becky is almost always engrossed when making parcels and presents. The planning matches her educational needs.

SUPPORTING HER SCHEMA AT HOME

At home it is nearly Christmas time. Becky's envelopment schema has led her to make up lots of parcels. She enjoys cooking with mum, but is only interested in covering the cake with butter icing and chocolate buttons.

Becky received a pram for Christmas, but rather than use it in the traditional manner, she was more interested in filling it up and covering it with a blanket.

Her mum's diary 4.1.98

'Becky's Christmas present from nursery was very successful. Four rolls of Sellotape and a big roll of paper. She then proceeded to cut out all her Xmas cards and wrap each one into a parcel. 27 in total!'

13.3.98

'No nursery today – I gave her a roll of brown paper and some Sellotape and left her to it – by bedtime, there was a huge pile of parcels for Alice, William and Sheree.'

BECKY ENGAGES WITH THE WHOLE CURRICULUM

Physical development – Becky is using her senses and physical actions. When Becky began wrapping parcels, it was all on a sensory motor level. She enjoyed the experience of playing with paper and Sellotape while learning and developing new skills.

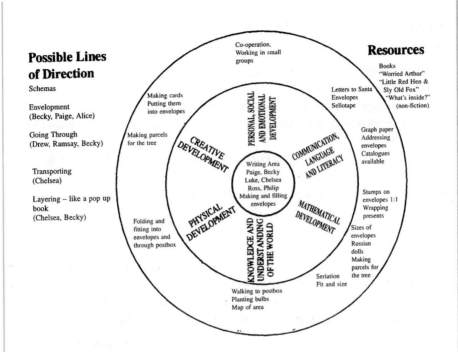

Figure 8.6 Becky's PLOD chart

Communication, language and literacy – Becky's parcel making became more intricate. She began to work at a symbolic representation level. Her parcels and presents became gifts and messages for different people. She wrote the names of her family and friends on each parcel, using upper and lower case letters appropriately. Becky is developing her emergent writing.

Knowledge and understanding of the world – Initially, Becky was making simple transformations by screwing up paper to make a parcel. She is now able to make complex transformations – she plans angles, makes corners, estimates size and fit, and positions and coordinates different surfaces.

Mathematics – Bending the paper when wrapping parcels involves spatial concepts and estimating how much paper is needed.

Personal social and emotional development – Becky is thinking of others, and communicating with them.

Creative development – She is making something of her own for each of her special friends.

PROVISION FOR AN ENVELOPER

How do we support, extend and challenge Becky's thinking in nursery?

- We ensure that there is enough choice of provision, e.g. Sellotape, paper, string, hole punch, stickers, etc.
- We encourage her to make her own decisions about what to use.
- We are interested in and supportive of what Becky is doing and try to extend her interests.
- We allow Becky to wallow in the experience and give her plenty of time to organise her thinking and carry out her ideas.
- We try to protect her space, so that she can use the provision optimally.

The school is not isolated from society but an integral part of it. The school has both the right and the duty to make this culture of childhood visible to the society as a whole, in order to provoke exchange and discussion. Sharing documentation is a true act of democratic participation.

(Rinaldi, 1998, p. 122)

Increasingly, the documentation we produce at Pen Green contributes to the wider debate between parents, early years educators, politicians and policymakers about critical issues in early childhood education.

CHAPTER 9

Growing Together Groups: Working with Parents and Children from Birth to Three Years of Age

Colette Tait

In this chapter we outline the development of Growin0g Together groups, which run each week for parents with children from birth to three years of age. These groups evolved as the result of the three-year research project, Parents' Involvement in Their Children's Learning (PICL). In the PICL project, workers from the nursery met alongside parents whose children attended the nursery. The workers and parents watched video vignettes of the children in the nursery, and the workers shared theoretical frameworks with parents. Parents were able to share their specialised knowledge about their own child, and together workers and parents could dialogue and try to understand each child's development. The discussion generated in these study groups informed the nursery planning session on a weekly basis, and also impacted upon what the parent provided for the child in the home.

How Growing Together evolved from PICL

After the PICL study groups had run successfully for three years, we wanted to try to extend this work. We wanted to set up a study group for parents with younger children (from birth to three years). We wanted to provide a forum in which parents and workers could study the younger children's development, once again using video material and the four key concepts that we had successfully used in the PICL project:

- involvement (Laevers, 1997);
- well-being (Laevers, 1997);

Figure 9.1 Parents and children at Growing Together

- schema (Athey, 1990); and
- pedagogical strategies (Whalley and Arnold, 1997a).

This is how Growing Together grew out of the PICL programme, but there was a big difference – parents were going to attend the group sessions *with* their children (Figure 9.1).

When we initially developed Growing Together, we spent some time thinking about what our aims were. We came up with a list of aims for the group:

- to give parents a chance to play with their child;
- to help parents understand more about their relationship with their child;
- to dialogue with parents about their child's development;
- to encourage reflective parenting (through reflecting on video material);
- to facilitate parent-to-parent support (we have found that close and supportive relationships between women develop during Growing Together groups);
- to validate the feelings women are experiencing when they are suffering from post-natal depression (PND) (if women attend group sessions when their children are aged 0–3, then, statistically, there will be quite a high proportion of women suffering from PND at some time during their attendance); and
- to reinforce helpful attachment experiences through modelling, video feedback and discussions.

Once these groups had been set up, it became apparent that something was missing. The four key concepts were very useful in terms of child development. However, as parents were sometimes bringing very young infants, we felt it was critical to look closely with the parents at the relationship between them and their child. Because of this, we found it useful to draw on a number of psychoanalytic theories:

- holding (Winnicott, 1965);
- containment (Bion, 1962);

- attachment (Bowlby, 1969); and
- companionship (Trevarthen, 2002a).

Psychoanalytic theories

Holding

The concept of holding describes the emotional holding parents can give their baby by holding him or her in mind (Winnicott, 1965). So when, for instance, you put your baby to bed and leave the room, he or she understands that you are still there for them – you are not abandoning them. They have learnt to believe this from the way you have responded to them both physically and emotionally since birth – they understand that you are holding them in mind.

Understanding the concept of 'holding' also has an impact on the way that the group is run. Staff involved in the sessions have planning and reflection time each week; we do this to try to make links between the weekly sessions, ensuring that we hold parents and children 'in mind'. If a parent has not attended Growing Together for a couple of weeks, we phone them. Once again, we believe that this process of 'making contact' lets parents know we are concerned about them even though we have not seen them; that we are holding them in mind.

Containment

The concept of containment describes the parent taking in the baby's distress, understanding it and responding so that the baby feels emotionally looked after and contained (Bion, 1962).

So, for instance, when children are grieving (and they could be grieving about something that appears very small to us – losing a toy or the death of a pet) parents who are able to 'contain' their children will allow them to express all the range of emotions that they feel – their feelings will not be dismissed, and the adult will not deny the child is having these feelings.

This concept also informs our practice; we try to ensure the Growing Together groups run regularly and that there is consistency in the staff that attend each session, so that parents and infants can be confident that they will engage with the same staff. We try to ensure that the sessions are not cancelled or moved to a different place. Again, we believe that this structure in the provision helps parents feel emotionally contained.

Attachment

The concept of attachment describes how adults and children form and develop reciprocal relationships (Bowlby, [1969] 1991). With secure attachments, children can thrive; without them, children tend to struggle in relationships and learning, and to have a reduced sense of their own agency. From contemporary attachment theorists, we learned that adults who were insecurely attached to their own parents, and who have not reflected on their experiences, sometimes miss opportunities to perceive and interpret their children's attachment signals and may wish to inhibit them (Charlwood and Steele, 2004). In our Growing Together sessions, we approach this issue by video recording babies' attachment invitation signals and parents' responses or missed opportunities to respond (Tait, 2004), and we discuss these video vignettes with parents.

Companionship

Colwyn Trevarthen has shared with us the concept of companionship (Trevarthen and Aitken, 2001). An effective parent–infant exchange can have the quality of a conversation between equals. Staff in the Growing Together groups recognise how this companionship relationship develops and record on video moments when parents, demonstrate responsive reciprocal relationships. Staff also build warm and responsive relationships with parents, who often use the group for extended periods of time.

What's happening now?

Pen Green staff offer three Growing Together sessions each week. These sessions are run as drop-in groups for parents with children aged from birth to three years of age. We use these theoretical concepts to underpin our practice, and we aim to encourage positive parent–child relationships. Each group lasts for an hour and a half. Two of the groups meet on the Pen Green campus, and one at a clinic in the town centre. The room we are based in at Pen Green and the room at the health centre are not purpose built – they are multipurpose rooms, and quite a lot of time and effort goes into setting up the room for the Growing Together group.

In Growing Together, we need to get the balance right. We need appropriate play provision for the children, as well as a warm and welcoming atmosphere for their parents. We do this by ensuring that the provision remains constant for the children; there are always sand, water, dough, a train set, trucks, and a small tent with a tunnel for the older children. We also set up a baby area with a large mirror, treasure baskets and beanbags for the infants. Among all this play provision, we have soft, comfortable chairs for the parents, and we always offer parents a warm drink on their arrival.

All three groups are highly staffed by workers with different backgrounds and skills – child development, psychotherapy, parent support, and health. Generally, from eight to 18 parents with children attend any one session, making the ratio of workers to families quite high. This enables workers to get to know families well, and provide a consistent and supportive atmosphere.

Although these are drop-in groups for anybody to attend, we do try to encourage members to attend regularly, as this type of continuity helps to provide a safe and secure environment for both parents and children.

Crèche provision

We are also able to offer a crèche for the Growing Together groups at Pen Green. This means that a parent with a child three years or older could put that child into the crèche, and then attend the Growing Together session with the younger child. In some instances, parents with two children aged from birth to three have come along to two different Growing Together sessions and have put each child in turn into the crèche. This means that parents can have some 'one-to-one' time with a child if they desire.

What makes Growing Together different from other toddler drop-in groups?

During the sessions, we video film parents, children and workers. We may film a child at play, or a parent/child interaction. We then use a computer system (set up in the corner of the same room) to view the film we have just made. One of the workers and the parent who has been filmed will watch the video material together and discuss it. The video can be watched at normal speed, and also one frame at a time, so they can get a really close-up, 'in-depth' look at what has gone on (Figure 9.2).

At this point the worker may introduce some theory (either from child development or psychoanalysis – the seven key concepts) if it seems appropriate. By discussing theoretical concepts with parents, we are able to begin to dialogue; we have a shared language with which to discuss the video material. The parent is then able to select a sequence of still images from the video material, and choose some language to accompany the images.

Figure 9.2 Watching video material together

At the end of the session, the parent is able to take away a copy of this 'portfolio'. We believe this process encourages reflective parenting, and reinforces positive experiences.

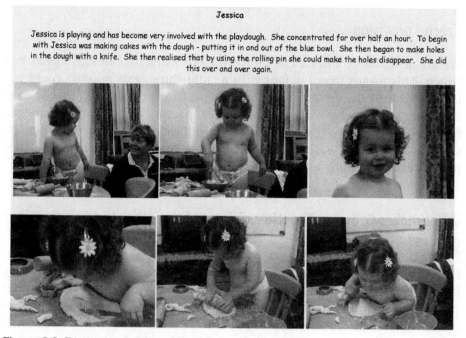

Jessica

Jessica is playing and has become very involved with the playdough. She concentrated for over half an hour. To begin with Jessica was making cakes with the dough - putting it in and out of the blue bowl. She then began to make holes in the dough with a knife. She then realised that by using the rolling pin she could make the holes disappear. She did this over and over again.

Figure 9.3 Discussing Jessica, alongside her mum, Kirsty

Jessica's portfolio

Throughout the discussion about this piece of video, the worker, alongside Kirsty, Jessica's mum, would have thought about how deeply involved Jessica was, what her well-being was like, and what Kirsty's role was in terms of supporting Jessica's play. Kirsty was able to sit alongside Jessica, encouraging her and providing appropriate language to support her play.

This is the kind of informal way in which we would begin to introduce these concepts to parents attending Growing Together. In the following section, we introduce two families, using case study material, to illustrate how they have used the Growing Together groups, and how the concepts shared in Growing Together have affected them.

A case study: Emily and Sophie

This case study focuses on Emily and Sophie who have been coming to Growing Together for 7 months. At this time, Sophie is 2 years and 4 months old, and Emily is 19 weeks pregnant. In this case study we tell you a story which took place over a 4-week period for Sophie and Emily. For each week we report:

- the events that happened;
- Emily's feelings, in her own words; and
- how the concepts of holding and containment influenced our responses as workers to Emily and Sophie.

> **Holding**
> The concept of holding describes the emotional holding parents can give their baby by holding him or her in mind (Winnicott, 1965).
>
> **Containment**
> The concept of containment describes the parent taking in the baby's distress, understanding it, and responding so that the baby feels emotionally looked after, contained (*Growing Together Booklet*, 2002; see Bion, 1962).

Week 1

Events

It was midway through the Growing Together session (each session lasts for an hour and a half). Sophie was busy playing with the tunnel. Emily stood up and, without saying anything to Sophie, walked toward the door, to go to the toilet.

Sophie looked up and saw her mum Emily moving toward the door. She began to cry. Emily heard her, turned, went back to Sophie, picked her up, and took her to the toilet with her, without speaking to her. Emily reflected on how she felt when this happened:

Emily's feelings

'I felt upset that Sophie was upset. I felt guilty that I was leaving her – I also felt pissed off that I never got a minute to myself. The biggest feeling was guilt, but it made me feel so special. I felt really needed. Although it was hard most of the time, I felt really needed.'

Holding and containment

We have a reflection and planning time each week – keeping links between sessions, holding parents and children in mind. This week in our staff reflection time we thought about how upset Sophie was when she realised Emily was about to leave the room.

Week 2

Events

Once again, Sophie was playing when Emily stood up and walked toward the door. This time she actually left the room. Almost immediately Sophie began to cry. Tracy (the worker) went over to Sophie and told her where Emily had gone. Sophie continued to cry. She asked Sophie if she wanted to go and find Emily. She said yes and lifted her arms up. Tracy picked her up and carried her out of the room and waited outside the toilet. Sophie was still crying. She talked to Sophie about her mum being behind the door in front, and Sophie began to settle and stopped crying. Emily came out of the toilet and took Sophie from Tracy's arms, saying, 'It's really difficult to leave her. She's like this all the time.' Sophie appeared pleased to see Emily.

Emily's feelings

'When I came out of the toilet I felt awful – I felt wretched. I was thinking you might think I am a bad mother. I thought, you might think I was doing something wrong, because why would she cry like that? But I thought, well you might see what it is like for me. I was envious toward other parents – I didn't know anyone who had a clingy child like Sophie. I would compare her to other children.'

Holding and containment

At the end of the session, during reflection time, Tracy explained the event to the staff team. We talked about strategies we could use in future weeks to support Emily and Sophie. The weekly sessions provide a setting for Emily where she can feel 'held' if we are able to support her and listen to her.

During the session, Tracy was able to contain Sophie's feelings by noticing her distress, understanding it, and providing her with help and comfort. Allowing Emily to talk about her difficulty in leaving Sophie was also a form of containment for her.

Week 3

This week we had an outside consultant, Penny Lawrence, in the session. Penny was gathering material for a video that is to be part of a Growing Together Training Pack, and she filmed what happened this week when Emily left the room.

Events

This week's events mirrored the events from week 2. Emily left the room. Sophie pointed to the door and started to cry. Sophie walked to the door and tried to open it. Colette responded to Sophie by going over to her, crouching down, and asking Sophie if she wanted to go and find her mum (Figure 9.4).

Sophie lifted her arms, and Colette carried her out of the room, to wait outside the toilet. Sophie calmed much more quickly this week. While standing outside the toilet, Colette spoke to Sophie about how her mum was behind the door (Figure 9.5) (in a similar way to that in which Tracy had, the previous week).

Figure 9.4 Colette asks Sophie if she wants to go to find her mum

Figure 9.5 Colette speaks to Sophie about her mum being in the toilet

Emily came out of the toilet and once again took Sophie into her arms (Figure 9.6). As we went back into the group room, Colette said to Emily, 'It might be helpful to tell Sophie where you are going … she may still get upset, but at least she will know where you are.' Emily did not respond.

Emily's feelings

'I felt awful still, I felt guilty for leaving her … but I never got a minute to myself … I knew she (Colette) was right (to say about telling Sophie where I was going). My mum had said it as well.'

Holding and containment

Colette was able to contain Sophie's feelings. She responded to Sophie's distress in an almost identical way to the way in which Tracy had responded to Sophie the previous week. The reflection and planning time each week enabled us to keep links between the events that were happening, and hold both Sophie and Emily in mind.

Figure 9.6 Emily takes Sophie into her arms

Between weeks 3 and 4, Emily had reflected on what her own mum and Colette had suggested. She had decided to try telling Sophie where she was going when she was about to leave her. We saw Sophie behaving very differently on week 4 from the way she had behaved in previous weeks.

Week 4

Events

Sophie was playing with the train set. Emily told Sophie that she was going to the toilet. Emily left the room, and Sophie continued to play with the train set, without becoming distressed. Sophie left the train set and walked over to Tracy and took her hand. She said, 'Lady come.' She pulled at Tracy's hand. Tracy stood up and Sophie, still holding her hand, led her to the door. Sophie led Tracy to the toilet door and then said, 'Mummy in there.' Sophie did not cry. Emily came out of the toilet and asked if Sophie had been crying. Tracy explained what had happened.

Emily's feelings

'This week I told Sophie I was going to the toilet. I said to her, "Mummy's going to the toilet and I will be back in a minute." I thought "I wonder if she will come wandering out?" I'd thought about it and tried it during the week and it had been working. When I came out of the toilet and saw you standing there, and you told me she had fetched you and hadn't cried, the biggest thing I felt was relief. What I was doing was working – I was getting somewhere with her.'

Holding and containment

At this time Tracy talked to Emily about the concepts of 'holding and containment', in relation to what had happened for her and Sophie over the last four weeks.

It would appear that through this process Emily had begun to reflect on one aspect of her relationship with her daughter Sophie. She had begun to tell Sophie when she is about to leave her for a few moments, and to reassure her that she will return. As a result of this, Sophie appears to have come to some understanding, over time, that when Emily leaves the room she is not abandoning her, but that she will return shortly. Sophie is safe and secure in this knowledge, and Emily is much happier too.

Emily reflected once again

'It's changed my life – I don't know why I didn't do it sooner, and now I do it all the time. Now I can leave her. I tell her where I am going. Before when she was clingy she would cry when I got back, but now she is happy and everything is normal. (Emily talked to us about how her relationship with her partner Alan has changed, but most of all how Sophie's relationship with her dad had changed. Now Alan takes her up to bed and reads her a story.) 'He enjoys it, it is his special time. He now feels more bonded with her. It is lovely. I sit and watch *EastEnders* in peace or eat a bar of chocolate on my own. I was worried about how demanding she was, especially when the new baby arrives. I feel a lot more relaxed about the baby... everyone has commented on it, my mum, Alan's mum, Alan.'

A case study: Heidi, Ethan and Leah

This case study is about Heidi, who attended Growing Together for several years before becoming a worker within the group. Heidi first came to Growing Together four years before, when her son Ethan was three weeks old. There was building work being undertaken at the centre at the time and the group was being housed in a temporary mobile. 'The group was in the mobile when I first came ... it was just nice to get out. We were filmed, it was lovely ... it made me feel special about him. I knew one of the group leaders as she worked in the nursery and so it made it easier for me to come ... there was a friendly face, somebody who knew my name and my history already.' Heidi continued to attend the group regularly, and two years later had a baby girl, Leah, and continued to come to Growing Together.

To begin with, Heidi joined the group to 'socialise with other mothers ... to get out of the house and meet with other people in the same position as me. As Ethan got older and began to get interested in things in the group, I found myself playing more and more with Ethan ... and then when he got older, I had more time again to talk with other people at the group.'

Heidi talked about the filming that happens in Growing Together: 'The filming is really good, and looking back is really good. Ethan and Leah both like to look at the pictures and show their dad what they are doing.'

Ethan's interests

Ethan spent a lot of time both at Pen Green and at home playing with train sets (Figure 9.7). Heidi reported that Ethan loved watching Thomas the Tank Engine videos, and playing with his Thomas crane. He had enjoyed watching the video and seeing the crane being used to pick Thomas up when he was derailed! Heidi had also taken Ethan on a trip to see Thomas the Tank Engine, and had taken him on a train.

Ethan loved playing with the train set at Growing Together and returned to it week after week (Figure 9.8).

Ethan's portfolio

Ethan

Ethan is very involved with the trains at Growing Together. He repeatedly pushes the train around the track and stops in the same place. He then reverses the train back around the track. At one point he said to his mum, Heidi, that he was going 'backwards'. When he came to the bridge he pulled the train very slowly as he knew from previous experience that if he pulled it quickly it would come apart.

Figure 9.7 Ethan involved with the train set

During the discussion with Heidi about the video of Ethan playing with the train set, she commented, 'I knew that Ethan liked playing with certain things, trains being the number one thing, but I didn't realise the significance of what he was doing in terms of schemas. I just thought he enjoyed playing with trains, but when you watch the video and do it frame by frame, you can see his expressions, his concentration and how involved he is.'

Heidi was also fascinated by the things she spotted in the video that perhaps were missed in the session. 'You also catch the little bits ... like when he puts the two opposing magnets together and then he does it again.'

Figure 9.8 Ethan propelling the engine around the track by utilising the opposing magnetic forces

Heidi appreciated watching the film alongside a worker and learning about different theoretical frameworks. 'You've got someone there to look at it with you who knows about these frameworks. I could then look for different things and think about why he was doing particular things. You then use that way of thinking to look at how he is playing in other areas.'

Myke, Ethan's dad, was able to see what Ethan was doing at Growing Together. Heidi reported that previously Myke sometimes thought that what Ethan was doing was intended to 'wind him up', but then, through being introduced to schemas, he said that he understood him more and looked at what he was doing differently.

Heidi said, when thinking about schemas, 'It's a compulsion to do it and to stop them would be bad for the child. I think for Myke to not say no to him and watch what he's done has been good, as he's seen how much he's progressed ... I think Myke enjoyed it too – hearing and seeing what Ethan was doing, and it helped him to play the way Ethan wanted to play. As adults, you think things should be done a certain way, but once you understand, you go with what the child wants to do.'

Leah's experience

Leah was a very contented baby, and for about a year Heidi brought both Ethan and Leah to the group (Figure 9.9).

Figure 9.9 Heidi brought both Ethan and Leah to the group

Heidi was able to take Leah along with her to spend time with Ethan, and was also able to leave Leah with friends in the group if she wanted to spend some time alone with Ethan.

As Leah got older, she used the group very differently from Ethan. She tended to move around the room, accessing all the provision. Leah also spent a lot of time watching people. On this occasion when Leah was filmed, she was engaging in a social interaction with other adults who attended the group. Leah was 18 months at this stage, and had been interested in trying to get herself dressed for some time. She spent a lot of time trying to put this doll's sock on and off her foot.

Leah's portfolio

Leah - Growing Together - 11-11-05.
This is the first week that Leah has approached other adults at Growing Together and engaged in a social interaction.
Leah is very interested in the sock she wants to put it on , then take it off.
    At home she does this all the time with hats, socks and Ethan's pants.No sooner are they on when she wants to take them off again.

Figure 9.10 Leah engaging in a social interaction

Through watching the film and then taking stills, Heidi said, 'This makes you realise you've got to be aware of what you're doing and how what you are doing really affects your children.'

Moving on

Leah was offered a place in the Pen Green nursery when she was two years of age. In our reflection time at the end of one of the sessions, we spoke together about the possibility of asking Heidi to become a worker in the group. There has been a long history at Pen Green of asking parents who have used groups effectively, to become group leaders, with appropriate support and training. We all thought that this was a really good idea, and soon afterward approached Heidi.

'When they first asked me, I was apprehensive. I thought I'd really like to do it, but I was worried about how it would be, being in a different role.'

Heidi has been working in the group for six weeks now and says,
'I still find it strange because when I was a group member I didn't interact with all the people in the group, so I don't feel able to easily approach everybody now, but I am aware that my responsibilities have changed. I really like interacting with the children in the group – I had a lovely time at the sandpit with Ethan and Liam making sandcastles. They were reacting to me, laughing and really engaging with me … they wanted me to be involved in their play … it was lovely. I'm enjoying what I'm doing.'

Finally ...

Growing Together is a drop-in group, running each week, in which parents can gain emotional support and spend time with their child. The group seeks to encourage positive parent–child relationships, and uses video material to encourage 'reflective parenting'. We have found that both the child development concepts and the psychoanalytic concepts are useful concepts to share with parents. This sharing of concepts is instrumental in building up a shared language with which to discuss both children's development and parent–child relationships. The psychoanalytic concepts also affect the running of the sessions. Spending time as a staff team planning and reflecting each week helps us to keep links across the weeks, and we are better able to support parents and children effectively.

CHAPTER 10

Deepening the Dialogue with Parents

Eddie McKinnon

In this chapter, the focus is on the researcher developing a deeper relationship with parents through sharing journal material and through video analysis sessions.

> The teacher is no longer merely the-one-who-teaches, but one who is himself taught in dialogue with the students, who in turn while being taught teach... . They become jointly responsible for a process in which they all grow... . Here, no one teaches another, nor is anyone self-taught. People teach each other.
>
> (Freire, 1996a, p. 61)

This quotation from Paulo Freire encapsulates the way in which parents, nursery workers and researchers are encouraged to work together at the Pen Green Centre. Each one of us, whether parent, worker or researcher, has his or her own relationship and roles in relation to the child being studied. Each of us cares about the child but, necessarily, in different ways and to different degrees. We all have our own perspective on the work we are jointly involved in and on each other's place within it.

Parents' love for their children will always be fundamentally personal and qualitatively different from the fondness that a family worker develops for a child while in his or her care. The family worker's knowledge and understanding of the child will be informed by professional training and will be of a different nature from that of the parents. The researcher's relationship with, and understanding of, the child will be of a different nature from that held by both the parents and the family worker. The researcher adopts a position which is less connected to the child than either the parents or family workers. The thing that unifies us in our work is a common desire to come to a better and deeper understanding of the child with whom we all interrelate in such complex ways.

At Pen Green, this structure of relationships is achieved by a continuous triangular dialogue about the child involving parents and family worker, family worker and researcher, and researcher and parents (Whalley, 1997b; 2001; Arnold, 1999b; 2003).

This triangulation of perspectives, in which each participant's knowledge about the child is shared, enhances everyone's understanding of the child (Easen *et al.*, 1992, pp. 282–96). For this sharing of knowledge to be effective, each person involved has to understand the value of the contribution that they themselves make and to appreciate the contributions of the others: the family worker accepts that the parents are the experts on their child; the parents are not inhibited by the family worker's professional understanding; the researcher, while appreciating the personal and professional expertise of the others, will have confidence in their own ability to provide something of equal value.

The significance of this kind of collaboration is highlighted in the work of Jordan and Henderson (1995), who argue that the assumption underpinning interaction analysis is:

> that knowledge and action are fundamentally social in origin, organisation and use…expert knowledge and practice are seen not so much as located in the heads of individuals but as situated in the interactions among members of a particular community.
>
> (Jordan and Henderson, 1995, p. 41)

At Pen Green, the 'particular community' consists of the parents, family worker and researcher, who dialogue and share what they know and believe they understand about the child, fulfilling Patrick Easen's view that:

> The roles of professional experience and parent's everyday experience are seen as complementary and equally important. The former constitutes a 'public' (and generalised) form of 'theory' about child development, whilst the latter represents a 'personal theory' about the development of a particular child. An interaction between the two 'theories' as ways of explaining a child's actions may produce an enriched understanding as a basis for both to act in relation to the child. Only through the combination of both types of information could a broad and accurate picture be built up of a child's developmental progress.
>
> (Easen *et al.*, 1992, pp. 282–96)

Dialoguing with parents – the research context at Pen Green

During the 1990s, staff at the Pen Green nursery were interested in developing a 'shared language' with parents about child development concepts. If real dialogue was to take place, it was vital that staff and parents had a shared conceptual framework so that they could really discuss 'the ways in which children learn and how adults can effectively intervene to support and extend children's learning' (Whalley, 2001, p. 15).

Training sessions were set up to help parents find a focus for their observations of their children at home (Tait, 2001, pp. 36–56). The work of Susan Isaacs on observations and intellectual growth and Ferre Laevers' involvement scale were shared and discussed with parents (Isaacs, 1936; Laevers, 1994a). This knowledge and understanding provided parents with the necessary foci in terms of their children's behaviour. Parents quickly saw how useful it would be to video record and note in their diaries those times when their children were deeply involved in some aspect of their play. Written information and taped images could then be shared with nursery staff. Pen Green had learned from the work of Chris Athey, director of the Froebel Early Education Project, that 'Nothing gets under a parent's skin more quickly and more permanently than the illumination of his or her own child's behaviour. The effect of participation can be profound' (Athey, 1990, p. 66).

The effects for both parents and staff at Pen Green were profound indeed. A full-scale research project was developed called Parents' Involvement in Their Children's Learning (PICL) which included:

- the establishment of study groups where child development concepts were shared with parents and applied to their children;
- training with video cameras for parents and the loan of one to use at home if required; and
- emphasis on the need for the continual exchange of information between parents and nursery staff via conversations and by recording the play behaviour of children in documents such as parents' diaries.

This model developed into 'the 'Pen Green Loop', in which nursery workers and parents regularly exchanged video material as a way of creating and maintaining an image-based 'dialogue' about a child that complemented and enhanced the verbal dialogue they engaged in. This process informed curriculum planning in the nursery, the extension of this work in the home, its further extension on return to the nursery, and so on (Whalley, 2001, pp. 140 and 148).

The value of using video as an important research tool to facilitate the process of dialoguing between parents, family workers and researchers is supported by Jordan and Henderson:

Only electronic recording produces the kind of data corpus that allows the close interrogation required for Interaction Analysis. In particular, it provides the crucial ability to replay a sequence of interaction repeatedly for multiple viewers – and on multiple occasions.

(Jordan and Henderson, 1995, p. 39)

Parents, family workers and researchers can all have copies of the recorded material, which they can view and analyse individually as well as watching and discussing together in dedicated meetings. This collective dialoguing can allow new insights to develop, behaviour can be 'seen' in a different light, and speech and actions can be reinterpreted in the light of the shared perceptions of others. Jordan and Henderson (1995) argue that this process can provide a 'balance' of interpretations, ensuring that the views of parents and workers are not 'outweighed' by those of the researcher: 'Collaborative viewing is particularly powerful for neutralising preconceived notions on the part of researchers and discourages the tendency to see in the interaction what one is conditioned to see or even wants to see' (Jordan and Henderson, 1995, p. 44).

Disagreements about what was said or done in the videotaped material can be settled by reviewing and rediscussing the recording, which becomes 'the final authority' in terms of what happened (Jordan and Henderson, 1995, p. 44). This approach has major advantages over written records of behaviour, as 'Errors of this sort are invisible in a paper-and-pencil record because there is no opportunity to go back and re-examine what happened' (Jordan and Henderson, 1995, p. 45).

Individually, and collectively, the videotape can be reviewed as many times as necessary to produce a definitive, agreed version of events. The material can be mined over and over again so that interpretations can be confirmed or refuted. In addition, the same sequence of actions can be looked at for different reasons; for example, to develop an understanding of the cognitive value for the child or how the child is affected emotionally, or to examine the nature of an adult's intervention in the behaviour. Jordan and Henderson argue that, 'in the course of repeated viewing … previously invisible phenomena become apparent and increasingly deeper orders of regularity in actors' behaviour reveal themselves...a video tape can be played in slow or accelerated motion, thereby exposing otherwise unseen patterns in the movements of persons or artefacts' (Jordan and Henderson, 1995, p. 52).

The advantages of this approach have emerged in some of the group work carried out with parents at Pen Green. For example, in the Growing Together groups:

> The video can be watched at normal speed and also one frame at a time. This enables the worker and the parent to look very closely at what has gone on in the video vignette. Parents often comment on seeing much more when they view the film a frame at a time. …The parent is able to bring their specialist knowledge about their own child into the conversation, and the worker is able to offer their theoretical understanding. …The parent and worker develop a shared language with which to think about the child.
>
> (Pen Green Research, Development and Training Base, 2004, p. 7)

John and his family

John's parents, Julie and Piers, agreed to John being observed as part of a research project at Pen Green, which took place between 2000 and 2004 (Pen Green Research Team, 2004). When this study was completed, John was 4.9 years old and had attended the nursery at Pen Green for two years. During John's first year in the nursery, Julie completed an Open College Network accredited course at Pen Green on involving parents in their children's learning. Julie shared much of what she learned with Piers, whose work commitments prevented him from attending any of the sessions. In John's second year at the nursery, Julie successfully completed a course of training at Pen Green and now works part-time as a worker in the crèche. Julie and Piers are both interested in the ways that John, and his younger sister Natasha play and how they learn about the world around them. Julie's commitment to understanding how her children developed was demonstrated when she agreed to keep a diary about John and his life with his family while the research work was proceeding. Julie's extensive and detailed diary proved to be an invaluable resource in terms of having a 'window' into John's behaviour with his family at home.

Since the research was completed, John has left the nursery and, now aged seven, is in Year 2 at a local primary school. John's sister Natasha is five years old and, having attended the Pen Green nursery for the last two years, left this autumn to join the Reception class at the same school as John. Piers is employed full-time by a local company that manufactures fixtures and fittings for the retail industry.

Julie and Piers provide a loving family environment for their children, and they believe in and practise a structured form of verbal discipline for their children that is intended to reinforce positive actions and discourage negative ones. John and Natasha have privileges withdrawn from them if they misbehave, accompanied by an explanation as to why this is taking place. For example, 'We try to encourage him to share by explaining that it is a good thing, and if he doesn't he will be punished by not letting him have a certain toy, or no sweets or stories at night. Sometimes it works, sometimes it doesn't. Sharing (or not) is a big issue with John' (Julie's diary, 19/10/03).

Julie feels that her knowledge and understanding of her children's development was greatly enhanced by attending the PICL groups at Pen Green; an entry in her diary exemplifies Julie's awareness of her son's schema development: 'John's just watching television at the moment. Spoke too soon! John has emptied the whole contents of his toy box out onto the floor. I'm not going to get annoyed because it is probably some sort of schema' (Julie's diary, 06/11/03).

John in the nursery

During his time in the nursery John integrated well. While John was popular with the children in the nursery, he had a small group of close friends, all boys (S, K and C). This came as no surprise to his parents; when Julie and Piers completed the application form for John to have a place in the nursery, their answer to the question, 'What do you think your child might enjoy most at nursery?' was 'Playing with other children. John is a very sociable child. He has no problems blending in with other kids' (Pen Green nursery file, 19/07/01).

John was and remains a strong and sturdy little boy, and he was very active during his time in the nursery. He was often to be found in the outdoor area on the climbing frame, playing with the barrels, pushing and pulling the wooden-block trolley, or pedalling around on the tricycles – usually very quickly! John had good relationships with the nursery staff, behaved well and responded positively to suggestions from staff about his behaviour, such as being asked to slow down in case he or someone else got hurt. On occasion, John engaged in solitary play, becoming deeply involved in exploring what he could do with sand and water, for example. However, John clearly enjoyed the company of his friends, and he engaged in lots of energetic social play involving physical games, and role-playing. Sometimes John was the 'leader' in the social play, and sometimes he was a 'follower' of one of his friends. John seemed to be entirely comfortable with this arrangement and the change from 'leader' to 'follower' appeared to be seamless for him and, indeed, for his friends as well. His family worker, Louise, noted some examples of this in her file on John:

> John and S were taking turns giving each other a ride in the big trailer all round the wood decking and back. There was lots of language and lots of laughter, and the play went on for quite some time.
>
> (family worker's file, 23/09/03)

> John was pretending to be a dog with his friends K and M. John has lots of special friendships. This includes his friends K, S, M, A, C and C.
>
> (family worker's file, 27/09/03)

> John and S were exploring the logs. They were jumping from one to the next pretending to be lots of different animals.
>
> (family worker's file, 07/11/03)

Julie and Piers were very pleased that John had made such good friends in the nursery, and they were also aware of how important these relationships were to John. Anticipating a visit to the Science Museum, Julie reflected, 'He is looking forward to it because S is going. S is John's best friend' (Julie's diary 14/05/03).

Julie's entry about the visit itself records the relationship between John and S in this way,

> He was so excited. S was in the car shouting, 'Come on John!' The two of them were talking and laughing all the way there. ...When we got on the train again John and S were great. ...They shared sandwiches and talked all the way there. ...At the museum John and S held hands which I thought was great. ...S kept farting and John kept saying, 'Mummy, I've farted'...he thought it was great to say this new word. On the way back on the train, John and S had a falling out. S had pulled John's hair and made him cry, so S said sorry and after a while John said, 'We're still friends, S, aren't we?' and S replied, 'Yes, John, we are.'
>
> (Julie's diary 17/05/03)

The importance of this particular friendship for John was recorded in Julie's diary when the family went on holiday: 'John was saying how much he misses S. He said, "I love S." John bought S a Spiderman from his own pocket money. He said, "S likes Spiderman, Mummy, doesn't he?"' (Julie's diary, 25/06/03).

When deciding about the primary school John should go to, Julie and Piers considered several schools in the area that were within buggy-pushing distance. They and John were delighted that the one they preferred was happy to offer John a place and that several of John's friends from the nursery, including S, were going to be at the same school.

Louise – John's family worker

Louise was John's family worker while he was in the nursery. She felt that she and John had a good bond but that John sometimes seemed a 'little distant' from her. Once again an entry in Julie's diary captured the quality of John and Louise's relationship:

> John has found three worms, two small and one big – he is so excited. He is now making a home for them. He wants to take it into nursery to show Louise. Also John and his daddy have gone down to the park to collect autumn things, e.g. leaves, twigs, cones, etc., to make an autumn picture for Louise.
>
> (Julie's diary, 20/10/04)

Louise found it endearing that John sometimes 'held her in mind' in this way (Winnicott, 1965). Louise accompanied families on the visit to the Science Museum, and Julie's diary entry records how John 'looked after' Louise, telling her, 'Put your hood up, Louise, or you'll get wet' (Julie's diary, 17/05/03).

Julie's diary

The diary which Julie kept during the period of research included entries for almost every day. It records the day-to-day life of her family with the focus on John and his behaviour at home and in the nursery. Many of the entries track John's behaviour toward his sister Natasha. For example,

> John has been shouting at his sister a lot today. He keeps pushing her away every time she wants to play with him, or if she has one of his toys, he snatches it out of her hand. We keep telling him off for it, telling him that he has to share his toys and if he can't, then we will take them off him.
>
> (Julie's diary, 28/10/03)

However, and in fairness to John, it needs to be pointed out that the majority of entries do not describe him behaving in this way but record the normal ups-and-downs of family life with two small children. Sometimes John can be very protective of his sister. For example, on a day when their cousin L was visiting, Julie wrote, 'Natasha likes to play rough-and-tumble with the boys, but John always pushes her away. But if L is playing with her, John pushes L away, shouting, "No, she's my sister!"' (Julie's diary, 02/11/03).

For Julie, the importance of keeping a diary can be seen from her feelings about it:

> Since starting the diary I have been able to see things in a different way – for example, when I read back I can see where we have made our mistakes or could have done things better or gone about them in a different way. We are learning all the time and John has an interest in the diary too – he likes me to read pages to him. When we read the diary together, John reacts to his behaviour described in the diary; for example, if John picks up a page where he has been naughty, then he responds by lowering his head and looking sad, but if it is a good thing, he will remember it and talk about it – he doesn't like being reminded of the bad things. Having kept the diary, we're more likely to let certain things go because they're a part of his schemas. Going to the 'PICL' group meetings has helped me to describe things about John and to write them in the diary. We have learnt so much as parents too. We have learnt so much about patterns of play, schemas, well-being and involvement. We see John in a different way now. We know that he is not being naughty when he plays with the water; he is just exploring containment by filling the cups up with water. We notice things more about John – how he does things, how he plays with Natasha. It also makes me laugh or think when I am writing about certain things John has said or done. I'm looking forward to John reading his diary – I want to see how he feels!

The value of the diary to me as a researcher was the way in which it provided me with a greater understanding of John and his actions, reactions and interactions when he is at home with his family. His behaviour and moods are vividly captured in Julie's diary with entries covering a period of many months. The diary also recorded the feelings of other family members in relation to John, especially those of Julie. My understanding of John as a developing person was enormously enhanced by having access to the diary so assiduously kept by Julie.

The research from September 2003 to July 2004

During this research, I carried out a tracking exercise with John over a full nursery session of three hours followed by six 30-minute video recordings of John's play and behaviour in the nursery. These were spread over a period of 10 weeks. Copies of the video recordings were given to Julie and Piers as the research proceeded, and a tape containing all six vignettes was given to John's parents when the recordings were completed. A tape containing three short excerpts from the original recordings was also prepared, showing three of John's emotional 'hot spots,' and a copy was given to Julie and Piers. The same tapes were also given to Louise, John's family worker.

Toward the end of one of the video sessions, Julie arrived to take John home (05/12/03). She habitually came a little bit early so that she could see what John was doing and gradually coax him to put on his coat and go home, making this transition as easy as possible. I mentioned to Julie how socially skilled John was and how well he shared the toys and equipment with his friends during their play. Julie giggled and said 'He's not like that at home with his little sister!'

Julie then went on to tell me that John was very possessive about his toys at home and that he got very annoyed with Natasha if she even so much as touched his things. Louise, John's family worker, was already aware of this and confirmed that John was not as assertive as many of the other children currently in the nursery. I became interested in why this should be the case. Was John being overassertive with his little sister as a result of not feeling confident enough to be assertive with other children in the nursery? Was he 'practising' being assertive at home as a way of developing the confidence to be so at nursery? I wanted to investigate this further, and so I liaised with John's parents and his family worker to arrange a meeting where we could all talk about John in relation to a piece of video taken from one of the storytimes which family workers in the Pen Green nursery have with their group of children at the end of each nursery session.

Parents, staff and researcher meeting, 5 July 2004

At this meeting, everyone with an interest in John was present;

- his parents Piers and Julie;
- his family worker Louise; and
- his researcher Eddie.

Everyone had been given a video copy of a story time session which Louise had conducted with her group so that it could be previewed before the meeting. We were also going to view it together during the meeting itself and discuss it in detail. The theme for this story time session was to explore the children's families, and they were invited to bring photos from home of family members, activities and so on. Louise knew that Piers and Julie were having difficulties at home with John in terms of his relationship with his younger sister Natasha. He was being very possessive with his toys, refusing to share them with Natasha and sometimes taking her things away from her. Sometimes John was overboisterous in his play with Natasha, and this often led to her being knocked over. Louise planned to use the story time session as an opportunity to talk to John about this, pointing out that it was all right for him not to want to share his toys, and allowing him to express his negative feelings about his sister Natasha. During the viewing a number of statements were made by parents, family worker and researcher, indicating, several areas of interest in terms of

1 the value of a shared video record of John's behaviour in the nursery;
2 the value of dialoguing between parents and workers;
3 how items 1 and 2 facilitate reflective parenting; and
4 how items 1 and 2 facilitate staff reflecting on their own practice and developing their understanding.

I have selected some of the comments made during the dialogue and grouped them together in order to illustrate these four points and make some analysis of them.

1 The value of a shared video record of John's behaviour in the nursery

Speaker/s	Dialogue	Commentary
Piers	1. I'm a bit concerned about some of the things he said about Natasha (John's sister) in the story time video; he said 'She slaps me' and then 'She spits at me' – she doesn't do these things.	This was said by Piers at the beginning of the meeting as a result of having been able to preview the parent's copy of the tape before we watched it together. ▶

Speaker/s	Dialogue	Commentary
Piers	2. I remember the bit of the video when John is in the barrel and he gets S's ball and then S gets upset – John is inside the barrel and S is telling him he wants the ball, and when John sees how upset S is he gives it back to him – he's aware of other people's feelings.	This comment referred to the tape of John's 'emotional hot spots,' which had been given to Julie and Piers several weeks before this meeting. Piers has seen how John behaves and reflects upon John's emotional awareness.

Analysis

1 This comment reflected Piers' own agenda as John's father; that is, what is important in the video material to him. The concern Piers expressed over how John described Natasha's behaviour to him allowed Piers to bring into the discussion what he felt to be significant. Piers had seen evidence of John's behaviour about which he was not happy, and he was able to say so. The shared video record enabled a parent to be an equal partner in the research process, not merely the object of it.

2 Piers recalled the videoed sequence showing John's empathetic response to S in some detail. John understands how his actions affect S and acts in order to assuage his friend's hurt feelings. Piers' comment showed how he interpreted this as a result of having access to the video record.

2 The value of dialoguing between parents and workers

Speaker/s	Dialogue	Commentary
Louise	In the nursery we've been encouraging John and other children to see that they can say 'No' to other children and be assertive. A few days ago we were out on the beach and John was playing with something – S came over to him and said to John that he wanted it, and even though S kept saying he wanted it, John stood his ground and kept playing with it. S went away but came back a few moments later and said,	Here, Louise shares this information with Julie and Piers in response to Piers' comments about John's awareness of other people's feelings. It indicates that the work done in the 'learning how to be strong' sessions has been having some influence on John's behaviour, and it was interesting information for me to have in the light of the questions which had occurred to me about John's behaviour at home contrasting with his behaviour in the nursery. Julie then sees John's behaviour at home as assertiveness and not of

'Sorry, John.' It was really good to see John sticking up for himself and not giving in.

Julie   A lot of the time John does that because he likes to please people, but at home he says 'No' a lot (so does Natasha!), so he asserts himself at home a bit.

Louise   Maybe he's trying out being assertive on his sister?

itself 'bad' behaviour. Louise then goes on to suggest that, while tentatively assertive in the nursery, he may be 'practising' standing up for himself with Natasha, who, as Julie has said, can be assertive in her own right.

Analysis

Louise reflected the concern of the nursery staff about John's reluctance to assert himself compared to other children in the nursery. However, the sessions which take place with the children about 'learning to be strong' seemed to have encouraged John to resist the pressure from others to always comply with their needs. Clearly, Louise was happy that 'learning to be strong' was having the desired effects. It is significant that, in the example given by Louise, John was not complying with the wishes of his best friend S. It is likely that this was a relationship which was strong enough for John to 'test out' in this way. John felt secure enough to be able assert himself with S, and S valued their friendship enough to return and apologise to John. In the same way, John may have been developing enough emotional security within the context of his family to be assertive with Natasha and develop his ability to say 'No' when he was unhappy with being expected to comply with the wishes of other people.

3 How items 1 and 2 facilitate reflective parenting

Speaker/s	Dialogue	Commentary
Piers	1. But John knows Natasha so well because they see each other for so much of the time, but with John going to school, soon they'll be spending much less time together, so I wonder how that will affect things between them.	In this excerpt of conversation, Piers reflects on the forthcoming changes which the family will experience and how this will affect his children and their relationship. Julie understands that the roots of some of John's feelings and behaviour are to be found in his having a 'rival' for ▶

Speaker/s	Dialogue	Commentary
Julie	Yes, at the moment John has to share me with Natasha, and for a long time he had me all to himself, so a lot of his feelings toward Natasha probably come from that.	her time and attention. Louise confirms Julie's feelings about John's jealousy of Natasha as someone who needs a lot of her time, and Piers clearly sees the same thing – that until Natasha's arrival John had Julie all to himself.
Louise	There's a lot of jealousy there.	
Piers	He doesn't have your undivided attention anymore.	
Louise	2. Couldn't you let him play in the bathroom if you were upstairs and around?	Here, in the context of some dialogue about John's behaviour at home, Louise suggests a way in which John's interest in playing with water can be facilitated while Julie and Piers can get on with other things nearby. Julie points out that John has caused considerable mess in the bathroom and kitchen when left to his own devices. On one occasion this led to Julie being so angry with John that she couldn't speak to him. Furthermore, John casually tells Julie and Piers when he has done this, knowing that he will be punished for it. Piers points out that John tries to shirk his responsibility for his own actions by saying that 'there's been an accident,' but, as Julie says, he doesn't seem to be perturbed by his own actions or what he knows will be the consequences for him. Piers says that, at these times the normal rules are invoked and John loses something he values. Julie expresses her concern that it is possible to become so angry about John's actions, and Piers does a bit of light-hearted speculation about how John might be extending and developing his schematic learning.
Julie	Yes, and we do, but he can't be left alone or he'll flood the place. Another time John had been trying to 'make a cake, Mummy', and the kitchen was a total mess and I was really angry with him and couldn't even talk to him for a while. He must know that what he's doing is bad and that he'll get told off for it – he even comes and tells us that he's made a mess! So why does he do it if he knows that he'll get told off?	
Piers	But John says that he's had an 'accident' or there's been an 'accident'! It wasn't him who did it!	
Julie	He's still quite pleased and proud of himself though!	
Piers	When it happens I try to stay calm and lay down the rules – like I'll tell John that he won't get a story at bedtime now or something like that.	
Julie	It's scary that you can get as angry, but when I saw the mess...	
Piers	Maybe it's a case of transformations versus boundaries!	

Analysis

1 In this excerpt, Piers and Julie discussed the changes which would occur when John went to primary school on a full-time basis, as opposed to a half-day in the nursery. They speculated about how the relationship between John and Natasha would possibly alter, as they will see less of each other during the day. Both Julie and Piers recognised that an important contributing factor to John's behaviour to Natasha was his jealousy of her as a rival for parental time and attention, especially that of Julie – she had been exclusively 'his' mum until the arrival of Natasha.

2 Here Louise made a suggestion as to how the inevitable stresses of allowing children to play and learn needed to be balanced with the needs of others in the family. This produced a conversation between Julie and Piers in which they discussed how John engaged in inappropriate behaviour while knowing it to be so. They also talked about how John, like many young children, introduced 'techniques of neutralisation' (Matza, 1964) into these situations, attempting to evade responsibility for his own actions and their consequences. Piers recognised his own anger at these times and his conscious decision to calmly apply the rules, while Julie expressed how frustrated she felt and recognised the need to control her reactions as well. Piers' and Julie's decision to have a clear set of rules for their children showed their understanding that John and Natasha are just that – children, who don't always act in the ways parents would like! They were conscious of the need, when necessary, to 'stand back' from what their children did and be 'the adults' in the situation – that is, those with the understanding and emotional resources to be able to deal with children's conflicts, inappropriate behaviour and so on. Piers then used the knowledge Julie had shared with him to conclude the discussion with a light-hearted reference to John's schematic development.

4 How items 1 and 2 facilitate staff reflecting on their own practice and developing their understanding

Speaker/s	Dialogue	Commentary
Eddie	One of the things I've heard being discussed at Pen Green is that it's also OK if a child doesn't want to share because, when we encourage children to share things we're forgetting just how important their own things	In this excerpt of dialogue, I rehearse my thinking about several discussions with various staff about how some children happily share their toys and other things with other children, while others are visibly more reluctant to do this. For ▶

are to them! How many adults would be prepared to share their own things with someone else? However, we expect little children to do this all the time with their brothers and sisters, their friends and even total strangers in many play situations. They are very attached to their own toys and other things and don't want to share them with anyone else. From what's been said, I'm picking up that John is becoming more assertive in the nursery (e.g. with S) and getting better at sharing with Natasha at home (e.g. his cars). In the nursery John plays in a very cooperative way with his pals and is very even-tempered.

some children, the things which they see as 'theirs' have a significance for them far beyond their importance as objects of play. Most small children have at least one thing which they clearly don't want to share with others. I then comment on what has been said about John becoming more assertive with his special friend, S, in the nursery, and that he will allow Natasha to play with all but his most treasured cars at home. I point out that, ordinarily, John's well-being is high, and he enjoys good relations with the other children in the nursery. Piers picks this up and compares John to other children who are not on such an 'even keel' as John; the other children 'know where they are' with John. Louise argues that the other children are able to 'forecast' how John will behave during their play and feel emotionally secure because of John's emotional consistency. I pick this up and reiterate the gist of Piers' and Louise's comments regarding the effects of John's behaviour being predictable for his friends.

Piers   John is generally a happy boy, and I think that his friends know he's always in a good mood – he's not 'up-and-down' like some of the others, so they know where they are with John.

Louise   Yes, and it really helps them to know how John is, that there's a consistency there – they can 'feel safe' with John because they know what he's like and how he's going to behave.

Eddie   The consistency in how he behaves means that his friends know what he'll do – there's a level of predictability about him.

Analysis

Here I reiterated ideas about children sharing or not sharing, and John's play and interactions being based on his equanimity of mood in the nursery. This prompted Piers, Louise and myself to think about how this promoted John's social relationships with his friends in the nursery. John's consistent composure ensured that the other children felt emotionally safe with John; his reactions were predictable, and he presented no threat to them in terms of behaviour which would have been 'out of character' for John.

At the end of the meeting, Julie and Piers both expressed their view that, in keeping the diary, they had developed an even better understanding of John and his behaviour and also that of Natasha. Keeping the diary had changed their understanding of their children's actions and interactions and how they treated them and, indeed, their own interactions with their children and how these affected all of them. Both Julie and Piers said that this was the most recent extension of their understanding, which had been enhanced by all of their interactions with the Pen Green Centre. Piers gave the example of how he used to get annoyed with some of John's behaviour and how he came to see things in a different light. For example, John would take out all the video boxes and join them together all over the floor in lines and walk on them. When Piers had developed an understanding of schemas, and specifically what John's schemas might be, he saw John's behaviour and actions in a completely different way; John was making pathways to walk on and follow, roads for his cars to travel along, and so on, not merely making a mess.

John's parents' reflections on their understanding of their son

In July of this year, two years after this meeting, I contacted Julie and Piers and asked them if they would be willing to tell us more about their understanding of their children arising from the research project and Julie's continuing involvement at Pen Green. They agreed to do this, and they were asked to reflect on three questions and then feedback their ideas and feelings. Julie and Piers' answers demonstrate that learning about key developmental concepts had been highly significant in shaping their understanding of their children and their ability to support their children's play and learning. This was particularly significant in the case of Natasha, whose development is delayed. Julie and Piers felt that they had a better understanding of this, and how to deal with it, than would otherwise have been the case.

1 Thinking back to that time, are there any occasions when your understanding of John's or Natasha's play and behaviour was enhanced by your knowledge of things like schemas, involvement, well-being and adult strategies?

By learning about the four key concepts, we can help to improve our children's learning by allowing them to make their own choices, letting them take appropriate risks, 'standing back' and letting them learn from their own mistakes. Schemas can introduce a whole new meaning of play. If you get to know what schema your child has, whether it's one main schema or a cluster, you can extend and enhance your child's learning and play. Learning about schemas at the PICL groups has made our lives much easier. For instance, John has a strong containment schema among others. Piers would bring home a large cardboard box from work. John would play for hours, containing himself, playing hide-and-seek, etc., until the box was flattened. Then he would use the flattened box for playing with his cars, making ramps and roads. John would become very involved in this play. Also, John would go to the bathroom and play with the water. Nine out of ten times, he would flood the bathroom. At first we thought he was just trying to annoy us and wind us up, but after attending the PICL group, we have come to realise that he is not out to annoy us, but is simply exploring his natural curiosity and learning. This made us more relaxed, and we could extend his play with a hose-pipe and containers in the garden. Since PICL, I have learnt that you do not have to spend a fortune on expensive toys. A box could keep your child entertained for hours and costs nothing at all.

2 Related to the above, were there any times when you responded differently to John or Natasha as a result? For example, joining in, giving them something, or going somewhere that you wouldn't have thought of beforehand?

Now we find it easier to find activities that they would really enjoy and become highly involved in, as we know that the higher a child's involvement, the greater the learning skills. Also, we are more relaxed about why John does the things that he does, like when we came to understand why he flooded the bathroom every day. Knowing that he has a strong containment and trajectory schema, we could find new resources that would encourage and enhance John's schemas in a new and improved, controlled environment. I think a good example of responding differently since knowing about the schemas and involvement of our children is our understanding that Natasha is about $2\frac{1}{2}$ years behind in development. Her concentration levels are poor, and she tends to flit about a lot. Learning about schemas has helped us to find different ways to extend her play and help her become more involved and engaged in her play and learning process. This had made a huge difference to her development.

3 Thinking back to the time when you kept a diary, did the act of keeping the diary change the way you thought about your children and yourselves as parents?

Yes, it did. Keeping the diary gave us an insight into finding out what improvements we could make as parents and what to focus on or change to make a difference to our children's global development. Also, having the diary means that we can look back on and see the differences we have made; to look back on our inappropriate decisions and make amendments as necessary. I think that sometimes John and Natasha were being naughty. They knew that they were doing things that would get our attention even though it was negative attention. Now, when we read back snippets from the diary, we realise just how hard they were pushing the boundaries. Now John asks a lot of questions about the diary and about his behaviour, and he recognises the difference between right and wrong. So I would definitely say it has made a big difference and had a huge impact on our teaching strategies.

Conclusion

I want to return here to the work of Paulo Freire because I believe that what he has to say underpins so much of what we try to put into practice at the Pen Green Centre. Freire has much to tell us about a number of fundamental things:

- the need to dialogue on equal terms with parents; we know that they are their children's first educators, and we believe they are committed to their children's well-being;
- that the process of developing reflective and reflexive parents, childcare workers and researchers is an iterative one – it is a 'two-way street' where everybody's knowledge and understanding has equal importance; and
- that to be successful, this work must be participative and collaborative and that the parents, children and childcare workers are subjects deeply involved and connected to the process, and not merely objects of study for researchers.

Hopefully, this account of our work with Julie, Piers and their children demonstrates that it is possible for parents, practitioners and researchers to work together in a spirit of equality of participation; for all involved to be reflective about their own actions and those of others, and together to develop a deeper understanding of the children who are the focus of our concerns. Paulo Freire's views on 'true dialogue' have much to teach all of us who are involved in the care and education of young children:

Men and women who lack humility (or have lost it) cannot come to the people, cannot be their partners in naming the world. Someone who cannot acknowledge himself to be as mortal as everyone else still has a long way to go before he can reach the point of encounter. At the point of encounter there are neither utter ignoramuses nor perfect sages; there are only people who are attempting, together, to learn more than they now know.

(Freire, 1996a p. 71)

CHAPTER 11

The Impact of Study Groups in Primary Schools on Children and Parents

Cath Arnold

This chapter draws on theory from child development, adult learning and psychoanalysis to demonstrate how parents became engaged in the process of change through becoming involved in their children's learning. Study groups in two local schools are described, with three case-study examples of how parents responded to the discussion groups and subsequently made portfolios about their children's special interests. These groups ran during 2002-3. In 2006, three parents gave us feedback about the long-term benefits of their involvement in the project.

Introduction

At the Pen Green Centre, we have worked with children and their families for 24 years. During our major research project, Parents' Involvment in Their Childrens' Learning (PICL) (funded by the Esmee Fairbairn Trust), 84 per cent of parents using the Pen Green nursery became involved in some way in discussing their children's learning with their child's nursery workers. One engagement method was to set up study groups for parents (Whalley, 1997b; 2001). Building on the work of Athey (1990), Bruce (1997) and Shaw (1991), we shared child development concepts with the parents during these group sessions. Parents also shared information with us about their children at home. Together, we applied these child development theories to their children's actions to help us understand what the children were learning. We began with a social constructivist view of pedagogy (Piaget, 1962; Vygotsky, 1978). Like Malaguzzi, we saw all children as 'rich in potential' (Malaguzzi, 1997, p. 117).

Our view of the andragogical process (the adult learning process) was that adults brought a wealth of knowledge and life experience to each learning situation (Allman, 1983; Knowles, 1970; Whitaker, 1986). Like Freire, we believed that, through dialogue, we could 'transform' our knowledge and 'name the world' together (1970, p. 69).

In our approach to parents, we were also influenced by the psychoanalytic literature. We knew that both parents and workers brought with them the 'ghosts' from their own early interactions with their caregivers to their current interactions with the children (Fonagy *et al.*, 1990). The ghosts referred to are within 'the conflicted past of the parents' that 'may interfere with their relationship with their child' (p. 116). We were also aware of Fonagy's finding that when earlier painful experiences are thought about and reflected upon, change can occur. Fonagy refers to this process as 'reflective functioning' (2001, p. 27).

These theories and the experience of setting up study/discussion groups with parents were the background to our research study of young children's emotional well-being and resilience. For many years, we had focused on children's cognition alongside their parents and workers. We wanted to find a new way of working with parents and workers in order to understand and to support the emotional lives of the children more effectively. This area was much more sensitive. One strand of the work involved setting up two study groups in local schools. I am going to share with you how the groups were set up. I am also going to tell you about the experiences of three parents who attended those study groups.

Setting up study groups

We were already running three study groups a week for parents using the nurseries on our campus. We also set up two new groups called 'Expressions' at the Pen Green Centre, specifically focusing on children's emotional development. For the second year running, we co-led study groups for parents in two neighbouring schools. We worked closely with the school staff by sharing information about key child development concepts. A member of our research team linked with a member of the Foundation Stage team in each school to facilitate the groups. We invited all of the parents of children aged 4–6 to groups called 'Understanding Young Children's Development'. Ten parents began to attend the weekly group in one school, and six parents attended the weekly group in the other school. We met one morning or afternoon a week in each school library. We sat on comfortable armchairs, had tea and coffee, and had a TV and video to use (Whalley, 2001). We introduced four child development concepts over a period of four months (Whalley, 1997b; 2001).

The concepts we introduced were as follows:

- *Well-being.* Laevers (1997) has developed signs and a scale to indicate the level of well-being in children. 'The level of well-being indicates how they are developing emotionally' (1997, p. 15).

- *Involvement*. Laevers (1997) has developed signs and a scale to indicate how involved a child is in an activity. 'Involvement only occurs somewhere between "being able to do something" and "not yet being able to do something".' (1997, p. 20).
- *Schemas* (Athey, 1990). 'Plans or schemas function as built-in hypotheses as to how things are...In humans, schemas acquire content from experience that modifies hypotheses' (p. 36). 'Schemas are patterns...children may try out the same action on a variety of different objects' (Pen Green Team, 2002).
- *Adult pedagogic strategies* (Whalley and Arnold, 1997). These are a set of indicators for effective adult teaching.

The parents have found the signs and scales helpful when reflecting on observations of their children.

We have now added the following concepts:

- *Containment*: The concept of containment describes the parent taking in the baby's distress, understanding it and responding so that the baby feels emotionally looked after, feels contained (adapted from Bion, 1962).
- *Holding*: The concept of holding describes the emotional holding parents can give their baby by holding him or her in mind (adapted from Winnicott, 1965).
- *Attachment*: The concept of attachment describes how adults and children form reciprocal relationships (adapted from Bowlby, 1991).

As well as these concepts from the psychoanalytic literature, we have also been heavily influenced by Colwyn Trevarthen's concept of 'companionship' and 'intersubjectivity'. Trevarthen describes the relationship that develops between adults and children, which is 'more than a dialogue' and more of 'an exercise in belonging' (Trevarthen, 2002a).

Each week our co-leaders, who worked with the youngest children in the schools, filmed three of the parents' children in school. Each child, whose parent came to a study group, was filmed on a rota basis. At the groups each week, we would discuss one of the concepts, and then think about and discuss how the theory related to our own experiences as children. We watched the video of the three children filmed in school that week. We then discussed each child's development and learning by applying the theory to each video observation. The parents were each given a diary to make written observations of their children at home. After Easter, we began lending the video camera to parents to film their children at home. So, each week, we introduced or discussed some of the theory. Each parent talked about their child at home that week; we watched video of some of the children in school or at home; and we discussed each child's emotional well-being, involvement and schemas, and how adults were interacting with the children. We also introduced the new psychoanalytic concepts when these concepts seemed relevant to the discussions.

The two parent groups were very different. In school (A), the parents focused very much on their children's development. All of these parents had been involved in study groups when their children were at the Pen Green nursery. In school (B), the parents talked at length about their own emotions and experiences of home and school, before beginning to think about their children's development. The group members discussed deeply personal issues at times. Issues of loss, separation and bullying were frequently discussed. There was a high level of trust and support for each other within the group. This was the first time most of these parents had attended a study group.

Making portfolios about children's interests

The adults were, over time, reflecting on their own experiences and learning about child development. Each parent was making a special study of their own child. In order to acknowledge the adults' learning, we approached the Open College Network, which accredited three units that we had written about 'theories of child development' and 'observing a child's development' (accreditation was at two levels). One way of providing evidence of the adult's learning was to make portfolios of each child's interests (Dahlberg, Moss and Pence, 1999; Pen Green Portfolios, 2000; Carr, 2001). Each parent approached the making of the portfolio in a different way. The process of making a portfolio made each child's development and learning more visible so that their learning processes could be discussed and more deeply understood (Dahlberg *et al.*, 1999, p. 153).

Parent case study 1 (2003)

Sharon began attending a study group in school (A). She had attended a study group at nursery and was interested in how her only son, John, was getting on in school. She also wanted to make a career change and go into childcare and education. She was particularly fascinated by John's emotional well-being. Sharon told me that when John was born she and John lived with his dad in Norwich. They decided to separate when John was two years old. She and John moved to Corby, as her parents lived in Corby. John's dad later moved to Colchester. Sharon described her relationship with her ex-partner as 'difficult at first'. She said they did not have 'good communications at first because I was feeling pretty much upset and did not want to talk to him'. However, she says that they 'got over it and now we go from strength to strength... . Whatever John needs, we sort it out between us. If anything is wrong with John, we talk about it and try and work out between us how to sort it out.' John goes to his dad's every other weekend and also in the school holidays.

Soon after John and his mum came to live in Corby, he made a good friend, Elliot, who went through nursery and the first year of school with him. 'They'll fight and bicker for a few minutes and then be best buddies.'

Sharon told me, 'The only time his well-being was down was when he had chickenpox. Six weeks ago, he broke his wrist – that didn't faze him at all. He's got his dad's girlfriend's family and also my partner's family. They all adore him. He's a happy, loving and sociable child.'

Sharon decided to make a portfolio about John's well-being. 'I just kind of went through the notes I had in my diary and just sort of watching John myself, I realised he's got such high well-being – I thought I would do it on that. He's creative ... got very high self-confidence and self-esteem. ... He's very good at being in touch with himself as well as other people. ... If he finds he's not happy with something, he will say. ... or he just won't do it. He will tell other people about it.'

I asked what attracted Sharon to the group. 'Mainly I wanted to make sure he was settled and he was happy, and I could see the evidence through watching the videos of John at school and through talking. I was a little bit concerned that he was going into school early, because he was only just four and I did not want to think that he was getting pushed into it too fast'.

I knew that the group was important to Sharon because, at the beginning of the year, when she was working in a shop 20 minutes' walk from the school, she would arrive out of breath, having run up the road. During the year, Sharon began working at a local nursery but negotiated Thursday after-noons off so that she could continue attending the group.

After the interview, Sharon added that she valued the fact that the video clips of each child were copied for each parent to keep. Sharon said that she wanted video of John at nursery and at school to show him when he is older. She also wanted to make a portfolio so that he could see what she did when he was little. Sharon also appreciated being able to show the portfolio to his dad.

Sharon was keen to learn about the theories and able to apply them to John. Although John is a very happy and optimistic child, Sharon did not assume that he would be like that at school. She wanted evidence of his enjoyment of school. Sharon realised that it was important for John to be assertive and to be able to say when he was not happy with something. It was also important for John's educators to know about his lifestyle. John demonstrated his resilience. His parents seemed to foster that resilience by:

- communicating with each other about John's needs;
- valuing his friendship with another child and with several adults;
- expecting him to be assertive and to express his dislikes as well as his likes; and
- being interested in his emotional well-being.

Where are they now? – 2006

John still attends the same school and is doing very well. Sharon is very proud of his recent school report, 'He's doing brilliantly at school. Nothing seems to faze him. All of his teachers love the way he helps other children understand lessons.'

Sharon is now a school governor. This is her second year. 'I saw the opening advertised in the newsletter. I asked John what he thought – he said Yes, so I went for it. I wanted to have an understanding of what's going on.'

Looking back, Sharon appreciates attending the groups both at nursery and when John was in Foundation Stage 2 in school. 'One of the reasons I went to the group was that I was worried John was suffering on the inside. My relationship with John has come on in leaps and bounds since then. I know when he's having a bad day just by the way he holds himself...without the group, I think I would have had a hard time understanding what makes John happy or sad. Also, I wouldn't have had as much feedback from the school staff.'

John still visits his dad, just during the school holidays but talks with him on the phone regularly. Sharon and her new partner got married recently. At the end of the wedding evening, John took the DJ's microphone and said, 'I just want to say – I love my mummy and I'm glad she's met Tim'! Sharon was very moved by this.

The next big decision for Sharon is which secondary school to choose for John. 'I'm a bit nervous about him going to another school. I'll go and look around and try to ensure that he gets the same attention as he is getting in his primary school.' Most important to Sharon, 'I'd like him to go with some of his same friends, he started school with...in fact, Elliot's been his friend since nursery.'

The day Sharon came to see me, she had been interviewed for a job as classroom assistant for Years 1 and 2. She mentioned that she'd done the course on 'understanding young children's development' and knew about and was interested in emotional well-being.

Parent case study 2 (2003)

Caroline's only daughter Billiejoe was in Foundation Stage 2 class in school (B). Caroline had briefly attended a study group two years earlier when Billiejoe was in nursery, but did not sustain her involvement. Caroline said that she found attending this group both 'enjoyable' and 'painful'. She told me that going to the group and discussing emotions 'makes you sit and think about what's happened'.

Caroline described this group as 'more personal.' She went on to say that she felt she 'could have said anything at the group and nobody judged anyone else'.

Caroline realised that sometimes her daughter's well-being was low. Billiejoe went through a particularly difficult time when she had chickenpox.

She said she felt ugly, she thought that no one would talk to her, she hid her face with a hat so no one would see her face.

Her well-being was low, between level 1–2 – I know this because:

her eyes were dull

she cried and became anxious

clinging to one person

worried about what other people said and thought

she needed adult support to help her start to feel her old self.

(Billiejoe's Style, a portfolio)

On another occasion, Caroline observed that Billiejoe's well-being was high (level 4) when she was 'feeding the birds'.

I know this because:

she was scared at first but quickly relaxed to enjoy herself that she did not want to leave

her face showed how much she was enjoying herself, wide-eyed and smiling and calling us to look

she showed the confidence to go in and try a new experience and coped well.

(Billiejoe's Style, a portfolio)

On one occasion, Billiejoe had had a bad dream 'about an alien'. Caroline's friend suggested asking Billiejoe to draw the alien. Billiejoe was able to express her ideas about her dream by drawing the alien and has never dreamt about it again. Caroline reflected on this process and compared how this had helped Billicjoe, with herself writing a poem about her own feelings. She had expressed her feelings in words, to get them from 'inside to outside' herself.

Caroline has found talking about Billiejoe's well-being particularly helpful. She talks to her boyfriend and to her mother about Billiejoe's well-being now. She says she notices it now. 'Her well-being has been a bit scattery this summer.'

Caroline says that her boyfriend Paul wanted to come to the group. He wanted to know whether there were any other men there. There were none attending this group, but some men attended the groups within the Pen Green Centre. Caroline reported, 'I wouldn't stop him from coming'. She is 'looking forward to doing another set of observations and adding to the portfolio.'

Caroline thinks she will be able to communicate with Billiejoe's new teacher by showing her the portfolio.

When I asked about anything Caroline did not like about coming to the group, she mentioned a parent who was so preoccupied with her own issues that she was unable to focus on her children at all. The other parents wanted to help but found her difficulties frustrating.

Caroline enjoyed making the portfolio although 'it was hard'. The best bit was 'putting the final touches to it and feeling I've done it!'

Figure 11.1 Case Study 2: Caroline and Billiejoe

Where are they now? 2006

Billiejoe is now eight years old. She has a baby sister Jorjalee, who is nearly one, and the family are expecting another baby in November.

Caroline went on to make a second portfolio about Billiejoe. This time she observed and identified the curriculum areas Billiejoe was most interested in. Caroline helped Billiejoe follow up her interests at home; for example, 'although Billiejoe has a good collection of books, our old next-door neigh-bour gave her some very old books...She also has some books that belong to her Great Gran, that are to do with sewing and flower arranging. She likes reading her old and interesting books, as well as her story books.'

Caroline continued to support Billiejoe's emotional well-being. When her Grandmother's dog died, Billiejoe was very upset. 'Both Billiejoe and Dad cried for hours...she planted a plant in Mum's back garden in memory of the dog.'

One major change that has occurred is that Caroline and her partner decided to send Billiejoe to a different junior school from the one attached to the infant school she attended. They said that they 'wanted her to do as well as she could'. So, after considering Billiejoe's well-being and also look-ing at the Ofsted reports on the schools, they approached another school in the area. Caroline said that when Billiejoe first started school, she was a single parent who worked. She sent her to the nearest school because that was most convenient for her at the time. Caroline and her partner approached the process very differently when it came to choosing a junior school for Billiejoe. Caroline said that this was partly because of being with a partner, but she was also influenced by the many discussions she had had in the parent group. This time she was able to exercise some choice.

Billiejoe said she was 'a bit frightened going to a new school'. Luckily, she had a friend there whom she knew from outside school, and that has helped. Things are going well, and Caroline feels 'more confident to speak to her new teacher'. Caroline says, 'I was adamant that if it came to it, I'd teach her at home. I think I'd have to go to school to learn new maths as it's changed drastically since I went to school.'

When Jorjalee was born, both parents wanted to do things that involved Billiejoe. As they live in a Sure Start designated area, they asked their family visitor whether Caroline could learn baby massage at home so that Billiejoe could be involved. Eventually, the Sure Start Team managed to send someone to their home for a number of weeks. Billiejoe learned baby massage alongside her mum and was very excited when a certificate came through the post to her, as a recognised masseuse.

The parents regularly attend Friday assemblies at Billiejoe's junior school and are pleased that it is relaxed enough to take Jorjalee. They are already thinking about which secondary school will suit Billiejoe best and which nursery to choose for Jorjalee.

Billiejoe is now a very confident, articulate girl who is very much in touch with her feelings. When she grows up, she 'wants to be a singer and do a magazine and be an artist'.

Parent case study 3 (2006)

Tina came to live in Corby from London when her only child Zoe was two years old. Tina is a single parent and her sick mother lives with her. Tina had previously worked in hotels for 15 years and admits she knew very little about young children. When she arrived in Corby, she felt lonely and isolated. She lives in a Sure Start designated area, and a Sure Start family visitor came to visit. Tina discussed how she was feeling and said that she was thinking of a career change to become an early years worker. The family visitor encouraged her to ring round the local schools to see whether she could do any voluntary work. Tina began volunteering in a local school with a nursery attached. She began a classroom assistant course, through which she gained an Advanced Learning Support Certificate at the end of her first year. The nursery teacher encouraged Tina to begin her NVQ. The Sure Start project supported her in this by paying for childcare and transport. Tina had to travel to college in the evening in the next town, and, for a single parent with a young child and disabled mother, this took great effort and determination.

Tina continued to volunteer and also became a dinner lady at the same school. After Zoe began attending nursery, Tina was sent a leaflet about the parent group. She began attending and also going into the nursery more often to observe Zoe (Figure 11.2). Tina says 'It helped me in my relationship with Zoe. I had brought Zoe away from everything she knew. At two she blamed me. She would shout at me and say, "I want a new mum"...I thought it would be wonderful, but I was anxious and would not let her do things. ... That group helped me to realise that if I didn't let her experience things for herself, she wouldn't learn.'

Tina reflected on her own learning. 'I learnt to listen to her – she's an individual. The parents in the group talked about feelings. 'I built up a lot of trust in the other people...I realised that all of Zoe's unhappiness that year was down to me. It was my moods and how I felt and how I dealt with it...it was to do with me and Mum and what's going on in the house. ... She can now express herself more.'

Figure 11.2 Case Study 3: Tina and Zoe

Tina also gained a greater understanding of how Zoe was learning. 'I got more involved with what she was doing. ... When she was interested in something like stones, I'd walk to school each day with stones in my pocket. ... She connects everything with stones. ... She liked sticks, and I'd let her collect them and she'd spend hours painting them in the garden. It's about letting her do what she's interested in, rather than pushing what I think she should be doing. ... I wanted her to go into school and have a good education. Now she's in there, I think I want her to enjoy it and to go at her own pace...it's not about being the best; it's about having loads of experiences and enjoyment.'

Tina talked about how attending the group had helped her relationships with the school staff. 'Julia (nursery nurse) was shy, and going to the group helped me to get to know her. I could already approach the teachers, but when Zoe wasn't enjoying reading, I went to see Mrs H.... If I hadn't attended the group, I would not have had as much confidence. Before, I might have said what I thought but I would have accepted what the teacher said. Now I'll persist and go back if I'm not happy.'

Tina realised that 'Talking to parents in the group helped me with talking to parents in the nursery. ... What really hit me, and I say that to parents in the group now, is that everything they learn before school, we teach them.'

Now Tina co-leads the parent group and is also employed a day a week in the nursery to encourage parents and children to share books. She is also still studying for her NVQ and still enjoying encouraging Zoe's learning. 'When we're on our way to school is the best time we ever have. At first everything was new to her – she's still like that now. She loves the birds, the flowers, blossoms, buds, seasons, etc. She talks about everything...what's happened at school...she'll count down days. She says, "Can we go that way?" It's about her making a decision. You can see the difference when I let her. In autumn, she collects leaves; in spring, she collects sticks to make an Easter tree. "That's fantastic!" she says.'

The parent groups

Five local schools are now running study groups for parents. Staff from Pen Green have helped to get them off the ground, but they are all running independently now. Around 30 parents from the schools have completed portfolios about their children so far. Each portfolio is highly differentiated in what its authors chose to focus on and in their ability to present. However, most of the parents used the concepts and applied them to their own children's actions. Some parents, like Caroline, reflected on their own early experiences and stated that they wanted their child's experience to be different and better than what had happened to them as young children, either at school or at home. This process links with 'reflective functioning', as described by Fonagy (2001). This may also be associated with each adult's capacity to be a friend to their child, described by Trevarthen (2003) as 'companionship'. Tina's description of walking to school each day is a good description of what companionship means.

So, providing a safe environment in which parents can explore and reflect upon their early learning, as well as their children's learning, may go some way toward meeting the parents' and children's learning needs.

From our perspective, the questions raised, while engaging in this development work, feed directly back into the research work.

Key questions, insights and implications

- How can we fully involve school staff and embed this way of working as part of the school philosophy?
- Does the group provide support for parents during a critical transition period (from nursery to primary school)?
- Does the portfolio serve as a tool for parents to use in engaging teachers or other professionals in getting to know their children as individuals?
- How can parents who get in touch with their own unresolved childhood issues be supported? (At Pen Green Centre, we are able to offer counselling and social work support.)
- How can workers who are 'containing' the pain of parents be supported? (Bion, 1962). (Again, at the Pen Green Centre, counselling and social work support is readily available.)
- What are the positive effects on the children of their parents having been in school once a week and seen their children on video in the classroom? (Can parents and children engage in more meaningful conversations about school because of the shared material?)
- Does attending a study group affect the relationship parents have with their child's educators at school?

CHAPTER 12

Developing PICL in Primary Schools: Beyond the Reading Record

Kate Hayward

This chapter looks at the gains that can be made in involving parents in a primary school by following Pen Green's Parents Involvment in Their Children's Learning (PICL) training programme. The programme was adapted for the school setting through a process of discussion, review, reflection and action. I consider the frustrations I had with the traditional school–home methods of communication and explore how, as a primary school staff team, we began working toward building real partnerships with parents. I describe how the child study, a central component of the programme, was a real turning point and a trigger for a critical review of our primary schools pedagogy. Through sharing key child development concepts with parents and watching video sequences of their child at home and at school, I go on to explore the depth of understanding that can be achieved through working together.

The one-way flow of information in schools

Often, communication between schools and parents on a regular basis is very one way. As a parent, my experience of the '10-minute slot' at parents' evening was rarely productive. I was pleased to be reassured that my children were generally happy at school, but I could not help feeling that there was more that could be shared. It was a case of going to be 'told' about your child, rather than being listened to and involved in sharing information in a true dialogue.

The reading record

In many cases, the only other regular communication between home and school in the earlier years is through the reading record book. For many parents and some teachers in this country, starting 'big school' is synony-mous with learning to read and write. The focus on literacy persists despite a curriculum guidance that sets out six equal areas of learning (DfES/QCA, 2000).

Believing children learn through their own experiences and build on what they know, most workers in the Foundation Stage are keen to broaden children's experiences in these important years (Bruce, 2005). Children learn best when they are intrinsically motivated and allowed to follow their own interests in all areas of learning (Laevers, 1997).

A two-way flow of information

As a teacher in a Foundation Stage/Year 1 split class in a primary school, I wanted to involve parents in all aspects of the children's lives at school. I wanted to get to know the children better, to understand their interests and previous experiences, and to share the joy of their discoveries with the impor-tant people in their lives. Most of all, I wanted the children to be able to 'take school home' and 'bring home into school' so that all their daily experiences had meaning, and these experiences were able to enrich their learning.

As Gordon Wells (1986, p. 222) explains, 'We are the meaning makers – every one of us: children, parents, and teachers ... the responsibility is clear: to interact with those in our care in such a way as to foster and enrich *their* meaning making.' Our challenge was to find a way for parents and staff to engage in this together.

Managing a dialogue with parents alongside everything else

I knew I had to go way beyond the reading record book, but how do you generate a dialogue with all the important people in up to 30 children's lives? Where was the time after setting up an exciting learning environ-ment; engaging with the children and other members of staff; and managing the busy schedule of observations, assemblies, registers, allocated sessions in the hall and class presentations to have time to talk? Managing the written messages about individual reading each week took up an enor-mous amount of time – was it possible to do more?

Being liberated from the reading scheme

The time pressures were huge, but I knew there must be a better way of working with parents. I was particularly troubled by the skewed emphasis on the reading record, as this meant that all regular communication between home and school revolved around a narrow, prescribed activity – the reading scheme.

As a parent, I knew about the pressures on the reading scheme. Through the experience I had with my own children, I felt restricted and fearful of 'not keeping up with the system', as this would disadvantage my child. Luckily, we were able to share many books and stories at home, and the reading cards and words we were given complemented the other things we did. However, I was aware of the tensions the hierarchical scheme created both within and between families. The reading book is the measure by which children and parents assess their child's competence compared to other children.

The whole reading scheme focus seemed, at best, to lead to unhealthy competition and, at worst, to set some children up to fail in their first year at school. In addition, parents who did not keep up with the programme were likely to be castigated as 'parents who do not bother with their kids'.

This all seemed to represent such a missed opportunity to me. The narrow concentration on the reading scheme book dismissed the importance of the other processes involved in learning to read, such as a love of stories and books, which is so important to foster at home (Whitehead, 2004). Above all, it did not allow a two-way flow of information about the child's learning in all areas.

Embracing other experiences

Even focusing just on communication, language and literacy, we could learn so much through sharing other home experiences. We know that participation in socio-cultural activities is at the heart of children's learning (Carr, 2001, p. 8). Children can make real connections through sharing favourite family stories and rhymes, linking written environmental language (such as signs) through experiences and trips, listening to grandparents' stories of the past, and talking about friends and family through looking at photographs.

My passion was to link family experiences with other areas of learning. Experiences that the children were having at home were central to their learning and should be built upon, not ignored. These might include explorations in the garden, on holiday or in the park; songs enjoyed with Grandma; jokes shared with Granddad; family hobbies and celebrations; and family thoughts on how we connect to our world spiritually. Did we, as teachers, really have a clue about all these things? Did we understand how really knowing children and helping them to make meaningful connections in their lives affects their emotional well-being and their ability to learn (Laevers, 1997)?

PICL training programme

Hearing about the 'PICL' training programme at Pen Green, I enrolled on the course. Luckily, I had a very supportive head teacher who understood the importance of involving families in our work and was committed to working with parents as partners.

Securing the support of colleagues and senior staff proved to be essential in terms of being able to take the work forward. This training programme has been developed at Pen Green from a research project on parental involvement, and it consists of two days' initial training followed by a programme of work in one's own setting and a child study. Those taking the programme are given support and encouragement in completing the work through an individual surgery and email contact. A further third day of training is included at the end of the programme to help students to reflect on how to continue to develop partnership work with parents.

PICL Programme

Training at Pen Green
Two days' training on:

- the principles that underpin our work with children and families; and
- four windows on learning:

1 involvement (Laevers, 1997)
2 well-being (Laevers, 1997)
3 schemas (Athey, 1990)
4 pedagogical strategies (Whalley and Arnold, 1997a).

Third day at the end of the programme to reflect on the process and to plan future development work.

Development work in your setting
Audit of current practice in terms of involving parents.
Action plan for organisational changes to improve involvement of parents.
Report on organisational changes and outcomes.

Development work with a family
Child study using video to observe and analyse a child's learning in partnership with their parents, using three of the four child development concepts studied.

Student support is given by email contact and individual surgery. Both aspects of development work are written up and submitted with the five-minute video used in the child study. The development work is marked in two stages with written feedback and support at each stage.

Initial two days' training

During the initial two days, we were guided through exercises that helped us to consider the principles that underpin our work in relation to children and parents. Using video case studies from the Pen Green nursery, we explored many different issues around working in partnership with the special people in children's lives. We looked at how we could sustain real dialogue with the families that was respectful, equal and meaningful (Easen *et al.*, 1992).

We were introduced to the work of the Brazilian community educator Paulo Freire, who recognised the need to respect others as equals if true dialogue is to take place:

> Value the contribution of others and listen to them with humility, respecting the particular view of the world held by different people.

> Get in touch with how much we need other people and have no fear of being displaced.

> Be humble; have faith in others and believe in their strengths.

> (Freire, 1970, p. 71)

This was inspirational. It made so much sense to me as a parent and as a teacher. As a parent, I wanted to be listened to and respected as an important influence in my child's life and as someone who knew my child best. I hear teachers glibly saying that the parent is the child's first educator but they often miss the point about parents being their child's most enduring educator (DfES/QCA, 2000, p. 9). As a parent, I wanted to be working alongside. As a teacher, I wanted to develop parent–worker partnerships so that all children could benefit from and enjoy the involvement of their families in their learning at school as well as at home.

Throughout the two days, the Pen Green trainers shared the struggles they had had at the centre through the early days. This 'lived' experience gave this course a real edge. There were many setbacks and difficulties at each stage of the research project and challenges that are constantly being faced at the Pen Green Centre each year. Learning from our mistakes and building on our own experiences were a key part of this training course. This gave me courage, as I knew that whatever happened would be useful, even if all I learned was never to repeat certain experiences!

We discussed all the various ways that information can be shared between home and school and related this to our own practice. These ideas ranged from open evenings to home visits. Having worked previously in a nursery, I knew the benefits of home visiting, and, despite having to overcome some concerns, I had successfully introduced an initial home visit before the children started school.

Sharing ways to develop a dialogue with parents

The transition process at my school had always been good, and the addition of the home visit complemented several school visits and visits to the feeder nursery. The children saw the home visit as reciprocal – they visited us at school and we visited them at home. Memories of these home visits lasted well into the year and were often referred to. Meeting the dog or the cat and other important family members allowed us to make important connections with the children at school.

Through sharing the ways we went about developing a dialogue with parents, we all learned from each other on the course as well as learning about the experiences at Pen Green. There were always refinements to try. For example, in terms of the home visits, I picked up the following ideas:

- Writing to the child individually to tell them when we would be coming.
- Taking the child's photograph at home and exchanging our photographs so that the child could talk about us to other relatives and friends at home and could remember us as special people at school.
- Inviting families to make, with their child, photo albums of their special people and places to share with us on the home visit (much more interesting and stimulating than the 'starting-school books' completed by the parents!)
- Arranging home visits throughout the year – not always possible but given the impact on the child's learning and their relationships with staff, something we should consider.
- Leaving the form filling to another occasion – the formality of the forms was a barrier to focusing on the child.

Every aspect that was discussed had possible enhancements, whatever the quality of our practice. The different ways that the work has been developed at Pen Green stimulated discussion and inspired possible developments in our own settings.

The idea was not to replicate all aspects but to take what we could from the ideas and the approach. It would be as inappropriate to 'do a Pen Green' as to 'do a Reggio' (Malaguzzi, 1998) or to transplant straight from New Zealand and 'do Te Whariki' (Ministry of Education, 1996). The ideas and understanding we gain from these particular contexts gives us the inspiration and tools to develop our work and to make it our own.

Audit of practice in terms of working with parents

Each aspect that is discussed is set out for teachers to conduct as an audit of their own practice with their staff team when they return to their setting. Having the backing of my head teacher was very important, as we were allowed time to work through the audit together.

We decided to include Key Stage (KS) 1 staff in our discussions as well. As a small, rural primary school, we had two classes, Foundation Stage (FS)/Year

1 (Y1) and Y1/Y2, involving a total of three members of staff, a learning support assistant and two teachers. A volunteer was also working with us while she gained practical experience for her Foundation degree. Working together in this way was in line with other exciting plans we had in terms of developing an early years department from the Foundation Stage to Year 2.

Our dream was to manage the learning in the department through workshop style access to resources and challenges, including sand, water, role-play and outdoor access for all children. These changes would be phased in, but we knew we needed the understanding and support of the parents if we were to manage this successfully. Developing real partnerships with the parents in the FS/Y1 class was an important first step.

Throughout the Pen Green training, we were constantly advised to reflect on and record all the possible developments, but to concentrate on only two to three areas that we could work on in a manageable way. We knew what was possible in the short term with the resources and time available. It is important to record our dreams for the future, and once we have gained a little momentum, we can begin to see how these dreams can become a reality in the longer term. The initial achievable first steps, however, are crucial.

The audit also gives us an opportunity to celebrate the work we are doing with parents that is very successful. We were pleased with the flexible way we were able to welcome children and families in the morning, for example, and the rich discussion that flowed between home and school in the home-school book relating to all areas of the curriculum.

However pleased we were, we still took note of possible developments and considerations. Had we actually asked parents if the flexible entry into school worked for them? Did assemblies curb this flexibility? Was it possible to arrange the school day differently? Did parents feel the home challenges suggested in the home-school book were appropriate? Did they find them a pressure? Did they feel free to comment on other experiences that they considered to be just as, if not more, important? Was it a schoolbook or a homebook? Could it be both?

We worked through every aspect of the audit, making notes on the things we wanted to research, the things we needed to note but could do nothing about in the near future, and the things we felt we could change for the better over the next few months. These things formed the basis of our action plan.

Action plan for organisational changes

After we had decided on the two to three areas we wanted to focus on, the programme then required us to make an action plan for the organisational changes that we intended to make in the short term. After lengthy discussions, we decided that there were three areas we wanted to do something about. We wanted to try to break down the formality of the school setting by asking parents if they would be happy to be on first-name terms. Although this was running against tradition, we felt that it was an important step toward working in partnership with parents as equals.

We also wanted to introduce a system of recording out-of-school routines for the children in our school. We had learned how keeping a record of the sometimes complex domestic arrangements for children at the Pen Green Centre allowed staff to have a greater understanding of the weekly rhythms for each child. We were also keen to invite parents to attend a study group to analyse the children's learning together through sharing video clips of their children.

ACTION PLAN

1 To establish first-name terms with all parents.
   Action: to ask parents during the home visit if they would be happy to use first names and to record the names of both parents and other special people in the child's life in the child's portfolio. To actively use first names through all informal communication with parents. To pass on a list of first names of parents, having gained their consent, to the KS1 staff.

2 To clarify information on the weekly out-of-school arrangements for each child.
   Action: to record with parents the routines for children in terms of staying at different homes or with different people at various times during the week.

3 To set up a pilot study group with interested parents.
   Action: to invite interested parents to look at video footage of children in the setting to analyse together what the children are learning.

Child study

The second component of the PICL programme is a child study. All participants on the course select a family they would like to work with and gain their consent, including that of the child, to work with them in analysing the child's learning. Four windows on learning are used for this analysis, as follows:

- well-being (Laevers, 1997);
- involvement (Laevers, 1997);
- schemas (Athey, 1990); and
- adult pedagogical strategies (Whalley and Arnold, 1997a).

Well-being and involvement

During the two days' training, we looked into these concepts in depth. Many practitioners are now working with Laevers' concepts of well-being and involvement, but even those of us who were familiar with these frameworks learned a lot from each other and the Pen Green trainers about how they could be applied.

We raised many questions. How do you moderate the use of these frameworks so that everyone is using them in the same way? How do you share these concepts with parents? Do you use Laevers' scales 1–5 or do you use the descriptions of high, medium or low levels of involvement or well-being? How do you analyse the involvement of children interacting socially? Is there a gender difference? Do we need to write our own descriptors?

Schemas

Schemas, or repeated patterns of behaviour, are becoming much more topical since their introduction into the Birth to Three Matters framework (DfES, 2002). At the Pen Green Centre, family workers have used schemas for many years to identify children's deep interests and to extend their thought and learning (Whalley, 1997b).

This work was inspired by the pioneering work of Chris Athey during the Froebel Nursery Project in the 1970s (Athey, 1990). Chris Athey, the researcher, and Tina Bruce, the teacher on the project, found that parents were quickly able to identify patterns in their children's play and to use this knowledge and understanding to make appropriate provision at home. At Pen Green, sharing this information between home and school in what is termed 'the Pen Green Loop' allows parents and family workers to plan for children's learning at home and at nursery (Pen Green Centre, 2000).

Adult pedagogic strategies

The fourth window that is used to analyse children's learning during the training is adult pedagogic strategies or adult style. This framework was devised following the initial research project at Pen Green funded by the Teacher Training Agency in 1997 (Whalley and Arnold (1997a). After study of the successful ways in which parents and staff engage with children and extend their learning, a list of these techniques are now used to enable adults to reflect on and enhance their approach.

Studying these concepts in great depth during the training allowed us to choose three of the four concepts, as directed in the programme, to share with the parents of the child we had chosen to study. I approached the family of a four-year-old boy in my class, Christie. Being careful not to impose, I explained that I would video Christie in school (Figure 12.1) and make written observations of his play. He was particularly interested in

Figure 12.1 Christie involved at school

construction and would spend long periods of time at the workshop bench. He would plan and design intricate models, and he was good at sharing his knowledge with other children and using his new skills.

Remarkably, the family were keen to work with me, despite having a very busy home life with three-month old twins and a three-year-old daughter. Christie's parents, Kirsty and David, voluntarily made observations of Christie at home and borrowed the video camera over a weekend. I encouraged them to video Christie when he was engrossed in his play, showing high levels of involvement. We looked at the video material together and decided to use well-being, involvement and schemas to analyse Christie's learning.

Well-being

During our discussion, I gave lots of examples of how a child's well-being may fluctuate over a day, and I outlined the signs of well-being and the well-being scale as described by Laevers (1997). I was concerned that Kirsty might have worries about the emotional impact on Christie of the birth of the twins, and I knew that this was an area that needed to be dealt with sensitively.

We discussed how the enthusiastic involvement of Christie by both his parents and his extended family and friends during the pregnancy and early baby care had really helped Christie to adjust positively to the arrival of his little brother and sister.

Kirsty felt that Christie's level of well-being sometimes dipped, and we discussed ways that we could support him at these times. Christie was often anxious during the transition time in the morning, and although he was happy to come to school, he often worried that he would only remember something important after his parents had gone. We devised a simple Post-it note reminder system to allow Christie to record any messages he was worried about forgetting.

The video footage I had taken in school featured Christie's project to create a knight's armour. We looked for signals of well-being during this video sequence. Christie was open to his friend's suggestions for creating this costume, and yet he had a clear and confident view of what he wanted

Figure 12.2 Christie's sense of pride

to do. He showed vitality and enjoyment and was confident enough to ask for help when the tape he was using became too difficult to handle. We felt that he showed a great sense of pride and achievement (Figure 12.2) at the end of the sequence when he entered into the character of the knight. He spotted a girl wearing a coronet and said, 'There goes the queen!'

Involvement

We talked through the concept of involvement (Figure 12.3), and its signs and levels. I outlined how useful these levels were in analysing children's deep-level learning in the classroom, and we talked about Christie's facial expression when he is really involved.

We considered the home video sequences and discussed how Christie had maintained his interest and concentration despite many other things going on around him (Figure 12.4). In his model making, he showed many of the signs of involvement: concentration, energy, composure, persistence, precision, and especially complexity and creativity (Laevers, 1997).

Christie had produced some amazing models at home and at school, and he was often the catalyst for others to engage in making models or in using a particular technique. In the school video sequence, he had been making the suit of armour for several sessions over three days. This highlights the importance of allowing children time to finish what they are doing, particularly when they are engaged in their own projects at this high level of involvement.

Figure 12.3 Christie involved in Sellotaping

Figure 12.4 Christie persisting with the Sellotape

Schemas

Christie had a cluster of schemas. These included envelopment, containing and connecting. Through our observations at school, we could see clearly how these schemas were coordinated and enabled Christie to explore many concepts through his play.

I was particularly fascinated by the way that Kirsty, through our discussion, was able look back at the things Christie used to do as a younger child and see the development of these behaviours. We looked at how Christie loved to wear cloaks and capes, enveloping himself in fabric and using tape extensively in his model making. Kirsty said that when Christie was a year old, at a time when she used to do a lot of sewing, he insisted on putting the tape measure around his shoulders all day like a tailor. At 18 months, he would often carry a soft toy with its tail draped over his shoulder around the house. At the time of the study, he was using Blu-tack at home to make capes and cloaks for his Toy Small World characters.

During the making of the suit of armour, Christie made a sword case out of card, which he used to envelop his wooden sword and eventually enveloped his whole body in the costume. In just this short sequence, we could see Christie operating at a level of functional dependency (making the case fit the sword), at a symbolic level (the costume represented a suit of armour), and at the level of abstract thought (Christie discussed his plans to make the armour and recalled the different types of armour he had seen in books) (Athey, 1990). Throughout this project, we could see that Christie was constantly revising his understanding of the concepts of size, area and measurement through making connections with his previous learning.

Christie had enjoyed containing objects in various containers long before he came to school. He used to carry a secret bag to nursery every day with his own selected items – usually a rope and a blanket, items that would enable him to explore his envelopment and connecting schemas wherever he went. Christie's rope play was extensive. When he was younger, he would spend many hours suspending his toys from the banisters on cotton threads and making spider webs with string around the house.

At school, he used various thicknesses of string and rope to tie between two posts, exploring the length and tensile strength of the materials. He would practise tying knots and making 'spider traps' for the gangsters in his stories.

Learning about Christie's explorations at home and at school gave us a much deeper understanding of Christie's learning. We could put his explorations into context and share the joy of his achievements in a much more meaningful way. Sharing the key child development concepts enabled us to share a language to describe our observations and to analyse what Christie was learning. This greater understanding enabled us to plan to extend Christie's learning much more effectively at home and at school.

Following his interests, Christie was intrinsically motivated and took his own learning forward with relish. His explorations allowed him to engage in all areas of the curriculum.

Parent's perspective

Kirsty

I was very pleased when Kate approached us and asked to study Christie. He was and still is a quiet-natured boy, but has always been very creative and productive, and so I relished the thought of finding out more about how he plays and how his behaviour and development are affected by his experiences.

The result for me was a much closer relationship with Kate, and a deeper mutual understanding of Christie as a whole. This left me feeling that Christie was very fortunate and that his needs and interests were taken fully into account during the school day.

Christie had a fantastic reception experience and has continued to flourish at school. He is aware that the study existed, and that he was sometimes videoed at school and home. I am sure that the extra information sharing that took place helped him to settle into school life and to get the most out of his early years experiences.

How the child study triggered a critical review of our pedagogy

Extending and supporting Christie in these developments, we saw how we could relate his learning across the whole curriculum retrospectively. We realised that we needed to start with the child and turn the planning cycle on its head. By following the child's interests, we could look back to record what we had planned. Our job is not to 'cover the curriculum' through disconnected activities in all areas of learning but to 'uncover the curriculum' in what the child chooses to do in a rich and supportive learning environment (Lawrence, 2004).

This child study was a revelation. The depth and joy of this exchange was staggering. If so much could be learned through sharing child development concepts and video footage with one family, how could we manage this exchange for all our children and families?

There are certainly many things that can be done. Sharing home-school scrapbooks and photo albums makes an enormous difference. Regular home visits would alter the balance, and open access to children's files would also help, as would just having time to talk. Time is a huge factor, but should we not be taking stock of what currently takes up our time? Are we always engaged in activities that would enable us to work with our children in such a meaningful and productive way as working in real partnerships with parents?

The PICL programme gave us the tools to enhance our work as reflective practitioners. The child study in particular opened our eyes to the need to work with parents in partnership if we are to maximise the learning potential for our children. We were able to make important changes through the small steps in our action plan.

Organisational changes

Simple measures such as being on first-name terms can begin to change the culture of a setting and the atmosphere in which we work. This step was warmly welcomed by parents. Many parents were known already by their first names but we made sure that all parents were treated with the same respectful informality. 'Hannah's mum' or 'Tom's mum' just doesn't convey the same message. Creating that openness to learn from each other allows us to plan for practical ways forward, things that we can do together that are effective and manageable in our own context.

We learned about the rhythms experienced by some children who stayed at different homes on different days and children's regular out-of-school experiences. This helped us to make connections with the children.

Pilot study group

Using video was another huge revelation. Eight parents attended the pilot study group. Being able to discuss issues arising from a short video sequence gave everyone a chance to 'see it for themselves'. The parents who attended the group were very enthusiastic. One mother commented, 'You don't tend to watch them do you, if they are quiet, but now I will!' Others found coming together to talk about their children really supportive. 'Talking about what we go through really helps – knowing others go through it, too.'

Using video with staff and children too

Sharing the video footage helped all of us to reflect on what was going on. We were able to return to parts of the video sequence to discuss points in detail. Children were able to discuss their learning while watching the video at home with other family members. We could take a sequence of stills from the video to document the children's learning, and we could also include the child's voice and the parent's comments. The possibilities were very exciting and everyone was having fun.

Working in this way releases the tensions of the 'teacher at the helm' model and allows everyone to share and extend the learning. The focus is on children in the context of all their daily experiences, building on what they know and are able to do. When everything is connected in this way, it all makes so much sense.

Head teacher's perspective

Earlier in this chapter, practitioners and parents have reflected on PICL and how this has had a positive impact in terms of the quality of learning and potential for the future learning of our youngest children. I am now in the happy position of being able to review the progress Christie has made and how this has shaped him as a learner. He continues to show a great interest in complex model making, but the size and scale of outcomes has increased considerably. He shows levels of deep engagement but also wishes to involve others around him.

Through PICL, we were able to reach out to our parents, and the parents were able to reach in to us. I have already talked about the benefits for Christie, but what about David and Kirsty? As their already strong links with the school have developed, David has been able to share his professional background by serving as an associate governor and also to share some of his leisure pursuits. I will long remember the day he came into school with all his photographic equipment and inspired the children. One week later, every child had produced a professionally lighted, staged and framed photographic image for display at an exhibition. Kirsty has also involved herself deeply in the life of our school, serving as the chair of our fund-raising committee and also vice-chair of the governing body.

I am so thrilled that our school has involved itself in the PICL process and would have little difficulty in recommending it to others without reservation.

To this day, we still draw benefits from the work that was undertaken at this time, and the quality of relationships with the parent body is the best it has ever been. Having established this relationship at the earliest possible opportunity, I can envisage the partnership growing, evolving and changing as the needs of the children change with age, maturity and experience. Above all else, we have found that by valuing and recognising the profound influence parents have on the life chances of their children, we can create a school where children are happy to be there, are motivated, engaged, curious, questioning, humorous and highly achieving, with a positive self-image and well adjusted to the demands of an ever-changing modern society.

Developing a Sustainable Approach

Margy Whalley

Transferring and using knowledge that derives from existing best practice is often problematic (Fullen, 2002). However staff and parents at Pen Green, working in collaboration with early years educators in many local authorities, have been able to develop a pedagogically grounded 'learning focus' (Jackson, 2001), which we have described as the Parents' Involvement in Their Children's Learning (PICL) Programme. This has resulted in staff groups in many early childhood settings developing and refining their own professional practice, and recognising the importance of home learning and school learning and the role of parents as co-educators.

We need in the next decade to embed this approach. Staff in all early years settings have to become cultural brokers and mediators. They have to develop a shared language with parents and a shared understanding about how children develop and how children learn, both at home and in the nursery. It is vital that staff understand parents' own theories about the development of their child and their child's learning at home. It is also essential that nursery staff share with parents their theoretical and practice-based understanding of children drawn from their observations of the child in the nursery setting. Developing this shared language requires consummate skill and continuous professional development. It takes time to develop reciprocal ways of working and to build on what the community has to offer. Working in this way produces outcomes that transform children's life chances.

Athey has described the PICL programme at Pen Green in this way:

> I cannot think of any other project involving so many people in so many different roles which functions as Pen Green is doing within a coherent and internally consistent view of education...the PICL programme reflects a set of consistent values based on mutual respect. The focus is on co-operation. Competition is confined to individuals trying to get better at what they are doing which is helping children to become successful and autonomous learners....Pen Green is revolutionary in its insistence on identifying and articulating positive learning for individual children and involving parents and extending those aspects in an educationally worthwhile direction.

> (Chris Athey, 2001, personal correspondence)

Bibliography

Abbott, D. (1998) *Culture and Identity*, Hodder & Stoughton, London.

Allman, P. (1983) *The Nature and Process of Adult Development*, Open University Press, Buckingham.

Anderson, K. (1987) in S. Anderson, S. Armitage, D. Jack and J. Wittner, Beginning where we are, *Oral History Review*, vol. 15, pp. 103–27.

Arnold, C. (1967) *Prejudice – racial, religious and class*, unpublished study, Kirkby Fields Training College.

Arnold, C. (1990) *Children Who Play Together Have Similar Schemas*, Pen Green Centre, Corby.

Arnold, C. (1997a) *Understanding young children and their contexts for learning and development: building on early experience*, Unpublished MEd thesis, Leicester University.

Arnold, C. (1997b) Sharing ideas with parents about how children learn, in M. Whalley (ed.) *Working With Parents*, Hodder & Stoughton, London.

Arnold, C. (1999a) *Child Development and Learning 2–5 Years, Georgia's Story*, Hodder & Stoughton, London.

Arnold, C. (1999b) *Georgia's Story*, Paul Chapman, London.

Arnold, C. (2003) *Observing Harry*, Open University Press, Maidenhead.

Athey, C. (1990) *Extending Thought in Young Children: A Parent–Teacher Partnership*, Paul Chapman, London.

Atmore, E. (1999) *Meeting the needs of young children through early childhood development policy*, Warwick Conference.

Audit Commission (1994) *Seen But Not Heard: Developing Community Health and Social Services for Children in Need*, HMSO, London.

Ball, C. (1994) *Start Right: The Importance of Early Learning*, RSA, London.

Barber, M. (1996) *The Learning Game*, Victor Gollancz, London.

Bartholomew, L. and Bruce, T. (1993) *Getting to Know You*, Hodder & Stoughton, London.

Bertram, A. D. (1995) *Adult engagement styles and their use in staff development*, Paper presented at the 5th European Early Childhood Educational Research Association Conference, Sorbonne, Paris.

Bertram, A. D. (1996) *Effective early childhood educators*, Unpublished PhD thesis, Coventry University.

Bertram, A. D., Laevers, E. and Pascal, C. (1996) Grasping the quality of adult–child interactions in early childhood education settings: the adult style observation schedule, in S. Rayna, F. Laevers and M. Deleau (eds) *What are the Educational Objectives for Pre-School Education?*, Nathan, Paris.

Bertram, T. and Pascal, C. (2000) *Early Excellence Centres: First Findings Autumn 1999*, DfEE, London.

Bettelheim, B. (1990) *Recollections and Reflections*, Thames & Hudson, London.

Bion, W. (1962) *Learning from Experience,* Heinemann, London.

Blakemore, C. (1998) Unpublished paper at Pen Green Centre Conference on Giving Children a Sure Start, November, Corby.

Blanden, J. (2006) *'Bucking the trend': what enables those who are disadvantaged in childhood to succeed later in life?,* Working paper no. 31, Department for Work and Pension, London.

Bowlby, J. [1969] (1991) *Attachment and Loss,* vol. 1, Penguin, London.

Bredekamp, S. and Shephard, L. (1989) How best to protect children from inappropriate school expectations, practices and policies, *Young Children,* vol. 44, no. 3, pp. 14–34.

Bright, J. (1998) *Provision for young children,* Implementation paper for the Cross-Departmental Review of Provision for Young Children, 26 February.

Bruce, T. (1997) *Early Childhood Education,* 2nd edn, Hodder & Stoughton, London.

Bruce, T. (1999) Seminar on pedagogic architecture, Unpublished paper presented at Pen Green in October.

Bruce, T. (2005) *Early Childhood Education,* 3rd edn, Hodder Arnold, London.

Bruce, T. and Meggitt, C. (2002) *Child Care and Education,* Hodder & Stoughton, London.

Bruner, J. (1977) *The Process of Education,* 2nd edn, Harvard University Press, Cambridge, MA.

Burk-Rodgers, D. B. (1998) Supporting autonomy in young children, *Young Children,* May, pp. 75–80.

Carr, M. (2001) *Assessment in Early Childhood Settings: Learning Stories,* Paul Chapman, London.

Ceppi, G. and Zini, M. (1998) *Children, Spaces, Relations, Meta Project for an Environment for Young Children.* Reggio Children, Somus Academy Research Centre, Milan.

Chandler, T. (1997) Daring to care – men and childcare, in M. Whalley (ed.) *Working with Parents,* Hodder & Stoughton, London.

Chandler, T. (2005) *Pedagogy and leadership. Research bursary on leadership,* Dartington 2005, Unpublished paper.

Charlwood, N. and Steele, H. (2004) Using attachment theory to inform practice in an integrated centre for children and families, *European Early Childhood Education Research Journal,* vol. 12, no. 2, pp. 59–74.

Cherryholmes, C. H. (1993) Reading research, *Journal of Curriculum Studies,* vol. 25, no. 1, pp. 1–32.

Dahlberg, G. (1998) Seminar held at the Thomas Coram Foundation, London, Unpublished.

Dahlberg, G., Moss, P. and Pence, A. (1999) *Beyond Quality in Early Childhood Education and Care: Modern Perspectives,* RoutledgeFalmer Press, London.

David, T. (ed.) (1994) *Working Together for Young Children,* Routledge, London.

Department of Health (1991) *The Children Act 1989: Guidance and Regulations, 2, Family Support, Daycare and Educational Provision for Young Children,* HMSO, London.

DfEE (1996) *Early Excellence – a Head Start for Every Child,* Labour Party, London.

DfEE (1997) *Excellence in Schools,* DfEE in 3681, HMSO, London.

DfEE (1998) *Meeting the Childcare Challenge,* HMSO, London.

DfEE (1999a) *Sure Start: A Guide for Trailblazers,* DfEE, London.

DfEE (1999b) *Early Excellence Centres. First Findings,* Autumn 1999, DfEE, London.

DfES (2002) *Birth to Three Matters: A Framework to Support Children in Their Earliest Years,* DfES, London.

DfES/QCA (2000) *Curriculum Guidance for the Foundation Stage,* DfES, London.

Drummond, M. J. (1989) Early years education: contemporary challenges in early childhood education, in C. W. Desforges (ed.) *British Journal of Educational Psychology,* Monograph Series No. 4.

Drummond, M. J. (1993) *Assessing Children's Learning,* David Fulton, London.

Dryden, G. and Vos, J. (1994) *The Learning Revolution,* Accelerated Learning, Aylesbury.

Dyson, A. and Desforges, C. (2002) *Building research capacity: some possible lines of action,* a discussion paper for the National Educational Research Fellow, February 2002.

Easen, P., Kendall, P. and Shaw, J. (1992) Parents and educators: dialogue and developing through partnership, *Children and Society,* vol. 6, no. 4, pp. 282–96.

Edwards, C., Gandini, L. and Forman, G. (1998) *The Hundred Languages of Children: The Reggio Emilia Approach – Advanced Reflections,* 2nd edn, Ablex, London.

Epstein, D., Elwood, J., Hey, V. and Maw, J. (1998) *Failing Boys,* Open University Press, Buckingham.

Epstein, J. L., Elwood, J., Hey, V. and Maw, J. (1996) *Partnership 2000 Schools Manual,* Johns Hopkins University, Baltimore, MD.

Faulkner, D. (1995) Play, self and the social world, in P. Barnes (ed.) *Personal, Social and Emotional Development of Children,* Open University Press, Milton Keynes.

Fletcher, C. (1999) Home and school myth: parents don't care, in R. O'Hagan (ed.) *Modern Eduational Myths,* Kogan Page, London.

Fonagy, P. (2001) *Attachment and Psychoanalysis,* Other Books, New York.

Fonagy, P., Steele, M., Moran, G., Steele, H. and Higgitt, A. (1990) *Measuring the ghost in the nursery: a summary of the main findings of the Anna Freud Centre – University College London, Parent–Child Project,* IPA Conference, London.

Freire, P. (1996a) *Pedagogy of the Oppressed,* Penguin Books, London.

Freire, P. (1970) *Pedagogy of the Oppressed,* Penguin Books, Harmondsworth.

Freire, P. (1996b) *Letters to Christina,* Routledge, London.

Fuerst, J. S. and Fuerst, D. (1993) Chicago experience with an early childhood programme: the special case of the Child Parent Centre Program, *Educational Research,* vol. 35, no. 3, pp. 237-53.

Fullen, M. (2002) *The Role of Leadership in the Promotion of Knowledge Management in Schools,* OECD Conference, 12–19 March 2002.

Gardner, H. (1991) *The Unschooled Mind,* Fontana Press, London.

Gewirtz, S., Balls, J. and Bowe, R. (1975) *Marketing Choice and Equity in Education,* Milton Keynes, Open University Press.

Ghedini, P., Chandler, T., Whalley, M. and Moss, P. (1995) *Fathers, Nurseries and Childcare,* European Commission Equal Opportunities Unit/Early Childcare Network.

Goldschmied, E. (1991) What to do with the under twos. Heuristic play. Infants learning, in D. Rouse (ed.) *Babies and Toddlers; Carers and Educators. Quality for Under 3's,* National Children's Bureau, London.

Goleman, D. (1996) *Emotional Intelligence,* Bloomsbury, London.

Greenfield, S. (1997) *The Human Brain: A Guided Tour,* Weidenfeld & Nicolson, London.

Gronn, P. and Ribbins, P. (1996) Leaders in context: post-positivist approaches to understanding educational leadership, *Educational Administration Quarterly,* vol. 32, no. 3, pp. 452–73.

Haggerty, M. (1996) *Using Video to Work With Te Whaariki,* Wellington College of Education, New Zealand.

Handy, C. (1997) *The Empty Raincoat,* Arrow Books, Reading.

Harding, S. (ed.) (1987) *Feminism and Methodology*, Buckingham Open University Press.

Hargreaves, D. H. (1996) *Teaching as a research-based profession; possibilities and prospects*, Teacher Training Agency Annual Lecture, April.

Harlen, W. (1982) Evaluation and assessment, in C. Richards (ed.) *New Directions in Primary Education*, Falmer Press, London.

Hendricks, A. and Meade, A. (1993) *Competent Children: Influences of Early Childhood Experiences*, New Zealand Council for Educational Research, Wellington.

Hobbs, R. (1998) Team building for staff at Pen Green Centre, internal training session.

Holman, B. (1987) Research from the underside, *British Journal of Social Work*, vol. 17, pp. 669–83.

Isaacs, S. (1936) *Intellectual Growth in Young Children*, Routledge and Kegan Paul, London.

Jack, D. (1987) in K. Anderson, S. Armitage, D. Jack and J. Witner. Beginning where we are, *Oral History Review*, vol. 15, pp. 103–27.

Jackson, D. (2001) *'The Creation of Knowledge'*, *Networks Collaborative Enquiry for Schools and System Improvement*, Paper Presented to CERI/OECD/DFES/QCA/ESRC Forum on Knowledge Management in Education and Learning, 18–19 March 2002.

Jordan, B. and Henderson, A. (1995) Interaction analysis: foundations and practice, *Journal of the Learning Sciences*, vol. 4, no. 1, pp. 39–103.

Knowles, M. (1970) Andragogy: An emerging technology for adult learning, in M. Knowles, *The Modern Practice of Adult Education: From Pedagogy to Andragogy*, Cambridge, Cambridge Book Company.

Laevers, F. (1993) Deep level learning: an exemplary application on the area of physical knowledge, *European Early Childhood Education Research Journal*, vol. 1, no. 1, pp. 53–68.

Laevers, F. (1994a) *The Leuven Involvement Scale for Young Children*, LIS and YC Manual and videotape, Experiential Education Series No. 1, Leuven, Belgium, Centre of Experiential Education.

Laevers, F. (1994b) The innovative project: experiential education 1976-1995, *Studia Pedagogica*, vol. 16, pp. 159–72.

Laevers, F. (1995) Lecture at EEL, Worcester College of Higher Education, September.

Laevers, F. (1997) *A Process-Orientated Child Follow Up System for Young Children*, Centre for Experiential Education, Leuven, Belgium.

Lawrence, R. (2004) Unpublished conference presentation, Pen Green.

Lazar, I. (1983) *As the Twig is Bent. Lasting Effects of Pre-School Programmes*, Consortium of Longitudinal Studies, Hillsdale, NJ.

Lee, V. and Das Gupta, P. (1995) *Children's Cognitive Language Development*, Open University Press, Milton Keynes.

Mairs, K. (1990) *A Schema Booklet for Parents*, Pen Green Centre, Corby.

Malaguzzi, L. (1993) For an education based on relationship, *Young Children*, vol. 11, pp. 9–13.

Malaguzzi, L. (1997) quoted in H. Penn, *Comparing Nurseries: Staff and Children in Italy, Spain and the UK*, Paul Chapman, London.

Malaguzzi, L. (1998) *The Hundred Languages of Children*, Ablex, London.

Malcolm, A. (1993) *Fathers' involvement with their children and outside work commitments*, Unpublished study submitted as part of the Diploma in Post-Qualifying Studies.

Marshall, J. (1994) Revisioning organisations by developing female values, in J. Boot, J. Lawrence and J. Morris (eds) *Managing the Unknown by Creating New Futures*, McGraw-Hill, London.

Matza, D. (1964) *Delinquency and Drift*, John Wiley and Sons, New York.

McKinnon, E. (2005) *Family life and family services – putting the jigsaw together*, Symposium paper presented at the European Early Childhood Research Association's Annual Conference, Dublin, September.

Meade, A. (1995) *Thinking Children*, New Zealand Council for Educational Research, Wellington.

Mezirow, J. (1977) Perspective transformation, *Studies in Adult Education*, 9 October, pp. 153–64.

Miller, R. L. (2000) *Researching Life Stories and Family Histories*, Sage, London.

Ministry of Education (1996) *Te Whariki Early Childhood Curriculum*, Ministry of Education, Wellington.

Moir, A. and Moir, B. (1999) *Why Men Don't Iron: The New Reality of Gender Differences*, HarperCollins, London.

Moss, P. (1992) Perspectives from Europe, in Pugh G. (ed.) *Contemporary Issues in the Early Years*, Paul Chapman in Association with the National Children's Bureau, London.

Mullins, L. (1989) *Management and Organisational Behaviour*, Pitman, London.

Nash, J. M. (1997) Fertile minds, *Time Magazine*, 3 February.

Newmann, F., King, B. and Youngs, P. (2000) *Professional development that addresses school capacity*, Paper presented at the Annual Meeting of the American Education Research Association.

NIAS (1993) *Primary Teachers Talking: A Reflexive Account of Longitudinal Research in Hammersley*, Educational Research Current Issues, Paul Chapman, London.

Nucci, L. and Smetana, J. G. (1996) Mothers' concepts of young children's areas of personal freedom, *Child Development*, vol. 677, 1870–86.

OECD (Organisation for European Co-operation and Development) (1997) *Parents as Partners in Schools*, OECD, Paris.

Oliver, C., Smith, M. and Barker, S. (1998) *Effectiveness of early interactions*. Paper for the Cross-Departmental Review of Provision for Young Children.

Pascal, C. (1996) Lecture at Pen Green Centre. Unpublished.

Pascal, C. and Bertram, A. D. (1994) Defining and assessing quality in the education of children from 4–7 years, in F. Laevers (ed.) *Defining and Assessing the Quality in Early Childhood Education (Studia Paedagogica no. 16)*, Leuven University Press, Leuven.

Pascal, C. and Bertram, A. (1997) *Effective Early Learning*, Hodder & Stoughton, London.

Pascal, C., Bertram, A. D. and Ramsden, E. (1994) *Effective Early Learning: The Quality Evaluation and Development Process*, Amber Publications, Worcester.

Pen Green (2005) Adult Pedagogic Strategies, updated by Pen Green Team, unpublished.

Pen Green Centre (2000) *Involving parents in their children's learning training pack*, Pen Green Research, Development and Training Base, Corby.

Pen Green Centre (2002) Portfolios produced by parents and workers on individual children and their special interests. Unpublished but available to purchase at the Pen Green Research Base, Corby, Northants.

Pen Green Centre/DfEE (1999) *Autumn term evaluation project: pedagogic architecture.* Unpublished paper.

Pen Green Research Base Report (2000) *Parent-led needs assessment.* Unpublished internal document.

Pen Green Research, Development and Training Base (2004) *Growing Together at the Pen Green Centre: Training Resources,* Pen Green Research, Development and Training Base, Pen Green Centre for Under Fives and their Families, Corby, Northamptonshire, UK.

Pen Green Research Team (2004) *A Research and Development Project to Promote Well Being and Resilience in Young Children,* Pen Green Research, Development and Training Base, Pen Green Centre for Under Fives and their Families, Corby, Northamptonshire, UK.

Pen Green Team (2002) *Growing Together Training Resources.* Unpublished and available from the Pen Green Research Base, Corby, Northants.

Pen Green Team (2002) *Understanding Children's Development.* Workbook for Parents on Four Key Child Development Concepts. Unpublished. Produced at the Pen Green Research Base, Corby, Northants.

Piaget, J. (1962) *Play, Dreams and Imitation in Childhood,* Routledge and Kegan Paul, London.

Plowden Report (1967) *Central Advisory Council for Education, Children and their Primary Schools,* HMSO, London.

Pollard, A. (1996) *The Social World of Children's Learning,* Cassell, London.

Pugh, G., De'Ath, E. and Smith, C. (1994) *Confident Parents, Confident Children,* National Children's Bureau, London.

Rinaldi, C. (1998) Projected curriculum constructed through documentation – Progettazione: an interview with Lella Gandini, in C. Edwards, L. Gandini and G. Forman, *The Hundred Languages of Children: The Reggio Emilia Approach – Advanced Reflections,* Ablex, London.

Rogers, C. R. (1983) *Freedom to Learn for the 80s,* Merrill, London.

Rutter, M. and Rutter, M. (1992) *Developing Minds,* Penguin, Harmondsworth.

Scott, P. (1996) He has seen the future and it gets harder: profile of Charles Handy, *Times Educational Supplement,* 29 November, p. 4.

Shaw, J. (1991) *An investigation of parents' conceptual development in the light of dialogue with a community teacher.* Unpublished PhD thesis, University of Newcastle-upon-Tyne.

Smiley, P. A. and Dweck, C. (1994) Individual differences in achievement and goals among young children, *Child Development,* vol. 65, pp. 1723–43.

Smith, T. (1990) Parents and pre-school education, in N. Entwistle (ed.) *Handbook of Educational Ideas and Practices,* Routledge, London.

Sood, N. (1999) *International perspectives and policy on early childhood provision,* Warwick Conference, April.

Stimson, J. (1995) *Worried Arthur,* Ladybird, Loughborough.

Strauss, A. and Corbin, J. (1990) *Basics of Qualitative Research,* Sage, London.

Strauss, A. and Corbin, J. (1994) Grounded theory methodology: an overview, in N. K. Denzin and Y. S. Lincoln (ed.) *Handbook of Qualitative Research,* Sage, London, pp. 273–85.

Sylva, K. (1994) A curriculum for early learning, in C. Ball, (ed.) *RSA Start Right: The Importance of Early Learning,* RSA, London.

Sylva, K. (1999) Linking quality processes to children's developmental outcomes, Keynote Lecture, Warwick Conference, April.

Sylva, K., Melhuish, E., Sammons, P., Siraj-Blatchford, I. and Taggart, B. (2004) *The Effective Provision of Pre-School Education (EPPE) Project. Final Report,* DfES Publications, London.

Tait, C. (2001) Getting to know the families, in M. Whalley, (2001) *Involving Parents in their Children's Learning,* Paul Chapman, London.

Tait, C. (2004) *Chuffedness,* Paper presented at EECERA Conference, Malta.

TES (2000) Early years shops save money, *Times Educational Supplement,* 25 February, p. 11.

Trevarthen, C. (2002a) Learning in companionship, *Education in the North: The Journal of Scottish Education,* New Series, no. 10, p. 16–25.

Trevarthen, C. (2002b) Training session with Pen Green Research Team, Corby.

Trevarthen, C. (2003) *Chuffedness: the motor of learning,* Conference talk, June 2003, Pen Green Centre, Corby.

Trevarthen, C. and Aitken, K.J. (2001) Infant intersubjectivity: research, theory and clinical applications, *Journal of Child Psychology and Psychiatry,* vol. 42, no. 1, pp. 3–48.

Vygotsky, L. S. (1978) *Mind in Society,* Harvard University Press, Cambridge, MA.

Weinberger, J. (1996) *Literacy Goes to School – The Parents' Role in Young Children's Literacy Learning,* Paul Chapman, London.

Wells, G. (1986) *The Meaning Makers: Children Learning Language and Using Language to Learn,* Heinemann, Portsmouth, NH.

Whalley, M. (1992) *A question of choice,* Unpublished MA thesis, Leicester University.

Whalley, M. (1994) *Learning to Be Strong,* Hodder & Stoughton, London.

Whalley, M. (1996a) Unpublished paper for EECERA Conference, Lisbon.

Whalley, M. (1996b) *Confident Parents, Confident Children: Group Leader Notes,* Open University Press, Milton Keynes.

Whalley, M. (1997a) *Parents' involvement in their children's learning.* Conference paper, November.

Whalley, M. (1997b) *Working with Parents,* Hodder and Stoughton, London.

Whalley, M. (1998) Getting fathers involved, *Basic Skills Magazine,* March/April, pp. 25–8.

Whalley, M. (1999a) *Leadership in early years settings,* Unpublished PhD thesis, University of Wolverhampton.

Whalley, M. (1999b) Unsettled times, *Nursery World,* 16 September, pp. 10–11.

Whalley, M. (2001) *Involving Parents in Their Children's Learning,* Paul Chapman, London.

Whalley, M. (2005) *Developing leadership approaches for early years settings: leading together,* PowerPoint (accessible on www.ncsl/.org.uk/media/f58/76/ communityleadership-together-Whalley.ppt#262).

Whalley, M. (2006) Leadership in integrated centres and services for children and families – a community development approach: engaging with the struggle, *Childrenz Issues, Journal of the Children's Issues Centre,* vol. 10, no. 2, p. 8.

Whalley, M. and Arnold, C. (1997a) *Effective Pedagogic Strategies, TTA Summary of Research Findings,* TTA, London.

Whalley, M. and Arnold, C. (1997b) *Parental involvement in education.* Paper for Teacher Training Agency.

Whalley, E. and Whalley, P. (1996) *Making schemas easy to understand*, Briefing paper
  for a conference at Pen Green Research, Development and Training Base.
Whalley, M. and Whitaker, P. (1999) *Leadership and Management in the Early Years*,
  MA Leadership Course Text, Pen Green Publications.
Whitaker, P. (1986) A humanistic approach to teacher in-service education, *Self and
  Society*, vol. 4, no. 6, pp. 276–81.
Whitehead, M. (2004) *Language and Literacy in the Early Years*, 3rd edn, Sage, London.
Winnicott, D. W. (1965) The theory of the parent–infant relationship, in D. W.
  Winnicott, *The Maturational Processes and the Facilitating Environment*, Hogarth
  Press, London.
Wittner, J. (1987) in K. Anderson, S. Armitage, D. Jack and J. Wittner. Beginning
  where we are, *Oral History Review*, vol. 15, pp. 103–27.
Wolfendale, S. and Einzig, H. (1999) *Parenting Education and Support*, David Fulton,
  London.
Yanez, Y. L. (1999) *Networking for children; empowering families for early education in
  rural and resourceless communities in Venezuela*, Keynote Lecture, Warwick
  Conference, April.

Appendix – Schemas

Schemas are 'patterns' of action that children demonstrate when they are exploring the world and trying to find out how things work. Children may try out the same action on a variety of different objects. They come up with their own working theories about how things work. They continue to test their theories or ideas. Sometimes they discover exceptions to the rules that they have established with their working theories.

As Athey (2004, personal communication) points out, 'A schema is a pattern of repeated actions. Clusters of schemas develop into later concepts.'

Here are some common patterns or schemas we have observed:

- **Trajectory** – lines that are moving, as in a jump. These lines can be vertical (up/down), horizontal (side to side) or oblique (at an angle). Trajectories can leave a mark or trail that we refer to as a line. You make the line by making a trajectory movement. Young children often place objects in a line, which is the 'figurative' aspect of the schema (Athey, 1990, p. 35). The movement is the 'dynamic' aspect (*ibid*.).
- **Heaping and scattering** – placing objects in a pile and spreading or scattering them in space is what some children constantly do. Children who enjoy scattering may like having lots of small objects to scatter. Sweeping up with a dustpan and brush may interest children who are interested in heaping and scattering. So might throwing bread or corn to ducks.
- **Transporting** – carrying objects or being carried from one place to another – a buggy or shopping trolley may be a favourite toy. Children who enjoy transporting, constantly find and gather things to move, and ways of moving them around, such as bags, buggies and shopping trolleys.
- **Envelopment** – covering themselves, objects or a space – tea towels, scarves or cardboard boxes may be popular play materials.
- **Enclosure** – enclosing themselves, toys or space – Lego, train track, blocks or cushions may be used when exploring this pattern. Children exploring enclosure often use cushions to surround themselves or like making pens for farm animals.
- **Rotation** – turning, twisting or rolling themselves or objects – ring games, globes, rolling pins, rollers and wheels might be played with when exploring this pattern.

- **Connection** – an interest in connecting or joining themselves to objects or objects to each other – construction toys, pegs, paper clips, string, Sellotape, locks and chains might help children exploring this pattern.
- **Going through a boundary** – making themselves or objects go through something and come out of the other side – tunnels, garlic presses, postboxes and fax machines might fascinate children exploring this pattern.
- **On top** – being on top or placing objects on top – climbing equipment or shelves they can reach may help children exploring this pattern. Young children seem to like to be 'on top' of the slide or to place things on top of their buildings to embellish them.
- **Containment** – putting themselves, objects or materials into different containers – a variety of bottles, bags and boxes help children to explore this pattern. Some young children spend hours at the sink filling and emptying various containers, repeating their actions, again and again.

Schemas can be explored in four different ways:

- Through our actions with feedback through our senses – we call this 'sensorimotor'. We never lose the ability or the need to do this.
- Through using one object to stand for another – we call this 'symbolic representation'. We replay our earlier experiences by using objects; for example, a child might hold a block near their ear to represent a telephone. We use words to represent our movements or objects. Georgia referred to 20p as a 'choo choo' because she could get a ride on a toy train at the supermarket for 20p (Arnold, 1999b, p. 67).
- Through understanding the effect our actions have on the environment, that is, 'if I do this, that will happen' – we call this 'functional dependency'.
- Through being able to think about people and objects in action without needing the objects to manipulate. Athey (1990, p. 68) says, 'Thought is where a child gives a verbal account of an experience in the absence of any material or situational reminder of the original experience.'

This whole section is from Pen Green Team (2007) *The Pen Green Framework for Engaging Parents*, unpublished training materials.

Index